Penny Arcade

Penny Arcade

OR WHAT DID YOU DO IN THE SIXTIES, DADDY?

SAMMY KING

First published in the United Kingdom in 2009 by
Bank House Books
PO Box 3
NEW ROMNEY
TN29 9WJ UK
www.bankhousebooks.com

© Sammy King, 2010

The Author hereby asserts his moral rights to be identified as the Author of the Work.

All rights reserved. No part of this publication may be reproduced, stored in a retrieval system, or transmitted, in any form or by any means, electronic, mechanical, photocopying, recording or otherwise, without the prior permission of the publisher and copyright holder.

Cover photography courtesy of Bruce Greer.

British Library Cataloguing in Publication Data
A catalogue record for this book is available from the British Library

ISBN 9781904408598

Typesetting and origination by Bank House Books
Printed by Lightning Source

To Mum and Dad – for granting me the opportunity to experience the joyous and frustrating idiosyncrasies of life

Contents

Acknowledgements	ix
Foreword by Roy Orbison Jr	xi
Preface: Sammy Who?	xiv
Chapter One: Pedigree	1
Chapter Two: Roots	15
Chapter Three: School Days	40
Chapter Four: Le Crunch!	45
Chapter Five: Elvis Presley . . . Who's She?	54
Chapter Six: *Ars Gratia Artis*!	70
Chapter Seven: King of the Road	78
Chapter Eight: Rock'n'Roll Days	94
Chapter Nine: The Dingos	106
Chapter Ten: The Voltaires	120
Chapter Eleven: Back on the Road Again	139
Chapter Twelve: Corridors of Power	156
Chapter Thirteen: Countdown to a Breakdown	169
Chapter Fourteen: A Spare Part in a Zeppelin Factory	188
Chapter Fifteen: 'Penny Arcade'	199
Chapter Sixteen: The Magic of 'Penny Arcade'	212
Chapter Seventeen: The Importance of being Independent	218
Chapter Eighteen: Too Much Too Soon?	224
Chapter Nineteen: Mandy	250
Chapter Twenty: Sweet Reality, and Back Down to Earth	264

Acknowledgements

I do hope you enjoy reading my book. If you do, then credit for it must be shared by those who, in one way or another, helped to make it possible.

It goes without saying that the support and encouragement of my wife Linda, daughter Amanda and my extended family sustained me throughout, but my heartfelt thanks must also go to the following good people:

Roy Orbison Jr; Barbara Orbison Productions/Roy Orbison Music – Tanja Crouch (vice-president); Reuben Davison; Joyce Stableford; Derek Neill; Terry Widlake; Bob Munday; John Leyton; Steve Etherington; Eric Holroyd; Bill Jessop; Bruce Greer; Garth Cawood; John Wagstaff/NOW Music; Camille Blackmore; Flair Theatrical Agency; Jo Jagger; Dorothy Doyle; Derek J. Lister; Carl Gresham; Dave Metcalfe; Derek Smith; Joe Kenyon; Colin Marchant; Dorothy Emsley; Eric Roper; Alan Clegg; Glen Stevens; Bernard Fenton; Doreen Fenton and family; Bernard Hinchcliffe; Jogger and Titch Anderson; Trevor Simpson; Goldie Armitage; The fans that have supported me over half a century; The doctors, nurses and auxiliaries of the NHS (orthopaedic, general and mental health facilities).

Last but not least my eternal gratitude to Jean, Dennis, George, Roz, Sue and Chris (the Black Bull Literary Society) for their unbiased critique!

Roy Kelton aka Roy Orbison Jr with Sammy.

Foreword

When I was six years old my favourite song by Roy Orbison was 'Penny Arcade'. I loved its bouncy, happy sound. Initially I thought the title was Penny RK. My nickname is RK, so I thought it was a song about me. Not understanding what the penny reference was about I asked my dad. He told me that a penny arcade is a gaming hall, much like the video-game rooms I loved at the time. I asked many more questions, 'Did the games only cost a penny?', 'What's a bagatelle?', and so on.

He told me all about the song and about how a man named Sammy King had written it. He spoke about Australia and, since the song was so hugely popular there, I assumed Sammy was Australian. I only found out much later that Sammy was British and part of an 'extended family' Roy had in Yorkshire, England. In the 1960s Yorkshirebecame an 'Orbison stronghold'. To this day Roy has more loyal fans there than anywhere else in the world. He and my mother Barbara lived in the area and became quite close to its people.

One evening, while Roy and Barbara were out eating dinner, Sammy introduced himself and gave Roy a tape of 'Penny Arcade'. This shows something of Roy's open spirit and something of Sammy's belief in his material.

Roy always spoke highly of Sammy's songwriting ability. The fact he never dropped 'Penny Arcade' from his live performances is telling. Roy also recorded three more of Sammy's songs, 'After Tonight', 'Say No

More' and 'I Got Nothing'. All are excellent and show a broad range of writing style.

I still find new meaning and forgotten memories when I listen to 'Penny Arcade'. Meeting Sammy King later as an adult was an honour for me. We got along like old friends immediately. He is a very nice man with a great love for music and Roy Orbison. His life with its ups and downs makes a great story. I hope you will enjoy reading this and learning about the man.

Thank you, Sammy King.

Roy Orbison Jr

MAJESTIC BALLROOM - BRADFORD

Thursday, Feb. 2nd

DANCING — 8 TO 12

GARTH B. CAWOOD PRESENTS

H.M.V.'s Top Recording Star—

JOHNNY KIDD

AND HIS PIRATES (Messrs. Shaking all over)

THE DINGOS
ROCK 'N' RHYTHM GROUP

PLUS

THE CRESCENT CITY JAZZ BAND

SOUVENIR SPOT PRIZES, ETC.

Tickets, 6/6

On sale at THE MAJESTIC or at ERRICK'S PHOTO SHOP, opposite Bradford Town Hall.

Preface
SAMMY WHO?

The rock'n'roll tour opened at the Southport Odeon. It was our job to open the show, and that evening I remember watching from the wings as the rest of the lads in the band checked their instruments behind the massive curtains. They were going to start with an instrumental number before I made my entrance and I could sense their nervousness.

Last minute instructions and reminders snapped back and forth as the lights were lowered and a buzz of excitement rose from the audience. Then the announcement boomed around the auditorium: 'Ladies and gentlemen . . . a new and exciting young group destined for stardom . . . The Voltaires!'

The crowd roared and screamed in anticipation, the adrenalin kicked in and the lads powered into their number. Spurred on by the crowd, the band played well above their potential – obviously inspired. They finished their number and the audience clapped and cheered.

Then it was my turn.

I was so nervous that my scrotum seemed to withdraw into my stomach to join the swarm of butterflies fluttering about inside. My mouth was dry and my knees were shaking. The announcer was standing next to me in the wings. I gave him the nod, and again the

PA system boomed: 'And now . . . introducing . . . Sammy King!'

Once again the crowd roared as the band played the intro to my first number, 'The night has a thousand eyes'.

I stepped into the lights. The spotlight caught the gold lamé jacket I was wearing and the girls started screaming – this was even before I'd started to sing! It felt so good. And even though the band was virtually unknown we were experiencing a taste of what stardom was all about. I milked the crowd for all they were worth, and they certainly got their money's worth.

What an experience it was!

We had arrived at the theatre earlier that day, and I'd just finished running through a couple of numbers with the lads. And on my way back to the dressing room I came face to face with Gene Vincent – the American rock star. Being a fan myself, it seemed incredible to me that I was actually in the company of someone whose records I had nearly worn out over the past few years. I was in complete awe of the man. I was also surprised to note that he had a calliper on one leg and walked with a pronounced limp. It was the first time I'd seen him in the flesh and his photographs gave no indication of his disability.

Oh God, I thought, as I limped towards him, I hope he doesn't think I'm taking the piss!

I sensed a slight tension in the air as we slowly limped towards one another like a couple of gunslingers in a western 'B' movie. His eyes began to narrow. They had a glazed look about them – medication? If it was, it didn't stop him glaring at me.

As we slowly passed each other he continued to stare at me over his shoulder. I think my uneasy smile helped to reassure him that I wasn't doing it on purpose. And anyway, no person on earth could have replicated the limp I had at that time.

The episode only added to the incredible atmosphere backstage. I found it difficult coming to terms with the fact that the rest of the artists on the show were famous too. Just being a part of it was so exciting. I glanced through a dressing room door, and Jet Harris and Tony Meehan, two of Cliff Richard's original backing group The Shadows, were talking. Don Groom, the drummer with the Innocents, was asking someone if John Leyton had arrived yet . . .

It was such a wonderful memory and it all happened back in the summer of 1963: just one of the many unforgettable experiences that

John Leyton, singer and film star. He is probably best remembered for the chart-topping 'Johnny Remember Me' in August 1961. I wrote two songs for him and played on various package tours with him.

Trying out the gold lamé suit look.

Gene Vincent.

Jet Harris and Tony Meehan

took place during my long association with the entertainment industry. So how did I come to be doing this in the first place? In truth I don't really know, because for as long as I can remember I never had any ambitions. All I ever dreamed about when I was a kid was playing football for Huddersfield Town and England. Showbiz . . . I never gave it a thought. I was always too shy. The fact is that I landed in it literally by accident, and I've had a rollercoaster ride through life ever since.

Although I made my mark in certain areas I'd be the first to admit that I was never a household name. This wasn't lost on me when I attended the annual Ivor Novello Awards bash at the Grosvenor House Hotel in London.

Stepping out of the taxi with my accompanying friends, we jauntily made our way towards the hotel entrance flanked by the barriers that held back the paparazzi and groups of noisy onlookers waiting for Take That – the new boy band – to arrive.

Two of my small entourage were already brandishing their invitations by the time I reached the entrance. 'We're with Sammy King,' one of them was telling a gorilla in a tuxedo.

'Sammy who?' grunted the giant.

'Sammy King,' they insisted.

Unimpressed, the colossus pointed out that our invitations were for entry at the lower door, and not the door for A-list celebrities.

So there followed an undignified retreat past the puzzled onlookers to a door down the side of the hotel that probably also served as a delivery entrance. And for the rest of our stay in London I was referred to by my friends as 'Sammy Who'.

I found it really amusing. But even though I wasn't afforded the privilege of using the same entrance as Elton, Sir Andrew Lloyd Webber and the other superstars, at least I'd earned the right to be invited.

For along the way, besides being a supporting act, I wrote songs for artistes that charted in Britain, the USA, Europe, Africa and Australia – including the one that was to change my life forever and is still as popular in the twenty-first century as when it was first recorded by Roy Orbison in 1969 – 'Penny Arcade'.

Although I've briefly touched on the adulation and the perks that go with stardom, to be honest I've always been more comfortable with the anonymity of the humble songwriter.

So what prompted 'Sammy Who' to write these memoirs?

Vanity, ego or profit? No, none of these. The true reason for this indulgence was instigated by a small pair of eyebrows, which belonged to my then teenage daughter Mandy.

One day I happened to mention that during my long career in show business I'd appeared on the same bill as the Beatles. She briefly looked up from the teen magazine she was reading and up went the eyebrows, then down, and then it was back to the magazine. That was it – a complete lack of interest

Is that all? I thought. Is that the only reaction I get to such a profound statement? Surely it merited some kind of recognition. Something a bit more encouraging than the raising of two adolescent eyebrows barely a quarter of an inch.

Feeling slightly miffed, I continued: 'I had a natter with Paul McCartney . . .' No reaction. '. . . and Ringo . . .' Still no reaction. '. . . and John Lennon glared at me a couple of times.'

'Hmm?'

Oh! A slight reaction – but she was still reading.

'It was back in the '60s,' I went on. 'A pop concert at the Queens Hall in Leeds, which used to be an old tram shed. There were between two and three thousand people there – a big crowd in those days.'

'Hmm?'

Aha! Vague interest. I began to pick up speed. 'I was well into my set, when all of a sudden girls in the audience started screaming. And I remember thinking, This is it! Fame at last. So I gave them the lot – hip swivels, crutch bumps, the sultry look – and still they screamed. What a feeling! I turned to face the rest of the band who were lapping it up too. Then, much to my disappointment, I realised what the girls were really screaming at. Paul McCartney was poking his head through the curtains behind us – and when he disappeared so did the screaming!'

At last I detected a faint smile – but she was still reading.

I know what it is, I thought, nursing my wounded ego. She's not really listening – she can't be. I decided to put it to the test. 'Would you prefer a present or money for your birth . . .?'

'Money please!'

So that was *that* theory out of the window.

When I was Mandy's age the only thing that mattered to me, was – me! I was far too wrapped up in myself to be interested in where my 'old man' came from or what he'd done. There would be plenty of time for all that later on. But the trouble is that this 'plenty of time' runs out. And, as I did, she'll find that the questions she might want to ask can't be answered because there's no one to ask.

So perhaps when Mandy is older she might welcome this opportunity to find out more about *her* 'old man' and, in doing so, maybe a bit more about herself.

Chapter One
PEDIGREE

Life began for me in a bijou terraced house in Batley, West Yorkshire, during the Second World War, on 25 September 1941. I hit the scales weighing 9 pounds exactly. Significantly my birthday falls exactly nine months after Christmas Day, so I like to think I was a deferred Christmas present to my mother. But I think she may have been a little bit disappointed at first when my 'spare' bit of umbilical cord was revealed. She really wanted a girl – and I was to have been called Susan. 'A Boy Named Sue' – now that wouldn't be a bad title for a song. Maybe this was an indication of what I was eventually going to aspire to.

By all accounts the midwife was late getting to our house when I was born. Apparently she had been trying to talk her previous patient out of calling her new baby girl Pearl, which was a popular name at that time. Trouble was – the young lady's surname was Button. We never did get to know the outcome, but I know for certain that the kid wasn't in our class at school – I'm sure I would've remembered her name!

But at least her name was pronounceable. I was baptised Alan Twohig. And I can hear you saying 'Alan *what?*' It's pronounced 'Too-hig' and originates from the west of Ireland, though some people can't be convinced. Over the years I've been asked if it was

Chinese, East European, Scandinavian, even Red Indian. So like most kids with funny names I occasionally got teased, but I didn't let it worry me too much.

There were signs, even back then, of my lack of ambition. When I was about five Dad asked me what I wanted to be when I grew up. 'Just big,' I answered, without even looking up from the picture I was colouring. Alas . . . this is something else I've never fulfilled – having only ever reached the dizzy heights of 5ft 3½in.

There are contrasting views as to whom I take after – my father or my mother. I like to think that I've inherited a little bit of the best of both of them. My flair for art and my great love of nature I definitely acquired from Dad, Edmond Patrick. Born in Eyrecourt in the county of Galway on the west coast of Ireland on 5 March 1905, he was the youngest of five Twohig brothers. He also had two sisters, Mai and Christine.

I've always been proud of my Irish heritage, and regret having never known my grandparents, Maurice and Elisabeth. Both died before I was born so I never got the chance to learn more about my Irish ancestry, especially the Spanish connection. Apparently when the English fleet routed the Armada some of the Spanish ships were chased and sunk off the coast of Ireland. Many of the Spanish sailors who survived went ashore seeking refuge, and never returned to their homeland. Some of them married into Irish families and, according to Dad, ours was one of them. Historians sometimes refer to these people as 'the black Irish', which I've always thought to be a bit extreme; 'olive' would have been much more suitable. This probably accounts for the reason why I'm completely at home with Spanish culture – from sangria to siesta and the Spanish guitar! The only aspect I can't come to terms with is bullfighting . . . bullshitting, maybe; bullfighting, never!

My parents

Dad was tall, very gentle and good-natured. I never remember him having hair, but despite this, and although he wore spectacles, the ladies always considered him to be a handsome man. He spoke with a soft Irish brogue, which never altered despite being exposed to the unyielding Yorkshire accent for more than fifty years. He was also a very intelligent man – college educated – blessed with talents he never fully used, a trait I've often been accused of myself!

Though he had many friends, he still enjoyed his own company

Mum and Dad: Edmond and Marion Twohig.

The Irish connection. Left to right: Dad, Uncle Pete, Mum, Auntie Rose, Cousin Mona, me and my brother Brian.

and frequently went off alone to indulge in one of his favourite pastimes – walking. He never used public transport, preferring to walk – having first donned his battered old trilby hat, which was always tipped to any lady he encountered along the way in gentlemanly fashion.

And, like all Irishmen, he was a great storyteller. In the years following the Second World War, when power cuts frequently plunged our house into darkness, my elder brother Brian and I would sit in the firelight glow and listen to Dad recounting the story of a little rabbit called Billy Bobtail until the lights came back on again. I used to tell the story to Mandy at bedtime when she was young; it was always one of her favourites. But I could never make it sound the same as Dad did. Perhaps it was because he always threw himself into the spirit of things by adding sound effects or whistling a catchy tune whenever Billy was on the move.

Although Dad told us many things about himself, I never felt that I knew enough about him, especially in the years before he met Mum. I knew he'd been employed at the Guinness factory in Dublin for a while and had tried his hands at many things before he came to England; but he never talked much about his childhood or adolescence. Maybe there wasn't that much to tell. Coming from a devout Roman Catholic family, it's more than likely that his studies and church duties took up most of his time.

I've worked out that he must have been in his late twenties when he left Ireland to seek a new life in England. His first port of call was probably London, but I'm not quite sure. I do know that he visited and worked in lots of places, for whenever a well-known town or city cropped up in conversation he always seemed to have first-hand knowledge of the place. And, more often than not, there was an anecdote to go with it.

This might have come from his time working 'on the gaff' – with a travelling fair. I don't know what he was actually doing, but I do remember him saying that one of his friends ran a hoop-la stall – a young man whose name was later to become famous to millions of holidaymakers: Billy Butlin of holiday camp fame.

I also know that he spent a lot of time in London. Dad loved London. I remember him telling me how excited he was when he first arrived there. He was really taken by the sheer size of the place; but it was a bit of a culture shock too. Exchanging the easy-going Irish way for the hustle and bustle of the heart of one of the world's greatest empires can't have been easy. And in those days the Irish immigrant was looked upon as just another navvy, fit for digging' – and that was all. But there was more to Dad than that, and he wouldn't have been daunted by any of it. He always worked very hard be it manual or otherwise, and he was prepared to take on any task. His education, charm and a willingness to please were the best qualifications for anyone setting out on a great adventure. And that's how he looked upon his time in London – as a great adventure. An adventure he was never too busy to tell us about.

Dad had this unforgettable way of gathering his thoughts together before he began a story. His head tilted slightly sideways and upwards and he stared towards the ceiling. Then, after a brief moment of reflective silence, a faint smile marked the beginning of the memory that was about to unfold.

He arrived in London with very little money, and most of what he had was spent on finding a place to live; the rest maintained him while he went in search of a job. So, having very little to spend on himself, much of Dad's leisure time was spent walking, taking in the sights and sounds of his favourite part of London – the West End. I never got tired of listening to him talk about the things he saw and did: seeing the historic landmarks and thoroughfares that he'd only ever heard about or read about in books; and experiencing the Underground for the first time – feeling the rush of air that preceded the train bursting from the tunnel, hearing the cries of 'Mind the doors', observing the syncopated sway of standing passengers clinging to the straps dangling from the carriage roof, marvelling at the escalators that seemed to ascend or descend forever. In his own inimitable way he described the cacophony of traffic competing for space in Piccadilly Circus, the clatter of horse-drawn wagons at odds with the ever-increasing number of honking motor cars, taxis and buses. And the sheer volume of people – enough to try the patience of a seasoned townie let alone a shy young Irishman. It must have been some experience.

When I visited London for the first time everything was there just as he'd said it would be: the buildings and monuments, the parks and thoroughfares. But among the mixture of emotion and excitement I felt, there was a small part of me that secretly wished I could have seen it as he had: the picture of London that was already engraved on my mind, the one he'd told me about, where style and elegance were not so easily compromised in the name of progress, and variety really was the proverbial spice of life. It really was a bit like seeing a film after reading the book. Let's face it, to a romantic like me a Ford convertible on its way to the Holiday Inn doesn't quite match up to a candle-lit landau en route to the Ritz.

But for each wonderful memory, doubtless others got away.

Quite by accident, we discovered that Dad had entrepreneurial connections in the West End. It came as a great surprise, because I felt sure it would be something he'd be bound to tell us about. I can't remember whether it was me or my brother who found the business card, lying at the bottom of one of the drawers of Mum's dressing table.

Printed on it was:

MARVON – the revolutionary new hair tonic!
Presented by E.P. Twohig Esquire.
Park Lane, London W1.

I mean, wow! Park Lane, W1! Impressive or what? We got the story from Mum. It turned out that he didn't really live there – he just paid to use the address. The practice was commonplace, by all accounts. But I'll wager the prospective buyers were more impressed by the address than the product: Dad was bald by the time he was thirty!

Everybody liked him. He had a great sense of humour, loved Irish jokes and always had a smile or a word for anyone he met. So great was his regard for the welfare of others, that a large part of his life was spent doing charitable works. Come rain or shine he'd be at our local church helping with whatever he could, or working tirelessly for the St John's Ambulance Brigade, which he served for many years. We were extremely proud when the Brigade saw fit to invest him into 'The Most Honourable Order of the Serving Brothers of St John of Jerusalem'. He travelled to London to receive his medal and illuminated scroll from the Duke of Gloucester. We were all extremely proud of him, so very proud.

My greatest regret is that I never got to grieve him properly when he died – primarily because when the time came his passing was tempered with a considerable amount of relief. The advanced stages of Alzheimer's had long since taken away the one person I had always looked upon as my hero. It took a long time for me to dismiss the image of what that terrible disease had done to a proud and wonderful man.

But in writing about him and recalling all these wonderful memories, I've finally managed to achieve a certain reconciliation, coming to terms with what I couldn't bring myself to do all those years ago. Like Mum, he's constantly in my thoughts – especially when I see my brother walk with the same gait or I find myself standing as he used to do, in front of the television with hands in pockets. Dad wasn't a rich man, but he left us with something all the money in the world couldn't buy – an example to live our lives by. I take great pride in the knowledge that no one ever heard anyone speak ill of him. And that, in my book, is the greatest legacy a man can ever leave his children.

So if there is any trace of flamboyance in my persona, it has to be attributed to my mother. She was a remarkable woman, and I adored her. Small, dark and raven-haired, she was very loving and protective. Though she was less than five feet tall, a tremendous drive and energy compensated for her lack of inches. She too wore spectacles but, like my father, she was considered to be very attractive. If anyone was born with the necessary requirements to take on the world of showbiz – or the world, for that matter – it was Mum. Being the centre of attention always seemed to come naturally to her. Wherever she went she always made her presence felt.

Mum loved music. She loved to dance, and taught herself to play the piano. I was fascinated by the way her left hand darted back and forth while her right hand calmly played the melody. She had a style of her own, but was obviously influenced by Charlie Kunz, one of her two favourite pianists – the other being Winifred Atwell. I was drawn to the piano like a bee to honey. Mum was aware of this, and was never too busy to show me how to play little tunes. It seemed to come easy to me – like most things I enjoy doing. And at an early age I was rattling off a rendering of 'Oh Will You Wash My Father's Shirt' with the utmost confidence. No doubt this made her very proud of me. But it wasn't long before everyone was sick of hearing Dad's shirt being washed umpteen times a night. Fortunately for everyone, I managed to learn the Harry Lime theme, 'Buttons and Bows' and a few other tunes.

Mum was born Marion Marsh in Liverpool on 24 April 1915. My grandmother, Maria, was employed in service at the time working as a laundress at a large house in Wavertree Road, Liverpool. A few years later mum's younger sister Evelyn, always affectionately known as Evy, was born.

For some reason Mum and Aunt Evy never talked about their father. Any mention of him was always met by a complete silence and indifference. There was much speculation of course but nothing much ever came to light, even after Mum and Evy died. Rumours that he was a Lascar seaman arose some years later, but we could find no proof to verify this – so who he was or what he did will always remain a mystery. The only relevant bit of information that we managed to uncover was that he never married Grandma!

Maria died before I met her so, like my other grandparents; I never got to know her. By all accounts she was a very imposing woman, slim, with a dark complexion complemented by jet-black hair that reached down to her waist. Her overall appearance could have been best described as 'gypsy-like'. I gather that she doted on my mother and never missed an opportunity to encourage her in her passion for dancing. Her dressmaking skills also ensured that Mum was never without a new gown for any important dancing competitions, which she frequently entered and on many occasions won.

I would have loved to have seen Mum in her heyday – even though it isn't hard to imagine. I can see her now gliding round the dance-floor in all her glory, dipping and sliding as if to say 'Get a load of this, you lot! This is how it should be done!' She loved to show off – and why not: she was good and she knew it. No, Mum could never have been accused of lacking in confidence.

I'm pretty sure that she must have been quite young when she left Liverpool – a thriving place at that time – to pursue her destiny. She worked at a few jobs on leaving school, including as a cinema cashier and as an assistant teacher in an infant school. She also worked in a large grocery store for a while alongside a young girl who became a singing star of the '50s – Lita Rosa, who sang with the Ted Heath Orchestra.

It was probably around this time that Mum decided that she wasn't ready for a conventional life and somehow found her way into the world of show business. How and where, is another one of those questions that will always remain unanswered, but I do know she was working as half of a mind-reading act with a guy called Hassan when she met Dad, who was some sort of stage-manager. And I also know that Dad was going out with someone else at the time – he was even engaged. It was their mutual love of ballroom dancing that brought them together, I guess.

That unwavering passion for dancing remained with Mum for the rest of her life. It even shone through when she was bravely fighting her losing battle with cancer. Even though she was too ill to dance, she would still be there to teach, to advise and encourage her prodigies. My fondest memories are of her telling me in great detail the impact she made when given the privilege of 'leading off the dancing' at some important ball or other. Coming from any other person I'd have felt embarrassed by the unabashed conceit – but Mum didn't see it that way. In her eyes, displaying confidence in one's own ability amounted to professionalism in its truest sense.

The Liverpool connection
The first trip I ever made to see my relatives in Liverpool was a strange mixture of excitement and apprehension. I was about six years old and painfully shy. I loved the train journey despite the fact that I suffered terrible travel sickness. Someone had told Mum that barley sugar would help to quell the nausea but it didn't. All it did was make the vomit taste a bit sweeter. That was the only aspect of the journey I didn't enjoy. How I envied Dad and my brother: they could ride backwards and not even feel dizzy. But once I'd thrown up I enjoyed viewing the changing scenery through the carriage window without distraction.

No sooner had we left the familiar sights of Mirfield and Huddersfield than we were plunged into the long, dark, noisy confinement of the Standedge Tunnel. As the train burrowed deep into the Pennine Hills a light came on in the carriage, but the bulb was so dim that the light it gave off wasn't much better than the candles we used during the power cuts, so I snuggled up to Mum for safety. Acrid smoke seeped into the carriage, which in turn made me feel nauseous again. It was also very noisy: every now and then there was a loud clatter outside the carriage and I tensed in anticipation of some impending tragedy. Later I learned it was only the wheels passing over catch points, which were situated at intervals along the track. Then, after what seemed like an age, the train finally burst into the grey light of industrial Lancashire.

As we wove our way through the giant cotton mills and chimneys I found the view strangely exhilarating: gazing down on the grey slated rooftops, peering into people's back yards crammed with all kinds of paraphernalia. Zinc baths hung from walls, large iron mangles with fat wooden rollers straddling corrugated peggy-tubs, bedsteads, bicycles – the list was endless. Some of the streets were festooned with washing hanging out to dry. I remember seeing women carefully raising the washing line with props to let a horse and cart through – it probably belonged to a coal merchant. It was all very reminiscent of what went on round our way.

And at that moment I began to feel the first twinge of homesickness within me. This was closely followed by an awful feeling of insecurity that wouldn't go away. It didn't get any better, and by the time we reached Liverpool I was ready to go back home. Mum remonstrated with me for being 'maungy' and I sulked. I'd already made up my mind that I wasn't going to like Mum's hometown.

Lime Street station seemed huge and noisy. It was very busy, and the chatter around me sounded strangely alien. At first I found the Scouse lingo incomprehensible. It had a kind of sing-song quality that was so different to the flat Yorkshire voices I was used to. Something about the people seemed different too: I hadn't yet been acquainted with the word 'cosmopolitan'. And I was soon to see my very first black person. Not that I wasn't used to seeing men with black faces – when the hooter blew at our local colliery there were hundreds coming through the gates – but the man I saw standing on that street corner in Liverpool was no collier. I was peering out of the front window of a tram we were travelling in. 'Look, Mam – a black man!' I blurted out. As I turned round to face her I was horrified to see that there were two more seated directly behind us – but they smiled, and didn't seem to mind; unlike my mother, whose face sported that well-known expression of 'shown-up again', so frequently displayed by mothers of small children.

We stayed with mum's sister at 81 Eden Street in Toxteth, a terraced house typical of so many in the surrounding area. Although it was quite a large house it always seemed smaller because of the number of people living there.

Aunt Evy was small and very much like Mum in appearance, but that's where the similarity ended. Whereas Mum always liked to be centre-stage, Aunt Evy took a more practical view of life and just got on with things. She was married to Thomas Fearon, a wonderful man and a typical Liverpudlian. He was small and stocky and always seemed to have a smile on his face. Uncle Tommy worked for the Liverpool Corporation Cleansing Department, collecting refuse and wit! He was so full of fun. Aunt Evy had a wicked sense of humour too, and I always remember their home being filled with laughter.

Cousin Thomas (who was always called Tucker to avoid confusion) was born a few weeks before I was. Quiet and studious, he always seemed to have his nose buried in a book; in fact he was generally referred to as the bookworm – with affection, of course. My cousin Linda came along a couple of years later. Delicately petite and as pretty as a picture, she was occasionally mistaken for a Chinese child, giving rise to suspicions that there might be an Oriental gene in our family . . . Grandpa again? Although of a quiet disposition she wasn't lacking in confidence. She could dance and sing and, like the rest of the family, had the inevitable sense of humour.

Grandma Maria had married eventually – not my unknown grandfather, but a man quite a bit older than herself who everyone referred to as Pop. Their marriage produced four children – John, Alan, Eddie and Elsie. Tragically Grandma died of cancer while still in her forties, leaving Pop unable to cope. By this time Mum had flown the coop, so it was left to Aunt Evy, already bringing up her own family, to take in her half-brothers and half-sister too. This meant the house in Eden Street had its fair share of occupants – and by the time we reached there people were swinging from the rafters.

Being of a shy and sensitive nature, I found meeting my relatives for the first time a bit overwhelming. After all I wasn't used to this kind of thing. Back home families tended to live in close proximity – in many cases in the same house. It was all very natural to them but it was a new experience to me. Secretly I was glad, of course, for it meant that when I returned home I'd be able to talk about aunts, uncles and cousins with the same aplomb that my friends did.

Aunt Evy and Uncle Tommy did a great job of bringing up their extended family. It's mainly thanks to their efforts that I consider myself having the best relatives anyone could wish for. Uncle Eddie felt more like my cousin than my uncle, I suppose because he was more my age and we had lots in common. And despite him calling me 'Alin', I was full of admiration for him, especially for his ingenuity. Nothing was impossible in his book; he was just about the most practical person I'd ever met. He could fix or make just about anything.

Uncle Alan and Aunt Elsie, being older, seemed to be out most of the time, and Uncle John went to live in Durban, South Africa, after the war.

As you can imagine, 81 Eden Street was a hive of activity from dawn till dusk. The constant flow of energy generated around the household sometimes got a little too much for me, and sometimes I sought solitude in the front parlour. I liked to be left to my own devices sometimes, and on one occasion it was to bring about my undoing.

Liverpool at that time seemed to be a massive place to me. Mile upon mile of terraced houses went on for ever. Each street looked the same as the next, so it wasn't a good place to get lost in – but guess who did? Me! My brother decided to go to Sefton Park with Tucker, Linda and Uncle Eddie, but I wanted to be on my own and decided not to go with them. Later, though, I changed my mind and decided to follow, thinking I knew the way. So I slipped away without telling anyone. And as I've just said, one street looks the same as the next . . . Hours later I was discovered lost and bawling my head off by a group of local urchins in the district of Dingle – where the Beatle Ringo Starr came from (he might have been one of them, for all I know!). Having the reputation for being a bit dodgy, Dingle was not the choicest place to be lost in at the best of times. But to their credit, and my relief, the gang of kids escorted me to the local police station and handed me over to a large policeman – but not before one of the kids had admired the snake belt I was wearing. He even asked me if I wanted to swap it for something. God only knows what he intended trading, as his tatty trousers were held up by a piece of string. Though I was grateful to him I had to refuse, because it had been bought brand new at Whitsuntide. And it would have been more than my life was worth to part with it.

I considered myself lucky to come out of the escapade unscathed. The policeman gave me a cup of tea and a biscuit and made a few phone calls. The only information I could give him was Aunt Evy's name and that she lived near Isis Street – the only street name I could remember, for some reason. Eventually Uncle Tommy came to rescue me and take me back to my frantic mum.

So there it is – my pedigree. I'm proud of it, even though it's not what you'd call an imperial bloodline – unless my mysterious granddad was descended from Genghis Khan. Both Mother and Aunt Evy had darkish skin tones, and there is more than a hint of the Orient in the family makeup. It's a pity we never found out who he really was, for I'd love to learn more about him – even though he didn't fulfil his obligations. I think it's a safe bet that Grandma wasn't the only woman he dallied with, so it's highly probable that I have more distant relatives than I'm aware of. Just think of it, I might have unknowingly met some of them on my travels. They might even have sung one of the songs I've written – or even be reading this. Nevertheless, by recalling a few relevant facts and laying bare the family skeletons, I've become more aware of who I am, notwithstanding the fact that in doing so I've also come to realise that I'm a bit of a mongrel. But being a mongrel doesn't mean I've led a dog's life. Although my childhood was fraught with illness and misfortune, I still managed to glean a great deal of happiness from it.

Chapter Two
ROOTS

Mum and Dad settled in West Yorkshire after Mum fell out with her showbiz partner Hassan. They'd been working on a promotion tour of large northern departmental stores. It was quite common in those days for manufacturers to engage artistes to perform in large stores in order to draw a crowd. Then once they'd got their attention the sales team took over. It made it easier to sell their products.

Anyway, artistic differences or whatever, Mum and her co-artiste parted company in Dewsbury. She and Dad took lodgings with a good-natured lady called Mrs Watts in the suburb of Eastborough, and they took over the Majestic Ballroom in Dewsbury, which later became known as the Galleon – a notorious dance hall in the '50s. Everything seemed to be going well for them for a while. Business was good, so good that they were able to move out of their lodgings and rent a comfortable house in Tate Naylor Street next to St Joseph's Catholic Church. It was here that my brother Brian was born on Burns Night in 1939.

The outbreak of the Second World War soon began to change things. Young men were called up, sent away for training and deployed to other parts of the country. Things were put on ration, prices began to rise and people began to prepare for the inevitable hardships that lay ahead. Business began to suffer, and consequently the ballroom failed, taking with it a large slice of my parents' income. As a result the house in Tate Naylor Street was no longer affordable, forcing a move to something a little less sublime. This turned out to be a small terrace house in Batley Carr, a close-knit community nearby.

As the war began to gather momentum the government sent out a call for more recruits. Dad went along – more in hope than expectation I expect - for he was born with a sight defect, which he probably knew would disqualify him from joining the armed forces. Having had his fears confirmed, he looked for other ways to serve, and eventually found a position with the ARP. He was posted to London during the Blitz, and was right in the thick of it when the bombs and doodlebugs were raining down. He probably faced more danger then than some of the other lads who were called up and sent abroad.

I know he encountered many horrific sights during the Blitz, but he would only talk about the lighter side of events. Like the time he and his mate were patrolling the docks when an incendiary bomb hit a massive six-storey warehouse. 'The whole place went up like a volcano,' he recalled. 'The flames must have been reaching a hundred feet high.' So his mate went to ring the Fire Brigade. When he returned, Dad asked him what they'd said.

'We've to do what we can till they get here,' said his mate, surveying the towering inferno confronting them. He then handed Dad a small bucket of water and a stirrup pump, adding, with more than a hint of sarcasm, 'So there you are, Eddie. Do what you bloody can!'

Another time his mate was ordered to guard a standpipe situated in the middle of a road during the blackout. Having stood there all night without encountering a single vehicle, he left it for a moment to take a leak, and immediately a lorry came round the corner and knocked it over. This appealed to Dad's sense of humour.

Batley Carr
Batley Carr was a small, tight-knit community straddling the border between Batley and Dewsbury. I've been informed by a local historian that Carr is an Old Norse word for 'wasteland' or 'land that nobody wants'. And originally it was left to refugees or destitute and misplaced people to settle there; it was also a stopping-off point for gypsies and travellers. But over the years, despite its humble

beginnings, it began to grow and thrive. At the turn of the century Batley Carr boasted thirteen pubs, over a hundred shops, a large social club, two churches, umpteen chapels, three schools, a library, park, cinema and half a dozen large mills. All of these were squeezed into an area less than a mile long and half a mile wide.

Textile mills were the mainstay of the Batley Carr economy and provided work for most of the community. There were also a number of colliers living there, many of whom were recruited from the Barnsley area to work the old pit at Shaw Cross, where the Dewsbury rugby league stadium now stands. The Barnsley influx probably accounted for the Batley Carr accent being much broader than the one spoken in the surrounding area. When I'm in full flow people often think I'm from Barnsley!

But though the pit provided work for some, textiles were the main industry, in particular the manufacture of mungo and shoddy. There were also, of course, manufacturers of quality woollens and cloths, and Batley can lay claim to supplying the cloth for all the Japanese army uniforms during the First World War: they were on our side then!

Shoddy, being cheap, was in demand. The raw material used in the making of shoddy was something the locals had in abundance – rags. So when we weren't wearing 'em we were selling 'em . . . which accounted for a feature that could be found in every neighbourhood – the rag warehouse. In those days bales of rags were brought from all over the country, many of them being dropped off at the local warehouse to be sorted before going on to the mills. So from time to time the warehouses had stacks of bales outside of them, which acted like magnets to the kids, who swarmed over them like bees. A mountain of bales was ideal for a game of King of the Castle, while oily bales set at an angle were great for sliding down; we always dragged a soft bale out to land on. We had to make the best of them while they were there, for the bales disappeared into the warehouse one by one, until eventually our adventure playground had gone. Sorters in the warehouse selected what was useful, and the rest was sent to a mill to be ground up, mixed with a fibre and spun into shoddy.

Another regular feature of the neighbourhood was the rag tatter. Tatters pushed carts, or in some cases old prams, around the streets, wailing 'Any old rags'. And people gave him rags in exchange for a few pence – or whatever he had to offer. Sometimes it was just a balloon for the kids or a goldfish – some of which lasted as long as three days! The 'better off' tatters had carts pulled by ponies: I remember one that was festooned with toy windmills, propellers on sticks that spun in the wind. 'How much are they?' the kids were asking.

'Ask your mammy for a few old rags and you can 'ave one,' was the reply. Then he sat back and let the kids do the rest. No wonder he could afford a pony and cart!

Horse and cart delivered most things in those days – even the milk. Our bell-ringing milkman arrived in a pony and trap complete with ladle and churn, and people carried jugs out or other containers to put the milk in: there were no milk bottles then.

Rington's delivered their tea in distinctive green and black vans drawn by horses, and a huge Shire pulled the big co-operative society wagon. It needed to be a Shire horse because the society wagon was laden with just about everything. It was virtually an emporium on the move, in essence the forerunner of the mobile shop. The teamster (the driver) didn't even have to shout or ring a bell to announce his arrival; the clatter of the hardware saw to that. Pots hit pans, crockery clinked together, and scrubbing boards clattered against the great zinc baths that hung from hooks at the back of the wagon. Yes, I can still remember the steady 'clip, clop, rattle, clank' sound it made as it rumbled down the street. Mum would send me out to buy pegs or black-lead for the fireplace when it stopped at the top of the yard.

Sometimes the old stallion unashamedly had a pee in front of all the customers – a sight that always made children giggle and men feel inadequate. If it did a 'number two' someone would fetch a bucket and shovel to retrieve it for use on the allotment later. You know the old joke:

'What does he want that for, Ma?'
'To put on his rhubarb.'
'Don't they have any custard in their house?'

Some of the horses were real characters too. My own favourite was Mickey, a big gentle dapple-grey Shire who worked for the railway. Mickey loved kids and whenever we fed him a sweet or a carrot he would scoop it gently from our hands with his huge lips. He always showed his approval by rattling his martingale as he happily chomped away. Every time he came into the street he stopped at the top of our yard, and if we didn't go out to him straight away he'd stomp his massive hoof impatiently. Once, when we were all late back from school, his handler left him nearby for a moment to deliver a parcel. He returned to find that Mickey had disappeared into our yard to look for his carrot. Not only that, he'd dragged his load in with him. Just how he managed to get the huge wagon through the small opening remains a mystery, but he did, and it took ages to manoeuvre him and his cart back into the street again. God bless you, Mickey, for such great memories.

I suppose hanging onto memories will always be associated with the older generation. But my generation was brought up to hanging onto everything anyway. It stemmed from making what little we had go a little further. We threw nothing away. The buzz-phrase in most households was 'It might come in useful later'. Recycling became second nature to us. Newspapers, wood, bottles, jam jars, tin cans: nearly everything was saved. Just about the only thing found in dustbins was dust, from the coal fire. This made the emptying of bins very dusty – hence the name dustbin man, I suppose. Everything had its uses. Take jam jars, for instance: we used to keep frogspawn and wild flowers in them. Then, when they became scarce, a deposit was placed on them and they became worth a few pence as a consequence. There was even a period when they could be used to buy entrance into the local cinema. Two half-pound jars could get you in to see a cowboy film; two one-pound jars could mean you watched it from a seat in the balcony! Sponsorship is nothing new . . . I like to think those films were brought to us courtesy of the Moorhouse Jam Company, Leeds.

Collins Cinema
Our local cinema stood near the bottom of Victoria Street. It towered over the rest of the buildings and was similar in style to many other theatres and cinemas throughout the north. The neat red brickwork was complemented at different intervals by lines of white-tiled bricks. And at the very top, underneath a crescent of imitation marble, the words 'Collins Cinema Companion' sat on a background of green tiles. Just beneath this was a row of small windows belonging to the projection room. These were usually kept open, and sometimes the booming soundtrack could be heard in the sweet shop opposite.

The entrance to Collins spanned at least half the front of the cinema. Wide stone steps led into a semicircular foyer, which funnelled patrons towards the central pay box. Everything here was tiled in green and white and the mosaic floor echoed every footstep. It was great for sliding on, but could be a bit hard on the eardrums if a large family turned up wearing clogs. I suspect the whole thing was an attempt by some obscure architect to put together a mock icon of a Middle-Eastern palace – a shining jewel set against the mundane backdrop of northern enterprise. Perhaps the Art Nouveau design was groundbreaking, but snotty-nosed kids called it the Bug Hut! OK, so it might have lacked the sumptuous facilities of the Leeds Odeon or the Playhouse in Dewsbury, but it did have a certain *'je ne sais quoi'*, which roughly translated into 'Batley Carr French' meant it was convenient and cheap. And the Odeon didn't accept jam jars.

Most of us kids looked forward to the Saturday afternoon matinées. Quarter to twelve and the scene outside Collins was like the gathering of the clans. They came from far and wide, pushing and shoving their way into the foyer to be first in the queue as the poor usherette tried to marshal them into orderly queues around the pay box. The excitement was exhilarating. Some of the younger kids were so impatient to get in they'd jump up and down in anticipation and wet their knickers – or trousers – in the process. At times it resembled a scene from the Black Hole of Calcutta. And the smell wasn't much better either: what a pong! It was a smell I always associate with the late 1940s – pee and stale biscuits tinged with the sweat. And as the temperature rose it got worse: on occasion a stray fart was as welcoming as a whiff of lavender. But what did it matter? A bit of pushing and shoving and a few nasty smells wasn't much of a price to pay – not when there were dreams to be fulfilled!

Because that's what was on offer: dreams. To us kids Collins was the magic portal into a world that could take us to places beyond our wildest imagination. That journey started the moment the house lights dimmed and a surge of anticipation and excitement filled the darkening auditorium. Row upon row of shining eyes was riveted to the screen as the projector flickered into life. A great burst of colour, a much-imitated laugh and Woody Woodpecker filled the screen to set the audience cheering. What a great start! Soon we were rolling with laughter at the slapstick humour of the Three Stooges or, my own particular favourites, Laurel and Hardy. Later we might fly to Mars with Flash Gordon, in a rocket ship that looked to be powered by sparklers, or marvel at the super-human powers of Superman. Batman was a big favourite too, as were Zorro and Sinbad, the swashbuckling sailor. Roy Rogers headed a long list of cowboys who fired guns that never needed re-loading. He was so tough that he could keep his hat on all through a fight – and then he'd go and spoil things by singing some soppy love song to a girl!

It was all great fun – and great value: two and a half hours of make-believe, and what did it cost? A jam jar!

But much as I enjoyed the Saturday madness, I preferred to go to the pictures in the evening, when there was usually a much wider variety of films on offer. I loved the Warner Brothers' gangster films and the lavish Goldwyn musicals. I drooled over the Hollywood beauties peeling grapes and eating mouth-watering chicken in swashbuckling spectaculars. Even at that early age, it was difficult to work out whether I was drooling over Betty Grable or the chicken – but as food rationing was still in force it was probably the chicken. Shame on you, Hollywood, for screening mouth-watering banquets when all we could afford was jam and bread for tea!

Shame on the Bickler family who owned the cinema too. They always seemed to turn the heating up and send the ice cream lady down the aisle when Gary Cooper and his French Legionnaires were sweltering in the Sahara desert. I mean, that's not playing the game is it? Not only were we parched, we were usually skint as well. Did they think we were made of jam jars?

But, as I said before, it was cheap and very handy. Well, handy for me anyway – I only lived in the yard across the road and could run home in eight seconds. In fact I once did it in four. I'd been to see Lon Chaney in *The Wolfman*. Gripping? Trouser-filling more like -- and it was so dark when I came out . . . there was also a full moon.

Early memories
Unlike my brother, who was born in Dewsbury, I was born on the other side of the track in Batley. Our house was one end of a row of four stone-built cottages. There was a sign on the wall that said Woolhill Cottages but we never used this in the address, which was 7 Victoria Street, Batley Carr, Batley . . . which I had to learn off by heart in case I got lost. (It cut no ice in Liverpool.) We only had two rooms (one up, one down) plus a cellar, so it could hardly be described as commodious. But it was all I knew, and it was my home for the first eleven years of my life. The downstairs room was small, but somehow we managed to squeeze in a three-piece suite, a

sideboard, a table, four chairs and a piano. Upstairs there were two double beds, a wardrobe, a chest of drawers and a dressing table. There wasn't a toilet in the house. Come to think of it, there wasn't one within fifty yards- and that froze up in winter! How we managed I'll never know, but we did.

Living conditions were primitive to say the least. Space and privacy were at a premium and the amenities were poor, but at least we had electricity. Many of the surrounding houses still had to rely on the old Victorian gas mantles to light their homes. Though groundbreaking in their day, they were considered by many to be dangerous in confined quarters. Their sole redeeming quality, as far as I was concerned, was that they were immune to power cuts. Like many others, when I was very young the darkness frightened me. Being a creative person I've always been blessed with a vivid imagination, and it often went into overdrive when the electricity meter ran out. A little click behind the cellar door was the signal for the room to be suddenly plunged into darkness, with the flickering fire sending sinister shadows dancing around the room. These liberated demons always disturbed me, and I'd sit with my eyes tightly shut, clutching anyone or anything near me, until the meter was replenished and the demons were dispersed. I hated power cuts.

Some of my earliest recollections may be slightly incoherent, but many are still very clear in my mind. One of the first things I remember is sitting outside the house one evening in a small wooden chair, looking at the stars above the brick air-raid shelter that stood in front of the house. Lights moved across the sky as aeroplanes droned overhead and I was fascinated by the noise they made. Even today the picture remains very clear in my memory. I must have been very young because I was dressed in a siren suit – a one-piece suit with a hood, so named because if bombing was imminent and the siren sounded a youngster or infant could be placed in it zipped up and carried to the safety of the shelter in seconds.

I was usually wrapped up anyway, because I was always a poorly baby – prone to just about every illness on offer. On top of the obligatory whooping cough, measles and chickenpox I had double pneumonia twice – which caused great concern. One time Mum, Dad and a nurse had to sit up all night with me. It was touch and go for a while and I nearly popped my clogs, but I pulled through.

Health care cost in those days: it was sixpence for a visit from the doctor. For treatments of basic illnesses people relied on

Me and my older brother Brian (left).

traditional remedies. I still can't come to terms with the notion that a sweaty sock filled with raw onion tied round your neck cures a sore throat. The only merit I can see in it is the probable isolation of the wearer – thus reducing the possibility of the ailment being passed on! The wide range of remedies for afflictions came from the unlikeliest sources sometimes. Even the local authorities helped to cure children unwittingly, by choosing to tarmac the roads when there was an outbreak of whooping cough: many of the older generation were convinced that the fumes from hot tar did you good. Being held over a smouldering tar barrel, along with other blighted kids, having your lungs opened up by the pungent fumes, frightened me to death.

On reflection it's a wonder some of the 'cures' didn't kill us. Cod Liver Oil, Fenning's Fever Cure and Indian Brandy tasted awful – straight from the Lucretia Borgia book of homeopathic medicines. Not to mention Cooling Powders, which tasted – and looked like – someone had taken a scraping from a plaster cast. Then there was the horrible thick yellow stuff called Emulsion: it looked a bit like paint but that's where the similarity ended, for it tasted far worse. And if you had a bad chest cold you could look forward to having your upper torso smeared in goose grease. The pong was unbearable. How could you hope to make any friends smelling like that? Even worse was having a bad chest *and* a sore throat. Can you imagine reeking of dead goose and sweaty feet soaked in onions? Pharmacy? More like farmyard.

Being a poorly kid, I was subjected to these eccentric concoctions most of the time – but I suppose I shouldn't complain: I lived to tell the tale. Maybe there was some substance to all those remedies after all. But while I'm not qualified to argue about their merits, there's one 'cure' I'll never come to terms with, not in a million years. It's the idea that brown paper wrapped around your ribcage prevents travel sickness. Motion sickness was the bane of my youth, a source of great misery. 'Don't despair' was always the cry. 'Brown paper will cure you!' Really? Could this be true? Who came up with the idea of brown paper? Why not white? Oh no, you'll honk all over the place with white. The only explanation I can think of is that a brown paper manufacturer dreamed it up when business was bad. Anyway, during my early years I was trussed up in it so many times that I should have been called Russell. Needless to say it never worked. Throwing up became second nature to me. I threw up in cars, buses, boats, trains – anything that moved. I even got seasick sitting in the cinema when I was watching a film about deep-sea fishing. The camera, aboard a trawler, was going up and down and up and down. I only saw fifteen minutes of the film and spent the rest of the evening lying on the settee at home green to the gills. But, God knows why, I kept faith with the brown paper. (My friend George's Uncle Frank told me that soldiers even wrapped themselves in it when they got posted. Do you think he was kidding me?)

Regardless of the occasional setbacks on the health front, everything seemed to be so uncomplicated then. People took nothing for granted and simply got on with life. Hardship seemed to be the norm, but it was comforting to know that no one had to face it alone. Adversity brought out the best in most people, especially round our way. And it wasn't uncommon for people to share what they had so that someone wouldn't have to go without, especially when children were involved. Although coal was rationed, it was common practice to give a bucketful from each household to a family with an ailing child, so that he or she could be kept warm. Or if the woman of a household was taken ill, the neighbours saw to it that her husband had a meal to come home to. And her children would be looked after until she was right again. People were very good like that: they looked out for one another. Great value was placed on community life – and this didn't only apply to times of crisis.

Parents often joined in with games in the street. It wasn't unusual to see a grown up mother of three re-living her youth by whipping a top up and down the causeway, or a couple of barrel-chested dads twirling a washing line so that the young ones could skip. And sometimes, usually in summer when the weather was good, the whole neighbourhood went on a picnic together. Each family took sandwiches, some water to drink and a bat and ball for recreation. I loved those communal picnics. They were spontaneous events and always a joy. We didn't have very far to go either, for we had a smashing little park in Batley Carr. Alternatively we could trek to Soothill and sit among the ruins of Howley Hall – conveniently flattened for us by Cromwell's army during the Civil War. It was a cheap day out. Other times we ventured a little further, catching the bus to Thornhill and walking down towards Horbury Bridge to Coxley Valley. I loved Coxley Valley. It was worth being sick on the bus. There was something magical about the area that was hard to define. Maybe it reminded me of the kind of place Enid Blyton –

whose books I read avidly – often featured in her 'Famous Five' stories. . . 'A secret valley teeming with wildlife and flowers. Dappled pathways followed the winding stream beneath the whispering trees . . .' It was so atmospheric. On a warm summer's day there was no finer place on earth to be. Everyone gathered in the meadow by the stream, laughing and talking and munching on sandwiches. In contrast to the 'lashings of ginger beer' quaffed by the Famous Five, bottles of water were placed in the stream to cool. And when they were removed, icy cold, and passed around to slake our thirst, they were better than champagne.

I also loved going to Wilton Park in Batley. It was one of the most popular places for miles around, and some Sundays, during the summer, it felt as if the whole world was there. Apart from the magnificent floral features and gardens, there were well-manicured bowling greens, putting greens and tennis courts to enjoy. But the main focal point was the large boating lake overlooked by the park café, which served cream teas on the terrace. Much as we would have liked to, we didn't bother with the rowing boats, because what little money we had usually got spent before we got into the park. The reason why lay in wait at the park gates – ice cream barrows. Standing in a row, each one sported the name of a dairy in brightly coloured letters: Spivey's, Providence and Crossley's, and the one considered by the majority of people to be the best of all: Caddy's. The ice cream was kept in a large round metal tub surrounded by ice in the centre of the wooden barrow. It spun in the melting ice when the man scooped up the ice cream with his wooden spatula. My mouth would be watering with anticipation as he pasted it onto the wafer cone. Such luxuries were few and far between, so I tried to make it last as long as possible. I always bit the bottom off the cone and sucked the ice cream through instead of licking it. After that we usually made for the swings, slides and roundabouts, which were always crowded. The paddling pool was popular too, but even on the hottest summer day it was freezing.

My favourite places in the park were the bandstands. I can remember two: one was near the park café overlooking the lake; the other was situated among the trees, half-way up the rhododendron-lined pathway that led to the park museum. It's more than likely that my great love of brass band music stems from the times I spent lying on the grass listening to the concerts in Batley Park.

The seasons of the year seemed to be more defined in those

days. Maybe it's my imagination, but for some reason those summers seemed to go on forever. Perhaps that's why they're still so firmly implanted in my memory and remain such a joy to recall.

The pace of life was much slower then – and why not? We weren't going anywhere in particular, and if we did we had all the time in the world to get there. We were just happy to be where we were and enjoyed what we had. The work ethic was taken seriously too. A hard day's work literally meant just that. After grafting all day at the mill some of the men popped into the Carr Hotel or the Junction Inn for the odd 'gill', to unwind after tea. Sometimes their wives joined them too, especially if they'd also been working, but only after first making sure that someone kept an eye on the kids if they were playing out. Usually it was Grandma Lees. She regularly sat on her doorstep at the top of the yard watching the kids play hide and seek, squat can and rally-o in the street. Most folk sat out on their doorsteps, drinking tea and chatting to each other. It was a common sight during the summer. Quite often, when I didn't want to join in any of the games, I sat next to my mother on the step, listening to the neighbours talking and laughing long into the evening. Those warm summer evenings were so atmospheric. The extended daylight also meant that I could stay up later than usual, which pleased me no end – for the bedroom was usually so warm that it was impossible to go to sleep anyway. Eventually dusk would fall and there was a brief moment of silence. The earth seemed to sigh in anticipation of the approaching darkness. It was a signal that my staying up time was about to end and I was about to be packed off to bed, protesting, 'It's not dark yet, Mam. But I'm not tired, Mam! Can't I just stay up a bit longer?' But this always fell on deaf ears and I had to be content to listen to the chatter through the open bedroom window until I eventually fell asleep. You know, it's a great comfort to me that these memories still evoke that same indefinable feeling of inward ecstasy that I used to think was exclusive to the young. Call me sentimental, but some memories are not for letting go of.

It was during one of these long summers that I taught myself to swim. The gang went to Dewsbury baths one day and, being a non-swimmer, I was alone in the shallow end. I remember being pleased with myself for ducking my head under the water and opening my eyes. The result was amazing! I had overcome my fear of going under water. For the next five minutes I bobbed up and down in the water, peering at legs of all descriptions gyrating and kicking in the strange green environment. After a while I thought, Water's not really *that* frightening – and it's only three feet deep. Oh what the heck.' Then I lay on my stomach on the pool bottom, and straight away I floated to the surface. I kicked my feet and away I went. It was as simple as that!

Apart from swimming, cricket was our other main activity during the summer holidays. Every other wall in the neighbourhood had some wickets chalked upon it. Batting creases were sometimes marked out by a line of dried white dog shit, squashed into the ground by the toe of a shoe. There was always plenty on hand too. (That wasn't meant to be a pun.) Whatever happened to white dog shit?

The national game quickly regained popularity with the masses after the war. Test matches were broadcast regularly, and the unmistakable voice of John Arlott could be heard drifting out of many an open window. I loved to hear him talk. He had a voice that brought to life names like Bradman, Stollmeyer, Bedser and Lindwall. You felt that you knew places like Lords and the Oval without even going there.

Our yard was well accustomed to the sound of bat on ball, and occasionally the shatter of a window. The cry of 'Pay for your own china' usually preceded a ball whistling towards a window. It distanced everybody from what was about to happen, and placed full responsibility on the poor unfortunate batting at the time.

Anyone passing by could join in the game and often did. The mainstay of all our sporting events usually arrived uninvited. The fastest runner, the best fielder, the noisiest and most enthusiastic of us all was also the smallest – and the hairiest. He was Laddie – Grandma Lees's dog. At the first sound of a bouncing ball her door would open and out he'd trot, ears pricked, ready for action like a gladiator entering the arena. His eyes would home in on the ball and remain riveted to it throughout the bowler's run up and delivery. He was a cricket coach's dream. And once the ball had been struck he was the first off the mark. Even if he was beaten to it his discipline remained intact. Those eyes never left the ball as it made its way back to the bowler. He knew from experience that he'd get his chance to field the ball – and he wasn't going to let any opportunity pass him by. It usually came when the ball was hit long and we were all too idle to run after it. 'Fetch it, boy!' was the cry. But Laddie didn't need prompting – he'd already be on his way. The streak of black and white lightning was in pursuit as soon as the ball left the bat. It was nice to have your legs saved, but like everything else in life there was a price to pay: getting the ball back. Laddie always felt that he was entitled to have a good chew before returning it, so it was usually soggy and dripping with dog saliva by the time we got it back, which didn't go down too well with the bowler – or the fielders for that matter. It's amazing how many dolly catches were missed when the ball was soggy. Batsmen didn't escape being 'gunged' either. Now and again Laddie spit splattered them if they played a backward defensive stroke to a fast ball: those sponge balls could hold gallons of the stuff! Even tennis balls could assimilate a fair amount of 'Laddie-gob', and they usually got punctured too. Despite all this sogginess, Laddie was a great dog – everybody loved him. And although our furry friend wasn't aware of it, his name was entered into the annals of cricket history. When we emulated our cricketing heroes by playing 'test matches' in the yard, my brother kept a scorecard. I can remember one entry that read 'BRADMAN caught LADDIE bowled WARDLE 2'.

Although Laddie was Grandma Lees's dog, us kids felt he belonged to us as well. In truth he was our unofficial minder. Being a crossbred border collie he retained those sheepdog instincts, which always came into action whenever a car or lorry came into the street. If children were playing in the road he barked and shepherded them to the pavement until the danger had passed. Only then did he return to lie in a sunny spot, maintaining a watchful eye over his flock. Laddie loved being part of the gang and we wouldn't – nay, couldn't – set off anywhere without him. As he was with us our parents never feared for our safety. As we grew older and became more independent, so Laddie was adopted by the next generation. Obviously he became less active as the years went by, but he never forgot any of us. The last time I saw him he was in his basket at Grandma Lees's house. He was so old he could hardly see, and it was an effort for him to move. But when I made a fuss of him he recognised my voice and wagged his tail as he gently licked my hand. I make no apologies for admitting to crying buckets when I heard that he died not long afterwards. He was a true friend, and I'm sure we'll meet again some day. Unlike some people, I believe that animals have a soul.

Chumps and fog and Worfolk's

After a good summer the main topic of conversation in the neighbourhood was usually about the winter that was about to follow. The older ones knew from experience that all good things came at a price, and a hard winter always followed an excellent summer. For much of the time autumn was an interim of much speculation and anticipation, a time for exercising a little prudence too. The nipping winds and shortening daylight hours served as a stark reminder of what was to come. Consequently many people viewed autumn with a certain amount of apprehension – but not me.

I was born in early autumn, probably on one of those bright crisp sunny September mornings I so love, which meant that I had a birthday present to look forward to. But for the majority of people it was a time for drawing in the reins. It was a good time to put a few bob aside for Christmas, and to stock up on winter fuel. Although coal was on ration, so-called duck eggs and briquettes (made by compressing coal dust into oval and square moulds) occasionally became available. It was a common sight to see a convoy of carts and old prams winding its way up Jack Lane heading for the pit at Shaw Cross to get some. I can still remember to this day George's Uncle Frank pushing a great pram-load, singing, 'Don't throw briquettes at me,' parodying the refrain 'Don't throw bouquets at me' in the musical *Oklahoma.*

Briquettes were slow burning and cheap, which made them very popular, but they were not very environmentally friendly. They polluted the atmosphere and contributed greatly to another bane of my early years – smog. I was quite happy to go out in those choking November fogs, but the pneumonia I'd suffered as a baby took its toll. Sometimes breathing was difficult and I was blighted by coughs and chest infections, which prompted the return of the dreaded goose grease smeared all over my upper torso. But, as the saying goes, you can't keep a good man down – especially during the run up to Bonfire Night. After I'd donned my balaclava helmet and wrapped a scarf around my mouth, I'd be away with the lads collecting old wood, branches, boxes, and paper – anything that could go towards making a bonfire. 'Chumping', as we called it (I don't know what it was called in other parts of the country), was one of the highlights of our year. In no time we'd gather together masses of branches and sometimes, if we were lucky, a few broken wicker baskets from the mill. These were always very oily and perfect for starting the bonfire. Often there was an old mattress or two or bits of old furniture that somebody had discarded, all piled high in the yard. As it was very choice tinder, extreme vigilance was needed to ensure that it stayed there, because gangs from other streets were inclined to come raiding at night and nick 'em. So we fashioned a den in the middle of it all, lit by a candle in a jam jar. There we sat until bedtime, guarding our chumps, ready to spring out and repel any raiders. The whole proceedings were conducted in military fashion, with patrols sent out to spy on other gangs and warn of impending raids. Sometimes we even went raiding ourselves, leaving a token guard in the den. It was like an ongoing mini-drama played out with a series of 'Who goes there?' 'Friend or Foe?' and the usual secret passwords. It was a load of fun.

Chumping apart, there was still the business of the fireworks fund to attend to. The token box we received from our folks usually lacked bangers, but a couple of weeks of Penny-for-the-Guying took care of that.

You know, I've always had a soft spot for old Guy Fawkes. If he hadn't been caught trying to blow Parliament to bits we'd all have been deprived of bonfires – not to mention bangers. Given the politicians we have to put up with nowadays, had he succeeded he could have done us all a big favour!

Bonfire Night was quite an occasion round our way. Everyone, bar the animals, looked forward to it. The men pitched in and built the bonfire in the centre of the yard, while the women busied themselves preparing food. The menu was mouth-watering – pie and peas, parkin, toffee apples and baked potatoes. Come six o'clock, and the evening sky in Batley Carr was tinged by the glow of several bonfires. A rocket would fizz over the rooftops coming from the direction of King Street as the distant crack of exploding thunderflashes, pom-pom cannons and little demons in High Street and Albert Street gathered momentum. For a laugh, one of our lads would set a jumping cracker off among the gathering and scare the little ones. Hastily a bag of sweeties would be dispatched to pacify the wailing youngsters, and a cuff round the ear was delivered to the culprit. Amid the commotion a wise head would see fit to light a multi-coloured firework and calm would be restored once more. Passers by stopped for a chat or to admire the fireworks and the kids got stuck into the pie and peas and stuff; and before long the party was in full swing. When the fire was nicely bedded in some of the men nipped to the pub for a swift pint. After all, it's thirsty work being a stoker!

Not only were occasions like these a source of great enjoyment, they were part of what held our little community together. And they were a great learning process for us younger ones. The foundations for self-preservation, discipline and respect for others – especially one's elders – all stemmed from the example set by wonderful people, whose efforts and experience are sadly viewed today as outdated and insignificant.

The days after Bonfire Night always seemed uninteresting. Efforts were made to keep some kind of momentum going by rekindling the fire to roast a few leftover potatoes, but by and large everything went flat. Christmas was a long way off, and the choking fogs that usually followed bonfire nights made outdoor activities arduous – apart from playing hide and seek! The only good thing was that if the fog was really bad I was kept off school. But once this novelty had worn off I was itching to be up and about again, even though there wasn't much to do.

Unlike today (when celebrations start in September) we never saw so much as a sprig of holly until a fortnight before Christmas. Many saw this as a time for reflection. Poppies appeared on lapels during the run up to Remembrance Sunday, and memories of the war were foremost in the thoughts of those who had lost friends and loved ones. Bonfire Night apart, November was my least favourite month, which is probably why God sent me my greatest gift of all to make up for it: Mandy was born on 17 November.

Fortunately the fog and gloom didn't last for ever, and soon our thoughts turned towards Christmas. Mum sometimes took me shopping with her to Dewsbury. It was only half a mile away, but we still had to get off the bus one stop early so I wouldn't be sick (I really was a terrible traveller). As the nausea began to subside I'd plead with Mum to buy me a Caddy's ice cream to settle my stomach. There was an ulterior motive behind this . . . To get to Caddy's ice cream parlour we had to pass Worfolk's toyshop, which gave me an excellent opportunity to drag Mum in and drop hints about what I wanted Santa to bring me for Christmas. I'd already written letters to him – but a little extra insurance wouldn't go amiss, would it? When I think of the letters I wrote and stuck up the chimney . . . in my best handwriting on Basildon Bond scrounged from my mother's writing pad, hoping to impress. I always wrote early, to give me a chance if it was first come first served. He never wrote back, of course: Mum said he was too busy. Sometimes I wondered if he ever received my letters, for a few weeks after I wrote I'd be sitting on his knee in J & Bs (a small departmental store in Dewsbury) and he'd say, 'And what do you want me to bring you for Christmas?' And I'd think, What's the matter with you? Didn't you even read my letter? The nerve of the man. So, once again, I'd remind him that I wanted a train set. After the usual 'Be a good boy and we'll see what we can do', I'd be mollified with a present from his helper – usually a young female junior from haberdashery – and would wish him 'Merry Christmas'. When I was outside I'd open the present, and find it was something they'd probably overbought the previous year. Still, it was better than nowt!

Throughout autumn the keyword was thrift. There may have been a few shillings to spare for a few fireworks for Bonfire Night, but usually money was only spent on essentials. Apart from birthdays, Christmas was the only time we could look forward to presents. There was little to choose from just after the war, so we were grateful for anything. And we were never disappointed. Mum and Dad always did us proud, which was more than could be said for some of the other kids. Some got very little and the occasional poor child got nothing at all. Things were so scarce that a battered old Dinky car, minus its tyres, was worth its weight in gold to anyone lucky enough to possess one. I wonder if a child of today would cherish an out of date video game with the same ardour as we did an old wooden bagatelle. Somehow I doubt it.

Come the first snow, everyone would be busy making new sledges or doing up the previous year's. Overnight the streets became war zones, where anything that moved was a target for a snowball. It was hell for the intimidated, especially during the winter of 1947 when the snow seemed to be around for ever. It gave the oppressors an endless supply of ammunition, and the oppressed perpetual torment! But the sledging was great that year, and there were still traces of an igloo we built weeks after the snow had gone.

It was great fun for us kids, but it came with a cost. The poor and frail suffered from these severe weather conditions. Coal was rationed and there was only so much to go round. And if you came off worst in a snowball fight, squelching home with your wellies full of water wasn't exactly exhilarating. Some nights were so cold that we went to bed wearing more clothes than we wore during the day.

Blankets on the bed were supplemented by a greatcoat if available, or an oven plate wrapped in a towel was placed in the bed to keep our feet warm. Biting frosts froze water pipes, rendering the taps and outside toilets useless. How we got round that problem I can't imagine. Perhaps it's just as well.

I don't remember much else about that particular year, perhaps because the winter seemed to take up so much of it. Indeed, if the custom of town twinning had been fashionable then Spitzbergen, or any other place within the Arctic Circle, would have been the obvious choice for us.

Yes, winter seemed OK at first – but it soon outstayed its welcome. Springtime was always my favourite season. It was so nice to get out of bed without shivering. The warm sunshine seemed to awaken a sense of adventure inside me. Outside the world seemed to come to life in the same way that we did after a long sleep – yawning, stretching and refreshed. This was the best time to go exploring. Going off in search of new horizons with my best friend George was always a source of great excitement. Eager to see what Mother Nature had on offer, we collected and examined her bounty with the same commitment as Darwin in his prime. The jam jars of frogspawn and bluebells triumphantly displayed on our windowsills bore testament to the success of our expeditions. Pond life always came under intense scrutiny, and the pond in Annie Webb's field was great for finding specimens. Bugs and creatures were carted about in tins and matchboxes, shown off to pals or used to frighten the girls.

Spring was a wonderful time to develop the imagination. A field became an American prairie patrolled by warring Indians, a copse a jungle in darkest Africa – to be entered at your own peril. Today, of course, parents are increasingly fearful about letting their children wander off unaccompanied, and getting close to nature is therefore discouraged. I'm so grateful I had that freedom. There was so much happening in spring that it was difficult to take it all in.

And so to church
Despite the lack of money, ethical behaviour, like simple toys, was highly valued. And though want and deprivation were widespread, theft was never considered to be an option by the majority of people. They were God-fearing, and usually attended church or chapel each Sunday to hear the 'good word'.

Being a Catholic I attended mass, which in those days was

conducted in Latin. Responding in a foreign tongue was like being able to speak a foreign language; the only trouble was that I didn't know what I was saying half the time. Nevertheless I enjoyed it. It was only when the service changed to English for the long dreary sermons that I tended to switch off. Learning to doze with my eyes open took a lot of practice. After all, the message was always the same: 'Fear God, and don't forget to fill the collection plate.'

When I was old enough to become an altar boy, things became more interesting. Looking suitably pious in a cassock and surplice, I took part in the services by ringing bells, moving great tomes, serving wine and acting as a gopher for the priests. I must have applied myself well, as I was selected to take charge of the thurible (the incense burner) when the bishop came to conduct the old canon's funeral. 'Whatever you do, don't let it go out,' the young curate stressed as he placed the smouldering charcoal into the censer before the requiem mass.

'I won't, Father,' I replied confidently.

Anyway, the service really dragged on as accolades to the old canon poured forth. My knees started to go numb as I knelt at the altar swinging the burner back and forth. Then panic set in as I noticed the puff of smoke getting smaller each time the censer came into view. I didn't think it would be prudent to leave the altar while the bishop was in full flow so I remained where I was and prayed. By the time His Grace came to use the thurible there was barely a spark in sight. One of the senior altar boys was dispatched to the sacristy to fetch some more charcoal. As the bishop waited, drumming his fingers together, the rest of the clergy looked nervously at each other and then at me. I looked towards the heavens – for divine help. Eventually we got the censer smoking again, and the bishop smiled at me reassuringly. Maybe among all the pomp and ceremony I served to remind him that some of us were, after all, only human.

I enjoyed my time as an altar boy. It made me feel important, while earning me a few brownie points with God at the same time. During the long sermons I sat in the sanctuary and viewed the congregation head-on, giving me ample opportunity to pursue another great pastime – people watching. Before long I had them all sussed out – well, nearly all. Some of those who considered themselves most holy turned out to be complete rat-bags; but most of them were OK.

Like the people, the mood of the church changed with the

seasons. Autumn and winter were approached with great solemnity, apart from Christmas, which had an atmosphere all of its own. In contrast spring and summer, which embraced the great festivals of Easter and Whitsuntide, were always very upbeat and exhilarating. The church was scented with masses of flowers, and there was always a buzz about the place.

Whitsuntide was considered by the Church to be a time of great significance. It was viewed as a celebration during which we reflected on every aspect of our spiritual renewal, but to us kids it meant renewal of a different kind. It was the only time we got kitted out with new clothes. The custom was that we showed off our Whitsuntide clothes to relatives and friends, for which we received a few token pence. Some kids saw this as a lucrative business opportunity, and I recall one lad showing his new clothes to just about every household in Batley Carr! If he wasn't a millionaire then he probably is by now. So on Whit Sunday the streets resounded to the squeak of new shoes shuffling back and forth as the children of Batley Carr went on parade.

Many of the churches and chapels held Whit walks. These colourful events were an opportunity for churchgoers to affirm their faith and celebrate the confirmation of their children into Christianity by walking in procession through the streets of Batley Carr and beyond. They were usually headed by a brass band – the sound of which prompted many to come out to line the streets. The band was usually followed by, in our case, men and women of societies within the church, like the Knights of St Columba, the Union of Catholic Mothers and the Children of Mary. Some carried elaborate banners and effigies of Jesus and Mary bedecked with ribbons and flowers. They were closely followed by members of the clergy, resplendent in their colourful vestments and attended by the altar boys and servers. Immediately behind them were the young boys and girls who'd just been confirmed. The girls usually wore white dresses and carried prayer books and rosary beads, while the boys made do with a white shirt, a red sash and grey trousers. It was a wonderful spectacle. The winding procession of Pentecostal white gave the chance for some to indulge in a bit of showing off, while giving others the opportunity to ascertain who used Persil and who didn't!

More often than not our Whitsuntide clothes were too big for us – to allow extra room for growth. Problem was that by the time they fitted us properly they were worn out, and we were due for new ones again. But it didn't always work like that. I remember one particular suit I had, a light gray pinstriped affair. One Sunday, instead of going straight home after church, I saw fit to go with some mates to ride bikes on the coal rally – a popular dirt track running alongside the local beck. It was also a spot where chimney sweeps disposed of surplus soot . . . Now I've never gone looking for trouble. I had no need to – it usually came looking for me. Inevitably I came off a bike and landed in a pile of soot – in my new Whitsuntide clothes. That was it. I was in *real* trouble. I decided to run away from home there and then, and for the rest of the day I hid in a den in the park. George came to tell me that my mother had been round to all my mates' houses looking for me. She was livid, and I had to go home. I sent him back with the message that I'd go home only if she didn't slap me. He returned assuring me that she wouldn't. So I returned and true to her word she didn't. Dad slapped me instead. The suit was a right mess but fortunately around that time a new technology had been introduced into the community – dry cleaning. The suit came back, as good as new and it hadn't shrunk an inch, which was remarkable in those days when usually anything that was washed shrank. But the suit must have been destined to fit someone smaller. A few weeks later, while visiting our relations in Liverpool, we crossed the Mersey to spend the day in New Brighton. We were in a pedal boat in the middle of a large boating lake when the heavens opened. By the time we reached the shore I was absolutely drenched and soaked to the skin. When the suit dried out the sleeves came half-way up my arm, and the trousers would have just about fitted a ventriloquist's dummy.

Maybe I should have saved it, as I worked with quite a few ventriloquists later in my career. The most notable was a young up-and-coming dude from London. He travelled up to work the Northern Club circuit to get some experience and I happened to be working the same club as him one evening. His first spot was a disaster: he couldn't get the audience's attention and they talked all the way through his act. As I was empathising with him in the dressing room afterwards, the concert chairman – resplendent in flat cap and muffler – came in and said to the young vent. 'They can't hear what the dummy's sayin' at the back, lad. So when tha' goes on again put its head a bit nearer t' microphone.'

Alas, the archetypal concert chairman is fast becoming extinct, much to my dismay. For when the crackling mike and bell is silenced for ever, who will be left to utter those immortal words 'Best of order, please!' – striking fear into the most disruptive audience. How will we ever replace the delightful innocence of the chairman who introduced an act called 'RIO' as R Ten? The short answer is we won't. So let us not forget these dedicated custodians of the concert rooms. I certainly won't; in fact there'll be many more stories to recount before this book is ended.

Whitsun and Easter apart, most Sundays were much the same. After church we went for a walk with Dad, sometimes through the park or maybe up to the allotments in the 'Rhubarb Fields' to buy a bunch of flowers for Mum. And by the time we got home dinner would be ready. I loved my Sunday dinner.

The aroma greeted us long before we reached the door, and beckoned us in like the sniffing Bisto kids. A quart bottle of dandelion and burdock always stood in the centre of the table along with four glasses. Although it was my favourite pop it never seemed to complement the Yorkshire pudding and gravy, and invariably gave me hiccups. Most of those around our way always had a good Sunday dinner. It was supposed to set us up for the week (Or for a month, where my best mate's Uncle George was concerned) We once watched him eat thirteen large Yorkshire puddings *before* he tucked into his dinner!

Though most things were in short supply we never went hungry; I guess we were lucky in that respect. Others were not so fortunate: poverty was no stranger to Batley Carr – the evidence was there for all to see. But some of the people were tremendously resourceful. One house I knew had no conventional furniture, just a few piles of old bricks brought in from the bombsite. A couple of wooden boxes standing on end served as cupboards, with a small piece of material draped in front of each to hide the meagre contents. The tap in the sink corner was missing and had been replaced with a large cork in the wall. The water pressure had been turned down slightly, of course, but when the bung was removed I had the rare privilege of seeing a kettle filled sideways!

I must confess that I had to smile years later when I saw a pile of bricks on a television programme offered up as a work of art in Tate Modern; more so when they valued it at umpteen thousand pounds. It bore a striking resemblance to the dining room table in the aforementioned household, which as far as I can remember cost nothing.

It would have been so easy for people to give up but no one did. Instead the hardships we endured bred a tremendous community spirit, which on occasions culminated in great acts of kindness and sacrifice, bolstering a will to succeed against all odds. And although I didn't realise it at the time, it helped to prepare me for what was to come later in life.

Chapter Three
SCHOOL DAYS

The first school I attended was St Joseph's Roman Catholic Primary School. My first day didn't get off to a very good start when I got into trouble for punching another kid in the mouth. He threw sand from the sandpit into my face, so I reciprocated with knuckles. Sister Maria Anunciata, the nun into whose charge I had been entrusted, made me stand in the corner until playtime – not a good start to my academic career! But I didn't hold it against her. She was very kind, very patient and a very good teacher.

I really enjoyed school – there was so much to do. I went armed with a nominal grasp of the three Rs, largely thanks to the card and board games our family played most evenings during the power cuts, so most things came pretty easily to me.

We got a small bottle of milk each every day, and at playtime we could buy Ovaltine or Horlicks tablets if we had any money. If not we usually took a small mixture of cocoa and sugar wrapped in a piece of paper. It was treated as a dip and dispatched to our mouths with a damp finger. And the state of some of those fingers makes me wonder why bubonic plague never broke out in Batley Carr! We were made to wash our hands in the washroom at regular intervals, but most of the boys didn't bother. The washroom was an awful place. Dark, and always crowded, its floor was usually awash with water

St Joseph's Junior school, 1947. I am in the middle row, right in front of Father Cox.

that had been squirted at us by the older boys. When the taps were in full flow they reached over and pressed their fingers under the tap, drenching us to the skin sometimes. The roller towel was always soaked as well, so I usually wiped my hands on my jersey – unless I was fortunate enough to be there when the towel was eventually changed (I could count the occasions when this happened on one wet, grubby hand). Not forgetting, of course, that all this took place amid the enduring, unforgettable fragrance of carbolic soap. But once I got into the swing of things a visit to the 'Wash Hole of Calcutta' became a bit more bearable.

    I soon settled into the routine, and even became friends with the boy I punched. He had the most vivid imagination of any boy I've ever met. His detailed accounts of his father not only driving railway engines but also letting him have a go had the rest of us green with envy. His storytelling (he was also of Irish descent) was so convincing that he had us all believing he had a magnificent train set in his cellar. It was steam driven, with toy porters who carried leather cases and guards who blew whistles. Not only that, but by a series of tunnels it was even connected to the main line near Batley Carr station. He described it in such detail that we were convinced he wasn't making it up. So believable did it all sound that a handful of train-lovers among us even turned up at his house one evening demanding to see it! His mother answered the door and, after listening with an expression of despair to the reason for our visit, duly summoned her offspring and cuffed him round the ear. I was so disappointed. It was a tribute to his glibness that I still wanted to believe it was there – even though his throbbing lughole told me otherwise. Now, of course, I know it was just the initial stirrings of the blarney latent in his Irish heritage. And years later it came into full fruition, for he became a distinguished college lecturer.

My first year in the babies' class, as it was known, seemed to pass quickly and without much further incident. Our day always started with prayers led by Sister Maria. Not being able to read very well at this time, we had to learn everything parrot-fashion, which led to all kinds of misinterpretations: 'Our Father who art in heaven, Hello be thy name . . .' and, in the Hail Mary, 'Blessed our farmer swimming' – which I was later to learn was really 'Blessed art thou among women!' The rest of our time was spent chalking on boards, colouring and painting. After all that we had our milk and were allowed to rest our heads on the desktop and go to sleep for a while.

It was a very relaxed environment, and we all felt safe and secure. Very little happened to cause any consternation, that is until we had our first encounter with the nit nurse, or 'Nitty Nora the jungle explorer', as she was affectionately known to the older children. When she first arrived she looked very impressive. I can still picture her standing in front of the class, resplendent in a starched white pinafore over a blue uniform. She set up her private examination room behind the small blackboard, in full view of seventy-five per cent of the class. One by one we were summoned to kneel on the coconut matting she had rolled out on the floor, ready to be searched. At first I didn't know what it was all about, and was a bit miffed when she gave a green card to some of the others and not to me. Later on, of course, I learnt the true significance - but fortunately for me when I did get nits Mum discovered them at bath time. With the aid of a fine-toothed comb and some French-sounding soap called Derbac I was spared the indignity of being green carded in front of the class.

Playtime was great. More often than not there was a game of football going on. Whenever I could I joined in with the older lads because it was more testing and earned me a bit of respect. It paid off in the long run, as I got picked for the school under elevens football team when I was only nine. This was a double plus for me because it meant that I could also get special dispensation to be excused from my class for away matches.

My first real test was against what was then the toughest school in Dewsbury. It was a cup-tie and was to be played on what was laughingly referred to as their pitch. The whole of their school turned out, and we were surrounded by a baying horde of hostiles. Some of the bigger lads in our side felt intimidated, but it was nothing compared with the treatment I received – being a lot smaller than the rest. Their team was a real rough outfit, and didn't even have a set of matching jerseys – which also added to our problems. Sometimes one of the spectators ran onto the field to make a tackle, and the trouble was that no one knew if he was a part of the team or not. All of this, of course, went completely unnoticed by their completely unbiased games-teacher, who just happened to be refereeing at the time. Anyway, we battled away and were losing by one goal to nothing with about five minutes to go. One thing I learnt quickly was that whatever I lacked in size I had to make up for with guile and resilience, so I developed what was considered the best aspect of my game – the ability to read a situation. This enabled me to cultivate a sixth sense that often saved my bacon and on this particular occasion the team's. I happened to be in the right place at the right time to boot in the equaliser with barely seconds to go. It silenced the jeering mob and infuriated the referee, who then gave the poor goalie a right bollocking for letting it in! The upshot of it all was that we had to replay them a week later on our pitch, and we gave them a right old stuffing.

Football had its lighter side, of course. Most of the schools we played against competed in the right spirit and there were some memorable moments. Like the time one kid turned out to play for us wearing his grandma's pink bloomers: his mother couldn't afford football shorts so he had to improvise. The funny thing was that he didn't seem to mind wearing them – but the rest of us died with shame. Another one couldn't afford boots so he had to play in wellies. He was a good player too, and he used it to his advantage – as it was a lot easier to dribble past opponents when they were immobilised with laughter. But when it began to rain his disadvantage was restored, as there are no studs on wellies. The pitch became so deep in mud that it began to resemble the battlefields of Flanders. The old leather ball became so heavy that it required more than a good swing of the leg to propel it anywhere. So if the ball came over from his side of the field we had to look twice because sometimes it was followed by a flying welly. Heading the old leather ball was bad enough but heading a welly? This didn't deter our vulcanised winger, however, and later on in the game while charging towards the goal to meet a cross his wellies got stuck in the mud, causing him to run out of them. Without breaking stride he carried on to score bare-footed. The whole school cheered as he returned to collect his wellies, which were sticking out of the mud at the same angle he'd left them.

I passed my scholarship in 1953 and couldn't wait to follow my brother to St Bede's Grammar School in Bradford. He was good at football too, and occasionally I went to watch him play for the school. He later went on to play for Bradford Schools and with a bit of luck could have represented England Catholic Schoolboys. He played alongside Mike Helliwell, who later played on the wing for Birmingham City and later England.

St Bede's wasn't just renowned for its sporting prowess. It also produced the author John Braine – writer of the classic novel *Room at the Top*, and was also the meeting point of four young men who got together to play music and later found fame as the pop group Smokie. Comedian Johnny Casson – another old boy – made his schoolmates laugh before going on to TV and theatre fame.

I couldn't wait to wear the green and gold jersey of St Bede's. The standard of football was so good that we had an A team and a B team in the same grammar school league. The A team were all picked from the second year and were a great side, while the B team were all like myself – rookies in their first year. The following year we moved up a form and most of us were promoted to the A team – I couldn't wait for the season to start.

Then a chain of events took place, which at the time seemed to be of no significance. But later on it set me wondering. I'd always hoped to pursue a career in sport, but madam fate thought otherwise. I missed the team photograph session owing to a bout of illness. This had happened the previous year in similar circumstances. It was as if I was never meant to have any kind of sporting recognition, because I was never present for any of the St Joseph's football team photographs either – even though I was captain one year. It is said that the Lord moves in mysterious ways, and knowing what I know now I wouldn't disagree. It was one of these mysterious ways that was to change my life forever.

Me and fellow patients of G ward in Pinderfields Hospital, Wakefield, where I spent two years in traction for a diseased hip. With us is the physio, Miss Muller.

Chapter Four
LE CRUNCH!

At the beginning of the '50s things began to go well for the family, perhaps too well. During the late 1940s Mum had rented a market stall in Dewsbury and began selling fruit and vegetables on Wednesdays and Saturdays, while Dad, after a couple of temporary jobs, finally secured a permanent position with Speights, a local lampshade manufacturing company. And by the time Princess Elizabeth had become Queen in 1953 the regular income had enabled us to move to a bigger house that was attached to an empty shop. Mum stocked it and began selling fruit, vegetables and a few groceries while still maintaining the market stall. Business prospered, Dad was happy in his job and both my brother and I were doing well at grammar school.

Now the saying goes that 'Into each life a little rain must fall'. For the Twohig family, and me in particular, it was about to become monsoon time.

Half-way through the school football season we were unbeaten and playing Grange Grammar, who were also undefeated. Their side included a boy who was tipped to play for England, and I was given the job of keeping him quiet. This I managed to do for most of the game, and we were winning by one goal. Then our goal was put under siege as Grange turned on the pressure, in an attempt to equalise. The ball squirted loose on the edge of the penalty area, so I slid in to clear it and somehow ended up between the goalkeeper and an incoming striker, who swung his foot at it and missed. I felt the full force of his boot connect with my hipbone. I was helped off the field muttering expletives, and that was that for the rest of the game. It didn't make me feel any better having to sit on the sideline and watch Grange equalise.

Over the weekend the dull ache I'd been experiencing developed into a pain that was so bad that even the vibration of someone walking past my bed reduced me to a quivering wreck. By Monday it was so severe that my mother summoned our GP, Dr Hinchcliffe. After his initial treatment failed to make any impression, a specialist was brought in to examine me. In the meantime my bed had been brought downstairs, as by now I couldn't even climb the stairs. The specialist gave me a quick examination, spoke briefly to Dr Hinchcliffe, and then gently led my anxious mother into the adjoining kitchen. Dr Hinchcliffe began to chat to me, but I didn't really listen: I could hear my mother crying, and I was more concerned about her. Presently she came back into the room, and in a vain effort to hide her distress she smiled and told me that if I wanted to play football again I'd have to go into hospital. She knew by this time, of course, that my football days were over, and that I'd have to undergo a lengthy stay in hospital. She also knew that the only thing that would get me through was the promise of being able to play the game I loved again. Everyone knew this, in fact; the only one left in the dark was me.

In due course I was admitted to Pinderfields Hospital, Wakefield, on Christmas Eve 1954. What a Christmas that turned out to be. I was taken into Ward G just as the rest of the beds in the ward were being wheeled out and taken up to the main hall for a Christmas party – but I was in so much pain that I couldn't have joined them anyway, and I was left alone in the empty ward, as a new admission being put next to the nurse's station. Eventually the rest of the ward came back from the party. The young kid in the bed next to me began to amuse himself by throwing his pillow into the air and letting it fall back onto his face. I tried to make conversation. 'I don't think I'll be in here very long – a week or two at the most,' I said with confidence. He seemed unimpressed. 'How long have you been in?' I asked.

He looked at me over his pink-framed national health specs and replied, 'Just over a year.'

I was a little more than taken aback. 'God, that's a long time!'

He threw his pillow into the air again. 'Oh, not really, some of the others have been in . . .' the pillow fell back onto his face and I didn't hear the rest.

'What?' I enquired.

'Over three,' he said, placing his pillow behind his head.

'Years?' I asked, disbelieving.

He nodded.

My mouth began to go dry. There was a matter-of-fact tone in his voice that did nothing to quell the fears that were already growing inside me. Maybe the problem I had was more serious than I had anticipated. My confidence began to falter. Just then an elderly nurse arrived on the scene.

'Do you want a bottle?' she asked.

My spirits lifted slightly. My throat was dry and I was about to get something to drink – or so I thought. 'Yes please,' I replied, and waited in anticipation. She didn't seem surprised by the 'What the hell do I do with this?' expression on my face as she handed me the receptacle. She called it a bottle, but it didn't look like any I had seen before. It was glass but that's where the similarity ended – and it was empty too.

She handed one out to each of the kids in the surrounding beds and they swiftly dispatched them under the blankets. Not wanting to appear conspicuous I did the same. What are they hiding them for? I thought. Have I been brought into a nuthouse or something? After a few seconds the bottle in the next bed reappeared. He held it in the air triumphantly, as did a few of the others.

'Who's done the most?' a squeaky voice further up the ward piped up.

So that's what it's for. Peeing in! I looked at them, all with bottles held aloft. How ridiculous they looked – as if they were about to drink a toast to someone. Cheers, I thought sarcastically. Long live Prince Urine.

It wasn't like me to be scornful but I was feeling very down. None of my family had ever been in hospital so I hadn't a clue what was going on. It was Christmas, I was in pain and I was missing my friends and family. The nurses were kind, though, and did everything possible to make me comfortable. Second nature, I guess – for they must have seen that same look of despair on the face of every kid who entered that ward. They were really nice. I think they really liked me too – because they didn't let me go home for another two years.

Life in the horizontal mode

For the first few months I underwent treatment to stop the infection in my hip joint spreading to other parts of my anatomy. I never found out what caused these problems, but if it hadn't been for penicillin I'd certainly have been a goner. My first instinct was to thank God for Alexander Fleming. But afterwards I thought... hang on a minute: if it hadn't been for God and His mysterious ways, I wouldn't be in this state in the first place. You know, I never realised this living business could be so complicated. And it could be painful too.

The area around my hip was swollen now and the pain was excruciating. The resident specialist came to see me, which did nothing to boost my confidence. I'd seen him make a right pig's ear of carving the turkey for the ward Christmas dinner. He was an old Austrian gentleman who was fast reaching his sell-by date. He prodded about with his bony finger and, as my screams began to subside, came out with the classic 'Does zat hurt?'

What do you bloody think? I thought.

He turned to the ward sister. 'Vee had better aspirate. Can you arrange for him to be taken up to the theatre, pliz.'

I had no idea what 'aspirate' meant, but the mention of theatre coupled with the memory of the turkey at Christmas dinner began to have the same effect on me as the word 'laxative'! The fear of not knowing what was going to happen to me took precedence over everything, and I don't remember much about the time between leaving the ward and entering the theatre. I do remember the anaesthetist, however. He wore the thickest spectacles I'd ever seen, and I remember thinking that with eyesight like his he'd have difficulty finding my arm, let alone a vein. But my fears were unfounded, for within seconds I was unconscious.

I awoke to find a young nurse peering down at me. 'I think he's coming round,' she said.

An older nurse joined her. 'Go and fetch a vomit bowl then. He'll probably want to be sick.'

How right she was. I retched until I thought I was going to turn inside out. Then as the nausea diminished I began to realise that the pain in my hip had decreased considerably. I also noticed that I had been attached to an intravenous drip.

'What's this for?' I asked the older nurse.

'It's to put some colour back in your cheeks,' she replied,

adjusting the bottle of blood above me. I have to admit that I did feel a lot better after a couple of pints of Dracula's Ruin, and my family were pleased when they saw the improvement in me. It also gave me fresh hope that I would eventually be returned to full fitness.

In the weeks that followed the discomfort could be described as bearable. Then a small swelling appeared on my thigh. It got bigger each day and then became inflamed. Eventually it burst, and horrible green pus oozed out of it. Years later when I cut a ripe Kiwi fruit in half it was like welcoming an old friend. And speaking of old friends . . . the Terror from the Tyrol came to examine it. He probed about inside the abscess with a metal implement – and I hit the roof. The young nurse in attendance was as distressed as I was. The old doctor seemed completely oblivious to pain – mine in particular. 'Shouldn't he be given a local anaesthetic?' the young nurse beseeched my tormentor. She did so with a measure of reluctance as old Hokey Pokey, as I had secretly christened him, was not above giving subordinates a good bollocking when he saw fit.

'Nonsense! He's a brave boy – aren't you, young man?'

I shook my head in disagreement.

'Not at the moment,' I squealed.

'Zer you are,' he said, and continued his poking about.

The nurse and I looked at one another in amazement. Maybe this was some kind of psychology he was trying. But it wasn't working: it was purgatory. Later I was amazed to learn that he was on *our* side during the war!

Not long after that I was transferred from a bed onto what was called a frame. It consisted of a metal framework roughly the shape of my body from the shoulders downwards, and padded with leather and reinforced straps that were positioned across the chest, pelvis and groin areas. The whole point of the structure was to restrict body movement. Before I was placed on it four huge sticking plasters, stretching the length of my legs, were attached and secured with bandages. At the end of each plaster was a tab, and after I was fastened onto the frame – legs akimbo – the tabs on each leg were pulled tight and tied off at the bottom of the framework, putting the hip joints into traction. Later the whole structure was secured to a metal trolley by brackets. These were high enough to leave a space in between the frame and trolley to receive a bedpan, which was really considerate as by this time the only part of my anatomy left able to move was my bowels.

This left me in a state of complete and utter dejection. My faith in God was called into question as I tried to come to terms with the misery inflicted on me. What terrible thing have I done to warrant this? I kept asking myself. I prayed and prayed but the answers weren't forthcoming. God didn't seem to be listening. Granted, I'd been no angel but I'd been no worse than others had. I made all kinds of promises to the Almighty, promising to be as good as gold in the future. 'Just get me off this thing soon,' I entreated. But all my pleadings fell upon deaf ears.

The only comfort I could draw from my predicament was that I was not alone. Looking around the ward half a dozen other kids – some a lot younger than me – were in the same boat. They seemed to have accepted it, which made me feel ashamed. Anyway, for the next eighteen months I didn't have much choice. One of the many things I came to admire about those kids was their tremendous spirit. They probably found their ability to laugh at their own situation was the best, if not the only, way to endure what many would consider unendurable. I remember watching a film show, which had been set up for us in the ward. The film was set in medieval times, and in one scene a man was being stretched and tortured on a rack. As we all lay empathising with the poor sod on the screen, a voice from the back of the ward observed, 'Huh! What kind of a frame is that? There's nowhere to even put a bedpan!'

'Probably crapped his self already,' somebody added.

Then they all joined in. 'Wonder what the food's like. Bet it's better than ours.'

'If they really want to torture him why don't they let Nurse Swallow sing to him?' This brought an outburst of laughter. Nurse Swallow was sitting among us and was not amused. But she didn't let it bother her; she was always in control. She was also very efficient, very middle aged and very unmarried. Completely dedicated to her vocation, everything she did had to be done by the book – which didn't make her one of the most popular nurses. But she was still a very good one nevertheless, and a lot of her talents went unappreciated. Unfortunately for her this included her singing. She really believed she had a wonderful voice, and despite protests from the older kids she insisted that her rendition of 'Alice Blue Gown' was an ideal lullaby to send the little ones off to sleep. Clasping her hands together she'd burst into song, and within seconds there was loud snoring; the whole ward appeared to be asleep. Undaunted, she'd waltz down the ward singing her head off until she finally disappeared into the office – at which point the whole ward reawakened and it was business as usual. I feel sure, though, that when they reflect on it in later years those kids will realise, as I did, that her heart was in the right place, and that her musical eccentricity could be put down to a swallow trying to be a nightingale – Florence, maybe?

The first time my mother saw me on the frame she did her best to remain calm. 'Why have they put you on this?' she asked quietly, trying her best not to look horrified. I knew she was hurting inside, but being a woman of great fortitude she wasn't going to let me see how upset she really was.

'It's supposed to keep my hip still so it'll heal quicker. I shouldn't be on it too long,' I lied.

'Will they take you off it when you go to sleep?'

'No, but it's OK – the lads say you soon get used to it.'

But I didn't – it took ages. I didn't sleep a wink for two nights; in fact I didn't get a full night's sleep for months, partly because of the discomfort of the frame and partly because of the injections of penicillin I was receiving – one every six hours, night and day for six months. I hated them. It wasn't the needle I feared: it was the after-effects. It felt as if someone had given me a kick, and after a while the muscle began to harden. Then the needles wouldn't penetrate it so another location had to be found. By the end of the six months there was only one muscle left that wasn't hard – and there was no way I was going to have that pricked!

Nurse Allen was the only nurse who gave painless injections. When she was on duty the sigh of relief could be heard a mile away. She had been a nurse a long time and was completely unflappable; her portly stature graced the ward with a calm dignity. She also had a dry sense of humour. One of the older lads, who was particularly well endowed, was 'making tents' as she passed his bed. 'Put your knees down. Matron's due,' she ordered.

'I haven't got them up,' he replied with a cheeky grin.

'Well, lie on your side then,' she fired back, without batting an eyelid.

It was round about this time that I began to look at some of the nurses with a little more interest – especially the younger ones. Some of the student nurses weren't much older than I was. I also began to notice changes to my body.

Every so often I was taken up to the X-ray department. To me it was like going on vacation. A change of scenery was a tonic, and meeting new people along the way was a bonus. My trolley was parked next to a mirror and I was quite surprised when I caught sight of myself. I was a bit taken aback. I hadn't seen myself for ages and somehow I looked different. My hair was longer and my face was a slightly different shape; I looked a bit more grown up. I experienced a strange feeling of vanity mixed with astonishment. Was this really *me* I was looking at? My reflection gave me a little shock – but soon I was going to have a much bigger one.

'Right! Let's get him on the table.' The young radiographer beckoned to the porter and the nurse who were with me. Between them they transferred me from the trolley onto the X-ray table. I was in good spirits; for I was no longer in pain and all seemed to be good in the world. Twenty seconds later the bottom dropped out of it. The radiographer had just aligned my pelvis with the camera and placed my legs together when the young nurse rather tactlessly observed, 'Oh look! One of your legs is shorter than the other one - nearly two inches.'

I was completely numb. She's got to be kidding, I thought. She *has* to be. Panic began to take hold. She's got to be having me on – but what a thing to say! I pressed my feet together tentatively.

'Keep still,' the radiographer's voice snapped from behind the screen.

My heart sank as I felt my right heel touch the top of my left anklebone . . . it was true. Any hopes I had preserved of getting back to normal were dashed as the awful truth slowly began to unfold. The realisation that my sporting prowess was behind me left an emptiness inside me such as I'd never experienced before.

The return journey from X-ray was of no importance to me. As far as I was concerned the world had ended, and they might just as well have taken me back to the city dump as the ward. Nothing mattered any more. Earlier I was in great spirits; now it was deep depression. I didn't really want to talk to anyone for a while, and I withdrew into myself – a lack of communication that was put down to adolescence. I was off-hand with those who were dear to me, and the remorse I felt afterwards made me feel even worse. I spent most of my time staring into space, wondering what was to become of me. Some of the younger nurses began to refer to me as 'the quiet one'. I wasn't really; I just wasn't interested in talking about anything. All in all nothing seemed to have any effect on me, until one day Nurse Margaret Elisabeth Hart walked onto the ward.

Beth, as she preferred to be known, was a student nurse. She was so pretty and had a presence that intrigued me. She looked at me in a way that no one had ever looked before. The first time she spoke to me I was completely smitten. We became great friends. One day I received a letter from her younger sister, who was the same age as me. Obviously Beth had been talking about me, which pleased me no end, and as a courtesy I wrote back. We exchanged letters and I was happy to show them to Beth. They only contained day-to-day stuff, which seemed to please her, as I sensed that she didn't want me to become too fond of her sister. She knew by this time that I was completely besotted with her, and I heard from other sources that she was very fond of me; but that's as far as it went. It was that kind of relationship – completely natural, and accepted for what it was.

Just being near to her evoked a feeling inside me that I'd never experienced before. She, in turn, seemed to enjoy being around me, and constantly fluffed up my pillow or tidied my bed. I occasionally stole a kiss, and she protested for the benefit of those around us. It fooled no one, of course; everyone knew she made no attempt to stop me. My first and only experience of puppy love was quite wonderful and, more importantly, it couldn't have come at a better time.

But the clouds of doom descended again when Beth was transferred to another ward. Though she still came back to see me, we lost touch after a while. She had a life outside the hospital that I couldn't share, but it didn't stop me thinking of her. For quite a while she was constantly in my thoughts. I'll never forget her – I don't think you ever do forget your first love. And there'll always be a special place in my thoughts for her, as she did more than bring much-needed meaning back into my empty world at that time: she also restored my faith in God. Once again those 'mysterious ways' were in evidence. Only this time He played His cards right and the ace up His sleeve was a young nurse from Horbury in West Yorkshire.

Chapter Five
ELVIS PRESLEY... WHO'S SHE?

How does that saying go? 'As one door closes another one slams?' No, that's not quite right – but as far as my ambitions were concerned this always seemed to be the case. Forgive me for sounding a tad cynical, but by the time you finish reading this account you might just understand why I tend to view life in general with a certain amount of scepticism. What's all this free will business we're told about? It wasn't my desire to end up in hospital with one leg two inches shorter than the other one, just as it was never my intention to make music my career. The older I get the more I feel inclined to subscribe to the theory that our destinies are pre-ordained by some mysterious power. Or in layman's terms - God. I've reached the conclusion that the only free will we're given is the right to like it or lump it!

Anyway, based on that theory, the mysterious power saw fit to place a James Dean look-alike in the bed next to me one day. Mick Shaw was a real ladies' man and the nurses loved him. Unknown to him (but not, apparently, to the mysterious power), his enthusiasm for music was the catalyst that eventually launched me into a music and showbiz career. His love of music, especially jazz, restored my own long forgotten interests. And although our musical tastes didn't always coincide, we still had a lot in common.

I talked Mr Moran – the male sister in charge – into letting me have a record player brought onto the ward. Thinking it would be good for morale, he gave me permission with the proviso that he could bring some of his Gilbert and Sullivan records in. Mick sent for his jazz records, and between us we just about covered the whole musical spectrum – from Bill Haley through Count Basie to 'The Pirates of Penzance'. One evening the assistant matron arrived unannounced to the strains of Bill Haley's 'See You Later Alligator', reverberating round the ward. I immediately turned it off as the flustered sister on duty dashed up to meet her superior, who by this time was half-way down the ward. The remainder of her round was carried out in complete silence. When the assistant matron had gone, the sister came over, and I feared the worst. That's the end of the music, I thought. But I was in for a pleasant surprise. 'Assistant Matron has told me to tell you to keep the volume down a little. By the way, have you heard that record by Elvis Presley?

'Elvis Presley . . . who's she?' I enquired.

The sister looked at me in disgust. 'Elvis is a man!' she informed me.

I'd never heard the name Elvis before, and it sounded like a girl to me. Either way it was a name I was to remember for the rest of my life. The record of course was 'Heartbreak Hotel', and I thought it was brilliant. Mick wasn't carried away with it, though, and suggested I buy another record called 'Basin Street Blues', by Louis Armstrong and the All Stars. This became very popular with the lads – partly because each musician on the record took a solo, and some of the lads made cardboard cut-out instruments and mimed to their respective solos. It might sound a bit sad but if you're stuck in bed with weights attached to your limbs for a couple of years, pretending to blow a cardboard trumpet now and again can be a real buzz. When the 'band' was in full swing ours was the happiest ward in the world.

I made myself some drums: two upturned biscuit tins with cardboard pads stuck to the bottom, a metal tray served as a cymbal and of course a couple of sticks. From that moment I was hooked. How the nursing staff put up with the noise I made is a mystery. But now I knew what I wanted to do; another door had opened. As soon as I got out of hospital I was going to buy some real drums.

Years later I worked on the same bill as Louis Armstrong, and when I went into his dressing room I fully intended to tell him about his other band – the G Ward All Stars. I was so in awe of the man that I could only blurt out a request for an autograph. He smiled and signed a photograph 'To Sam'. Then, with one of those famous wide-eyed sideways glances, he handed it to me, saying, 'You know, son, with a name like that you's ought to be black!'

The G Ward Co-Operative
Armed with a new incentive, I set about finding a way to get some money together that I could put away towards a drum kit. Being stuck in bed, my options were a bit limited. I managed to save some of my pocket money, but soon realised that it wasn't going to be enough. The only thing I had in abundance was time.

Naturally I always looked forward to visitors. My family only once missed visiting time, when a thick fog blanketed the whole of the West Riding and traffic was brought to a standstill. My mother was so determined that I was not going to be without a visitor that she rang one of her wholesalers who happened to live near the hospital, and threatened that he'd get less business from her unless he called by to see me for ten minutes; if he did there'd be extra business for him. He knew she wasn't serious, of course, but he came anyway and eventually stayed for an hour, which proved fruitful for both of us: he increased his business and I had a bit of luck. He brought a few comics for me to read and while I was browsing through one of them I saw an advertisement that read: 'Make money selling stamps to your friends and get yours free! Send now for catalogue.'

One of the worst things about long-term hospitalisation is boredom. If one of my wardmates found a good way to occupy his time the rest of us tended to follow suit. If someone built a model everyone built a model; if someone got a camera everyone got a camera; and so it went on. For some unknown reason no one had ever thought about collecting stamps, so I obtained an album and sent for the catalogue.

Before long everybody had a stamp album and they were buying their stamps from me. A kid called Dave, who was mobile, did my running about for a small consideration, and the money rolled in. The fad ran its course eventually, but not before I'd added a few coppers to the coffers. Towards the end one of the others went into business in competition with me, but by that time the demand was gone. This left me with the money and him with a massive collection of unsold stamps.

Around this time a new lad was admitted to the ward – who watched my enterprise with interest. His name was Jeff and he suffered from cerebral palsy. He was a quiet lad who kept himself to himself, and I always felt a little sorry for him because he never seemed to get many visitors. There was a wistfulness about him that could elicit pity from the most hardened heart. Occasionally we were allowed to have our beds pushed together to play cards or games, and one day I visited him. He told me that he came from Leeds and as we talked he brought out an unfinished wallet he was making at the occupational therapy unit. It was pre cut and all he had to do was sew it together. 'That looks pretty good,' I complimented him.

'Would you like me to make you one?' he asked humbly, lowering his head until his cheap glasses slid onto the end of his nose. I was caught off guard by the wistful look.

'OK then,' I said. 'How much?'

'Just a few bob for materials.'

How could I refuse? 'Right, Jeff, put me down for one.'

The doleful look immediately departed, and I realised I'd been witness to salesmanship of the highest order. The next day he was back with my wallet.

'By gum, Jeff,' I said in admiration. 'You've made a cracking job of this. The stitching's first class.'

'It was nothing,' he said casually. 'All I had to do was put on my doleful look and one of the staff did it for me!'

'You old fraud!'

'Well, it's no use being like I am and not being able to make use of it,' he said.

What a wonderful philosophy, I thought, and gave him ten bob. I must have been bonkers! I soon learned a lot more about Jeff. He lived with his elderly mother and it was painfully obvious that they were not very well off, which probably accounted for his lack of visitors and the empty drawers in his bedside locker. He was delighted with his ten bob, and had it changed into pennies so that it would look like more. Sometimes I was woken in the night by the chink-chink of pennies being counted in the bed opposite. He seemed to derive great pleasure from counting them over and over – and whenever the name Scrooge is mentioned, for some reason a vision of Jeff always springs into mind.

Seeing this as another possible source of income I decided to get some orders for wallets from the family and visitors who came to see me. Soon Jeff and I were in business together. We bought the materials direct, roped in a few of the lads to help with the cutting and sewing, and extended our range to include purses and anything else made of leather. Jeff was chief of sales and soon the orders poured in. He'd load up his wheelchair with swag and get someone to push him down to the hospital entrance. He'd lie in wait like a preying mantis ready to pounce. As the visitors arrived he'd put on his doleful look and in a pitiful voice beseech them, 'Would you like to buy a wallet, please, or a purse I've made?' Only someone with a heart of stone could have refused – and thanks to the warm-hearted people of the West Riding we did all right, thank you very much.

But all good things must come to an end, and our brief incursion into the world of private enterprise came to an abrupt halt. A surfeit of unmade wallets in the occupational therapy department caused great concern in the corridors of power: no one was making them any more, yet everyone seemed to be walking about with one. The ensuing investigation uncovered our thriving little business, and we were ordered to cease trading – but not before we'd pocketed a good few quid between us. It swelled my drum kit fund, and Jeff had a drawer that was literally groaning under the weight of copper. Some nights the chinking of pennies from the bed opposite seemed to go on for ever.

I often wonder what happened to Jeff. In fact, whenever I pass one of the many Pennywise superstores it sets me wondering if he's behind them. So if you're ever passing head office and you hear a chink-chink coming from the boardroom . . .

To an outsider the day-to-day life on a ward like ours would have seemed dull and uneventful, but as you've probably gathered by now this wasn't strictly true. Quite apart from my own experiences, some of the other kids had their moments too. One of them decided he was going to run away to sea after seeing a documentary on the TV – and he did just that! One night he got out of bed, dressed himself, said goodbye and disappeared through the French windows. The police caught him trying to board a ship in Hull. Then there was the rich kid brought in to recuperate after contracting polio. The son of an oil executive who operated between Britain and Venezuela, he was transferred from a private facility to our humble ward because of the availability of an iron lung. They were much in demand at that time and we had one unoccupied. It stood at the top of our ward, looking for all the world like a mini-submarine. I only remember it

LOUIS ARMSTRONG

Louis Armstrong. I worked with him at the world-famous Batley Variety Club.

Sitting at my first drum kit.

My early musical attempts were in a skiffle band, the Original South Side.

Lonnie Donegan. It was seeing Lonnie that made me want to play the guitar

being used once – in an emergency. (Most of the polio victims on our ward were there as the doctors and nurses tried to re-educate their damaged limbs.) It was also thought that the boy would benefit from the company of children, as he spent most of his time on his family's estate in Venezuela solely in the company of an armed guard, and not allowed to venture out of the grounds to meet other children. This was necessary, he told us, because of the kidnapping threat. Being in the company of the G Ward Gang afforded him this rare opportunity in complete safety. He was a really nice kid, completely unspoiled and beautifully spoken. He had a fair amount of ribbing from the Featherstone and Castleford lads, but this didn't upset him at all; he was happy just to be involved in any kind of relationship. It was a new experience and he was completely overwhelmed by it. He seemed to think it was worth being ill just to have a few mates!

One day a few of the kids were amusing themselves, firing matchsticks at toy soldiers from some cheap little toy cannons. The rich kid was enthralled by this and asked if he could join in. They let him play, and later that evening at visiting time he excitedly told his mother all about it. And when visiting time ended he informed us he was having his own toy cannon brought from home. It arrived the next day . . . some toy! It was a precision-built breech-loading howitzer, complete with tow truck, working searchlight and shells, and probably capable of dropping a shell with pinpoint accuracy from twenty yards. I'd never seen anything like it before, and have seen nothing similar since. He was only too pleased to let anyone have a go with it – and it goes without saying that he was the most popular lad on the ward.

When the time came for him to go home, he was really upset, and reluctant to leave his new friends. His parents, who were really nice people, were extremely grateful to us all for making him so happy and thanked us personally. I'm sure they realised that apart from the excellent medical care he received he also gained much from our company. Fraternising with children from all walks of life must have given him an insight into the rest of the world. Illness doesn't discriminate between rich and poor, and I'm sure he took note of that and many other things from his G Ward experiences. I hope he'll read this glowing testament to his character, and in gratitude donate an old oil well to me for my benevolence – or even that toy gun would do!

Back to the vertical
The day finally came when I was taken off the frame. Within an hour I'd shrunk from six foot odd to five foot three. It was marvellous to be in direct contact with a mattress again. My long-suffering body could once again appreciate the luxury of a cool crisp sheet. Metaphorically it was great to be in the car again as opposed to perched on the roof rack. Comfort was from now on going to be the greater part of the equation – or so I thought. I was awoken from my reverie by a familiar voice. 'Now zen, how are vee today?' The reappearance of old Hokey Pokey didn't exactly set alarm bells ringing – but I distinctly heard a loud tinkle. He pulled the bedclothes back, seized my leg and proceeded to jerk it from side to side, then up and down and around in circles. There wasn't any movement in the hip joint; it felt as if the ball and socket in my hip were fused together. 'Right,' he said, poking the thigh muscle of my other leg, 'Vee must build up zis muscle to take the weight of ze plaster of paris . . .'

'Oh no,' I groaned. 'He's talking pot legs . . . here we go again!'

'. . . zen vee can get you on your feet again.'

Hello, I thought. Maybe things aren't so bad after all!

Presently a pretty young Dutch physiotherapist came to see what could be done for my poor wasted leg muscles; there wasn't enough strength in them to kick a balloon let alone a football. She seemed to read my thoughts as I surveyed my stick-like legs. She started to work on the good leg. Her touch was exquisite.

'Never mind,' she said in perfect English. 'We'll soon have this leg back in shape.'

'Pull the other one,' I said, unconvinced.

'I'm not going to do anything with the other one,' she laughed. 'That'll be in plaster. You're making a joke, yes?'

I smiled back at her. She didn't realise we weren't talking about the same leg!

She had a wonderful technique, and muscles began to respond all over the place – I was fifteen after all. Before long my left thigh grew to resemble an oven ready chicken, while the poor right one remained like an oven ready glove.

I was taken up to the plaster theatre to get plastered, and guess who supervised the procedure. Yes, it just had to be my old Austrian amigo. I suppose he couldn't resist poking something in, even if it was only his nose. He had an uncanny knack of being able to inflict pain, albeit in an indirect way. While I was being positioned on the plaster table he began to mess about with the apparatus that was securing me. There was a metallic clang and the restraining boots, which my feet were fastened into, shot forward, pulling my groin into contact with an upright bar sticking from the centre of the table. My left testicle hit the side of my scrotum at about a hundred miles an hour. I let out a yell that was probably heard back in the ward. Now I'm positive he didn't do it on purpose and I'm sure he was just trying to help. But to me he was just trying . . . One of the theatre staff fiddled underneath the table to rectify the fault, at the same time probably looking to see if there was anything rolling about that belonged to me. Eventually they began to apply the 'pot'. It started just below my ribcage, around my waist, and stretched down to the toes of my right leg. As I lay there 'getting plastered' I began to think about going home for the first time. I'd never thought about this when I was on the frame, but now I was going to be partly mobile a tiny glimmer of light began to appear at the end of the tunnel.

Within a week the plaster had dried, and I was tried in the upright position. The first thing I did was fall over: I'd lost my sense of balance. But I persevered, and was soon hobbling about on a pair of crutches. My mother was beside herself when I asked her to bring some clothes for me. The only trouble was that nothing I had would fit me any more. We soon overcame that problem, and before long I was hopping about like a spring lamb. Now I was mobile again I was able to go out and explore the hospital grounds. It was like being a kid again, and I came to realise how much I'd missed the things I'd taken for granted – like the crackle of autumn leaves underfoot, the cool wind pinking up my face, even the hum of distant traffic. It felt so good to be part of the outside world again. I'd been away for too long – far too long.

Some of the kids got permission to go home for the weekend. I was given the option but declined. I'd already made my mind up that the next time I'd set foot inside our house was when I was home for good. But we still had some wonderful outings. By this time my folks had bought a car – a Morris Minor Traveller – and my brother, having passed his test, took us out for a spin. I was amazed at how things had changed in such a short time – or had they? Were things really so different or was it me? I began to think it was the latter. Maybe my life had been blinkered before, and the last couple of years had served to make me aware that there was more to life than football.

As the year drew to a close I concentrated my efforts on building up my strength and generally doing what I was told. I suppose I also quietened down a bit. Most of my friends had gone home, and the majority of those left in the ward were too young or didn't share my interests. I was feeling OK in myself, but the doctor wouldn't give me permission to go home until my blood count lowered. I had no idea what this meant or why it was so high. All I knew was that Christmas was round the corner and I was still in 'ossie'. The ward sister suggested that I take things easy for a few days instead of taxing myself: being on the move all the time could be responsible for my blood count being high. So I did what I was told, and virtually went into suspended animation. It nearly did the trick – but not quite. Mr Moran, the ward sister, came to see me with the results of my blood test. The look on his face said it all: it was still slightly higher that it should be. 'Do you want me to ring your mum and tell her?' he asked.

'No,' I thanked him. 'It'll be better coming from me.'

I was feeling very low. The prospect of another Christmas away from home didn't exactly fill me with seasonal cheer. Still, the staff always did their best for us, God bless 'em, and so I resigned myself once more to the inevitable. I was lying on my bed staring at the ceiling when I heard my mother's voice. She was trotting down the ward with my brother in tow, carrying a suitcase. 'What are you doing here?' I asked, wondering what was going on.

'I had a phone call telling me to come and fetch my lad home, 'cause they're sick of having him here,' she said, with tears welling up in her eyes. Mr Moran stood behind her with a mischievous grin on his face!

I left Pinderfields Hospital on Christmas Eve 1956.

Facing up

As we drove out of the hospital grounds I experienced mixed feelings for some reason or other. Initially I was excited at the prospect of going home, but as the old buildings disappeared into the distance I began to empathise with those I was leaving behind. There would be no respite for the staff. Theirs was an on-going routine of care and dedication. Even as I left they were attending a newly admitted patient – a young lad who, like me when I first arrived, probably had no idea what lay ahead of him. All kinds of thoughts began to run through my mind . . . Would he be subjected to old

Hokey Pokey's jabbing finger? Would he be sold bootleg wallets or stamps? Would he suffer the complete repertoire of Nurse Swallow's dulcet tones? All these thoughts should have made me smile, but they didn't. Perhaps it was because the lads I was leaving behind had wished me luck as I left. I knew only too well how they were feeling: the times I'd said the same thing, wishing that it was me going home instead of them . . . Now it *was* my turn and it felt so strange, a little bit scary to be honest. Somehow I knew that I had to put everything behind me and face up to what lay ahead.

The journey home didn't seem to take very long, probably because I was lost in thought for most of the way. I struggled out of the car and finally set foot (and crutch) inside the house. It seemed to be a lot smaller than I'd remembered it, possibly because I'd been used to the spaciousness of the ward – and I'd grown a bit too. Manoeuvring around the house sporting a large plaster cast proved a bit tricky at first but I coped. It took a while to get used to waking up at a normal hour after the six o'clock discipline of hospital life, but it was great to be home again even though it felt strange. I have to admit that at first I missed the hustle and bustle of the old bone factory. After all, it had been my home for the past two years and I felt a bit unprotected. No one cared how you walked or how severe your disability was in there. We were all in the same boat, helping each other through any difficulties we encountered. Now I had to find a way to leave all that behind and face a world that didn't understand what having a disability meant. In the past I'd often found myself staring at disabled people. Now that the role was reversed, how was I going to cope with being stared at?

To begin with it wasn't so bad, which was probably thanks to the plaster cast and crutches. People viewed them as temporary and didn't seem to bother about them much – it even gave me a certain air of machismo similar to that afforded to a wounded soldier on his return from a war. People who were sympathetic without feeling sorry for me pleased me no end: the last thing I needed was pity.

I somehow eased back into the slipstream of home life without the impact I'd first anticipated. Life for my family was getting back to normal as well, now that they didn't need to spend time visiting me. There wasn't much for me to do except sit around the house playing records or help a little in the shop, occasionally going to the local hospital for a check-up or physiotherapy. Then the time came for me to have my 'pot' removed – and what an embarrassment that turned out to be.

Anyone who has worn a plaster cast for any length of time knows that after a while the skin underneath dies and there's the dreaded itching. I'd been cocooned in mine for months and the itches had driven me mad sometimes. To ease my misery I'd pushed all kinds of things down the plaster to scratch the offending areas, and some of them I couldn't get back. Since the 'pot' stretched from my waist to my foot, getting down to the ankle was difficult: it took three lengths of Meccano bolted together. I actually achieved this goal, but not before losing quite a few bits of Meccano in the process. So when my plaster was eventually removed, the guy in the plaster room must have thought he'd opened a toolbox. Apart from half a Meccano set he also retrieved a couple of knitting needles, one and a half rulers and an assortment of pens and pencils. I left the room feeling a great deal lighter – and as I swung my crutches along the corridor I heard my 'scratching tools' being thrown into the bin – having declined the offer of their return.

I made my way back to the consulting room and waited. Before long the specialist and his entourage swept in, and I was placed on a table and surrounded. A lot of technical jargon was bandied about, X-rays were scrutinised and my leg was swivelled in all directions. Finally it was suggested that I should dispose of my crutches and transfer to walking sticks. Although this might be seen by some as progress, I actually found my mobility more inhibited. My hip joint was completely solid, which meant that to make any progress at all I had to lift my whole body with my left leg in order to swing my right side. I was left with an ungainly gait, and for the first time I became aware that I was being stared at. We're all furnished with a certain amount of vanity, I suppose, and I was no exception.

Eventually the walking sticks were discarded, leaving me with a very pronounced limp. Family and close friends scarcely noticed after a while, but I was very much aware of it, especially in public places. I used various little ploys to limit my self-consciousness, only moving when there was a distraction or pretending I'd hurt my foot when leaving a crowded room. It took ages – and a few pints – to walk across a dance floor on my own.

I needed to get my self-confidence back – and quickly. The recipe for that came courtesy of the G Ward co-operative and its past customers.

I began to look through the adverts for some drums. There was no way I could afford new ones so the sensible option was to buy a decent second-hand kit. The first ones I went to see were beauties but far too expensive. Then I spotted another that was within my price range; I was there before the ink had dried on the newspaper. It was slightly old fashioned, hence the reasonable price, but I didn't care. They were real drums and I wanted them! The man I bought them from, Syd Stephenson ran a local ballroom affectionately known as 'Stivvies'. He'd run many local bands in his time but had decided it was time to stop playing. His eldest son, Bobby, carried on the tradition, playing the drums professionally with the Ken Mackintosh Orchestra – a local band that made good. Their recording of 'The Creep' charted in 1954 and was a great success, which led to the band touring, recording and broadcasting for many years. Much later his other son Tommy and I became great friends.

The next few weeks were spent stripping down the drums and refurbishing them, in an attempt to modernise them. Soon I was driving everyone crazy as I learnt to play.

Sweeping the nation at that time was a style of music that had originated around New Orleans in the early twentieth century. It was skiffle – an uninhibited mixture of folk, jazz and the blues. Lonnie Donegan introduced it to the public with a string of hits that included 'Rock Island Line', 'Don't You Rock Me Daddio' and 'Cumberland Gap'. And the wonderful thing about skiffle was that it didn't only inspire kids to take up the guitar, but it welcomed improvised instruments like the washboard, tea-chest bass, comb and tissue paper and such, and you didn't have to be particularly musically gifted to join in. Soon skiffle groups were springing up all over the country.

My brother bought a guitar along with a few of our friends, and in no time we all got together to play. We bought a set of matching jerseys and formed the Southside Skiffle Group, and before long we were making a name for ourselves around the local clubs.

And so began my struggle for self-confidence and my introduction to the world of show business.

Chapter Six
ARS GRATIA ARTIS!

Now that I was getting about under my own steam it was suggested that I should be thinking about some kind of employment, and so I was packed off to the Youth Employment Office. They hadn't much to offer me really, chiefly because I hadn't much to offer them. I hadn't finished my schooling or taken exams, which meant I had no qualifications – so I turned out to be a bit of a problem for them. They sent me to a couple of jobs that involved office work. I was met by the sight of numerous people seated at desks in gloomy surroundings and scribbling away; most of them didn't even look up as I was shown round. I might as well have been invisible. I didn't fancy being chained to a desk at all, and deliberately flunked the interviews.

Where would I fit in? I was a real problem. So as a last resort, after noting that my best subject at school was art, they advised to enrol at Batley Art College. It turned out to be just what I needed: an opportunity to express myself without drawing too much attention to myself. But unfortunately that's just what I did.

My first day there I stuck out like a sore thumb. Wearing conventional clothes was definitely not the norm. Everyone dressed like vagrants or completely over the top. I felt as if I had a notice pinned to me saying 'Avoid me – I'm normal'. Some of the girls were friendly but most of the male students viewed my presence with total indifference – except one. He came in wearing a long grey raincoat, which had seen better days. He was small but taller than me (wasn't everybody?). A smouldering fag drooped from the corner of his mouth, emphasising the hangdog expression on his thin sallow face. When he took off his raincoat he was completely dressed in black. He took a long pull on his fag, sniffed, then looked me up and down. He expelled smoke as he spoke. 'What the fuck's them things on your feet?' He nodded his head towards my gold-flecked black suede shoes, which happened to be my pride and joy.

'Why? What's up with them?' I replied, slightly wounded.

The smoke began to envelop me. He sniffed again, took another drag, and spewed forth tobacco-flavoured words. 'They're a fucking abomination, that's what. Anyway, what's your name?'

I told him and he sniffed. I realised that he sniffed before and after everything he said or did.

'The name's Artie. Artie Banks. Here, have a fag.' He offered me a Capstan full strength. I took one and he gave me a light.

'God, these are strong,' I coughed.

'Aye, you need good lungs to smoke these.' He chuckled. 'Lungs like mine, I bet they're black and as tough as leather by now.'

I cringed, and my discomfort seemed to amuse him. I detected a slight twinkle in his dark piercing eyes as he told me, with a sniff, that black was his favourite colour. It didn't surprise me.

Artie was very much his own person and didn't subscribe much to the mainstream. But I soon began to realise that hidden behind his dark façade a very able and intelligent character was lurking. Well educated and armed with a vast knowledge of many things, when it suited him he was gifted with an eloquence that could hold its own in debates on any subject of interest to him, which in the main was beer, fags and the arts. I don't know why he took to me; he was very choosy when it came to friends. I was later to learn that he didn't mix much with others: there were those he liked, and the rest just didn't enter the equation. The next day I met someone he liked.

'Come and meet Prof,' he sniffed. He led me into one of the rooms in the college. 'Ah, there he is.'

I looked around the room and there was no one to be seen.

'Oi, Prof, look what I've found!'

A face appeared and looked down from the top of a very tall cupboard. About fifteen feet up there was a very unkempt figure, reclining and reading a book. He had a mass of thick wiry brown hair and a full beard. Peering over large horn-rimmed glasses he viewed me for a moment without making any comment. Then he looked at Artie. 'Got any fags?'

Artie threw him up a full strength.

'Ta,' he said, and lit it. He took a drag and went back to his reading.

'That's Prof,' said Arthur.

'So I gathered.'

Andy was another friend he introduced me to. He was small and slightly built like Artie, but that's where the similarity ended. His outlook on life was just about the complete opposite, but for some reason their friendship seemed to work – and work well. I liked Andy straight away. He was much more conventional than the others were, and though small in stature he had a tremendous presence. I first became aware of him when he breezed into the life class looking like a throwback from an old movie. Striding purposefully towards a cupboard in one corner, Andy removed his cloth cap to reveal slicked-back hair, which would have done justice to Douglas Fairbanks. He removed his double-breasted raincoat to reveal a well-laundered shirt and tie, polished shoes and conventional trousers with a precise crease. Considering the over the top informality of the art school he really looked a bit out of place, but it obviously didn't bother him. He opened the cupboard door and with a flourish placed his raincoat on a skeleton which hung inside (and was used by the class for anatomical reference), then closed the door. The whole routine was performed with great panache.

'Sorry I'm a bit late. The bus, you know . . .' He flashed a smile and fluttered his eyelashes, which were unusually long for a youth. It was a very winning smile. You know, the kind of smile that makes you want to smile. In fact, one of Andy's greatest qualities was his ability to smile no matter what. In all the years I knew him I don't ever remember him looking sullen. He had a wide range of interests, which ranged from listening to Tony Hancock and Eric Sykes to playing the trumpet.

A few of the other lads also played musical instruments, so I brought my drum kit and occasionally we jammed away at break time or at Art School functions. Derek Wadsworth, or Waddy as we knew him, was an excellent trombonist and all-round musician. It was obvious at the time that he was a bit special. On more than one occasion he sat in with some of the well-known jazz bands and more than held his own. In later years he ended up writing and arranging music for top London bands, and also wrote the theme tune for the successful TV series *Space 2000*. His CV has to be seen to be believed.

Sometimes we held dances in the art school. Most of the local top bands that were booked knew Waddy and were happy to let him sit in. So when the White Eagles Jazz Band from Leeds came to play for us Waddy had his trombone on hand. 'Do you think the drummer will let me sit in?' I asked him.

'Ask him and see.'

So after a few pints of 'liquid sophisticater' I moseyed over to the bandstand. The drummer – one of the best in the area – was carefully adjusting one of the cymbal stands of his very expensive kit.

'Mmm, nice kit.' I said casually. He continued to adjust the stand, totally oblivious to me. 'Any chance of me sitting in on drums?' I asked – with a hint of nonchalance.

'Fuck off,' he replied – without any nonchalance at all. That was my first meeting with Norman Emsley, who in later years became a very close friend and colleague.

Art school was a completely new experience. Best of all no one cared about or even mentioned my dickey leg. I was given the nickname Trog (short for Troglodyte) on account of my long hair, and even most of the staff used the name, such was the informality of the place. We got up to the usual student pranks, of course, which earned us regular reprimands from the college principal, and on one occasion from the chief constable when we 'borrowed' a large door mat from the town hall to use in our pottery shed.

But it wasn't all about having a good time. I worked very hard to reach the standards expected of me, and I like to think I did justice to the talents that were genetically bestowed upon me. I took to drawing like a duck to water – I'd always been able to draw a bit – and I found the history of art absolutely fascinating. It was only when I was introduced to the craft side of things that things began to go belly up.

'I think we'll try you with lithography, Trog,' one of the staff suggested. I was put into the capable hands of Joe Lee – who ran the lithography department and was the assistant principal, a man for whom I had a tremendous respect. He was very knowledgeable and dignified. Never rushed or flustered, he went about his work with an

Batley Arts College with Derek Wadsworth on trombone and me on drums. Derek, who has recently died, went on to be a composer and arranger of theme tunes (for example the TV series *Space 2000*). He played in the brass section on Dusty Springfield's 'I only want to be with you' and the Rolling Stones album *Their Satanic Majesties*: nothing if not diverse!

A recent picture of my Art College pals. Left to right: Derek Wadsworth, Pete Barraclough and 'Ned' Kelly.

air of calm that brought sanity back to the unconventional eccentricities of the madcap campus. So I entered his department filled with enthusiasm, hoping to broaden my horizon by learning the secrets of this great man. Why is it that my first days in any classes always end in disaster? Why? I was given two large flat stones, each with a smooth side. Before they could be used for printing purposes the two smooth sides had to be ground together in a circular motion, a mixture of fine sand and water in between them acting as an abrasive. This was supposed to leave the surface of both stones as smooth as glass.

So off I went, grinding away for all I was worth, and off went Joe for a cup of tea. I ground and I ground for ages. He hadn't told me when to stop so I assumed I had to continue until he returned. Eventually the grinding ground to a halt – I couldn't move the blasted things. The stones were well and truly stuck together. When Joe got back I showed him what I'd done.

'Why didn't you stop grinding when they were done?' he enquired politely, as was his way. His face went red as he struggled to prise the stones apart.

'Er, how d'you know when they're done?' I blurted out, feeling slightly stupid.

'Well, if the bladdy things weren't stuck together I'd be able to bladdy well show you, wouldn't I?' He turned to face the rest of the giggling class, raised his eyes towards heaven and uttered his favourite phrase, 'We've got a right one 'ere!' After a few more fruitless attempts to part the stones he decided to soak them in water. 'In all my years,' he went on, 'I've never known anyone stick bladdy stones . . .'

The entrance of Mr Byrd, the college handyman, interrupted him. 'Anything I can do to help, Mr Lee?' Mr Byrd, or Neb as we christened him, was one of those characters only a cartoonist could create. He was amazing. The first time we came across him he was kneeling behind a desk in the display department repairing something. He wore a flat cap with a massive neb – hence the nickname. Dick Battye, head of the department, introduced him to us. 'This is Walter Byrd, who's joined us as maintenance assistant.' He came out from behind the desk and only then did we realise that he hadn't been kneeling down at all!

'Eureka!' I cried. 'I've found somebody smaller than me!'

He peered at us through large horn-rimmed glasses that made

his eyes look bigger than they really were. His face broke into a broad grin as he greeted us. 'Pleased to meet you all,' he whistled. I couldn't believe it. He was too good to be true. He even made a whistling sound when he spoke the letter 'S'.

Everyone took to the little guy and nothing was too much trouble for him. He was conscientious, extremely versatile and also very strong, especially for his size. But even he, with all his tools and expertise, couldn't get those stones apart!

Years after I left the college I went back to a dance there, and out of curiosity I popped into the litho department to see if the stones were still there – and they were, still stuck together – probably left as a reminder of how not to grind litho stones.

I left the lithography department under a cloud. No matter how I tried I couldn't get the hang of things, and disaster followed disaster. I began to drive Joe Lee potty, which may have prompted him to refer me to Mr McAdam, head of the pottery section.

The pottery shed had a much more relaxed atmosphere and I was left to my own devices, free to express myself in what I found to be the most versatile and therapeutic medium of all. Mr McAdam was the archetypal absent-minded professor. His mind was constantly on creativity of the highest order, and for a while my presence went largely unnoticed – so I amused myself modelling figures and little pots. Occasionally Mac, as we called him, picked up something I was making and say, 'Yes, I can see what you're about.' I was pleased that he knew because I hadn't a clue myself.

One of the best things about the pottery class was the informality. No one minded if you took a peek at what they were doing and the senior students were happy to advise novices like me. On one occasion I watched with interest as the kiln was loaded up with pots and other pieces ready for firing. It was amazing how well packed it was: there wasn't room to put another thing inside by the time it was finished – except, perhaps, for a tiny pot in the bottom corner maybe . . . Hmm, I thought. I wonder what one of my little pots would look like if it was fired. When no one was looking I squeezed my best effort into the lower corner of the big kiln. That night the kiln was sealed and switched on, and I went home happy in the knowledge that I would be the proud possessor of a fired pot in the morning.

I was in the college canteen having a cup of tea when I first heard about the disaster. One of the senior pottery students came in cursing and swearing. 'Something fucking exploded in the kiln last night and a load of work has gone up the spout. Somebody can't have knocked up their fucking clay properly.'

'What does "knocked up their clay" mean?' I asked one of the students sitting next to me.

'It means getting rid of any air trapped in the clay before it's used. You see, if there are any air pockets in the clay when it's fired they expand and eventually explode.'

'Oh,' I replied, trying to look as innocent and interested as was possible. 'So how do you knock clay up?'

'Well, you just get your lump of clay and keep slamming it onto the stone slabs . . .'

I didn't let him finish. 'Oh, I've seen them doing that.' Then I left in a hurry before anyone got suspicious! So I should have knocked my clay up on the slabs in the corner of the pottery shed. It was strange how stone slabs crept into the equation again. I wonder if our family tree dates back to Moses.

Back in the pottery shed I commiserated with those who had suffered losses and thankfully no one put two and Trog together. I found my niche there eventually, and before long I was throwing pots as if it was second nature.

But careerwise I knew I wasn't going anywhere. The fact I hadn't finished my schooling was always going to thwart any aspirations I had of teaching art. I also knew my limits, and there was more chance of me becoming a van driver than a Van Gogh. I toyed with the idea of going to night school in order to get some qualifications, but there was no way I could see myself returning to the conventional discipline of a school classroom after the informality I had been used to. It would also have interfered with my music.

In the end the decision was made for me, following a boozy end of term session in the pub with some of the other students. The principal's Bond Minicar somehow found its way into the main corridor of the college – and rumour had it that he heard I was present at the event. When I received notice to appear before him at the start of the new term, and given that I was on a final warning anyway, I decided it might be more expedient to jump before I was pushed. And so I took a job repping for one of my mother's wholesalers.

Chapter Seven
KING OF THE ROAD

Fortunately this proved to be a good move for me, as I enjoyed the freedom of the road and meeting people. My self-consciousness was diminishing by the day. My Bohemian interlude at college had to take some of the credit as it taught me to view life from a whole range of different perspectives. I just didn't take anything seriously any more and was content to just breeze along and take life as it came.

So having passed my driving test at the second attempt, I was all set to challenge the world of commerce. I was seventeen and ready to test my new-found confidence on the conventional world. Having been used to the informality of the college, wearing a proper suit came as a bit of a shock to my system. The comfort level fell just short of that of a suit of armour.

Nevertheless I reported for duty on the Monday morning complete with empty briefcase, pen and pad, to await instruction. The prospects weren't good.

Midwoods was a small family business supplying sweets and chocolate to local shops and businesses. My boss was a honest, hard-working man constantly under pressure from the competitive big city wholesalers and their high-powered salesmen. He gave me a list of calls and a brief run-down of the customers. It didn't take an expert to conclude that his business was in dire straits. Owing to cash flow problems, the small salary I was offered was more of a token and amounted to little more than 'spend'. But that didn't bother me too much. I'd always enjoyed a challenge, and anyway I was earning a few quid working the clubs. So with an ego bursting with confidence and a brain full of teenage logic I set off to conquer the business world.

Having experienced confrontation and eccentricity by the truckload during my spell at art college, surely I could handle a few local shopkeepers . . . and it had been said I had a winning smile. So if all else failed all I had to do was beam. How little I knew! What I failed to consider first and foremost was that these were not ordinary shopkeepers. They were no nonsense, straight-talking, value for money YORKSHIRE shopkeepers. There was no 'going out of the back door' to tell you what they thought of you: you were told directly. Pussyfooting about was not part of their make-up; they shot straight from the hip. And talking about shooting, the first shop I went into saw the proprietor come out of his storeroom with both guns blazing. 'Who are you then?'

'I . . . I'm from Midwoods, sir,' I stammered — slightly taken aback, maybe because I couldn't believe I'd just called somebody 'sir'.

'And I suppose you've come for an order, 'ave yer?'

'I hope so, sir,' I simpered.

'Well, there isn't much chance of that, is there? Considering I haven't even got the last lot I ordered off your firm!'

Oh God, I thought. Nobody prepared me for this. I tried to pacify him. 'I'm new to the firm and not quite in tune with things at the moment, but I'll look into the matter when I get back . . .'

He interrupted me. 'And in the meantime what am I going to tell my customers? If they can't get what they want straight away they'll swan off somewhere else and get it — and sometimes they won't come back. And where does that leave me? I'll tell you where — waiting for your bloody firm to deliver it!'

He was obviously having a bad day and, true to form, my arrival was about as welcome as a singing telegram at a wake. He ranted on for the next few minutes, and my winning smile slowly accompanied the rest of my face on its journey to the floor. Eventually his rage began to subside, at roughly the same time as my chin reached my boots. His red face became less of a contrast with his white hair and moustache, and I began to sense a hint of humour. 'Look, lad.' He lowered his voice. 'I know it's not your fault personally, but I'm sick and tired of all the claptrap spouted by all you firms promising me this and that, telling me I can sell one thing or another . . .' He pointed to some shelves packed with chocolate I'd never heard of. 'Look at that lot. I've had 'em six months and I can't give 'em away. And the stuff I really want you've let me down with. I haven't time to concentrate on just sweets and chocolate . . .' He swept his arm around the shop, a large general store selling just about everything. '. . . I've got all this lot to think about as well.'

I knew what he was intimating. 'What you really need,' I patronised, 'is someone who knows what folk round here want and don't want.'

'That's right, lad.'

'Someone you can have complete confidence in, who wouldn't sell you any old thing just so as he could make his quotas up,' I went on.

'Exactly!' He nodded.

'Well, I'm from round here and I think I've got a pretty good idea of what folk like and dislike.' By now I was creeping so low that even a bus ticket couldn't be squeezed beneath my belly and the floor.

'I suppose you do have that in your favour,' he conceded.

My confidence was growing and I decided to play my trump card. 'Have you bought anything from us that you can't sell?' I enquired, hauling my winning smile back from the depths to help with the sales pitch.

'Now you come to mention it . . .'

I didn't let him finish. 'OK. I'll take it back and credit you for it. And that goes for anything else you get from me in the future.'

His eyes seemed to glow with satisfaction, and the tension eased. He beckoned me to sit down on the shop chair, which was provided for the benefit of the elderly and infirm. As I was feeling both of these by this time, I had no qualms about using it.

He made a cup of tea and we had a good chat. Initially he'd frightened me to death but the more he prattled on the more I liked him. Like all good grocers at that time he was conscientious, obliging and totally committed to his customers' requirements. His shop was packed with goods from every corner of the world – which made it a bit ironic that he couldn't get a jar of 'Yorkshire Mixtures' from his local wholesaler. The familiar aromas of bacon, freshly ground coffee and spices wafted past my nose as he went about his business clad in his spotless white overall and apron. He talked constantly to his customers with a practised ease, reminiscent of the conductor of an orchestra. After starting a conversation he gently eased anyone coming into the shop into it, a masterstroke that enabled him to serve more than one customer at a time, which kept everyone happy. Apart from anything else it made good business sense, as some people bought something extra just so they could hear the end of a juicy piece of gossip!

I spent over an hour with him. He talked about his son, who was a very talented bowler with the town cricket team. As it happened I'd been reading about him in the local press, and when I mentioned this to him he swelled with pride. We talked for ages, and by the time I left he'd not only agreed to reconsider his original order but he'd also added a few items to it as well. I left the shop feeling more than a little pleased with myself.

The rest of the day was pretty much the same story – orders short of items or not yet delivered. I had no illusions of the task that lay ahead of me. It was going to take a lot more than my winning smile to turn things around.

When I arrived back at base the boss seemed more than a little surprised that I was still in one piece, but by this time I was becoming quite adept in the art of survival. He was delighted with the results of my day's work and he seemed to cheer up a bit. But there were still a few problems to address. For instance, how were we going to supply the things we hadn't been able to get before? And what were we going to do with the stuff I'd brought back, the things our customers couldn't sell? I discussed it with my mother when I got home that evening and between us we came up with a solution.

Besides our shop, my mother had a thriving market business. During my lengthy stay in hospital she had diversified from greengrocery to concentrate on cut price sweets and chocolate: if the price was right she could sell anything. So it was decided that anything my customers couldn't sell would go straight onto her market stall at a reduced price. It worked a treat. Our customers could buy anything from me confident in the knowledge that it wouldn't be left on their shelves. And although my boss wasn't showing a profit on anything returned, at least he got some of his money back and kept his stock turning over. It also meant that Mum's stall could carry extra stock without additional outlay, as it was all sale or return. As for the problem of supplying things we couldn't get previously, this arose from the fact that the items in question were usually good sellers and on allocation. The manufacturers only allowed us so many with each order: when our quota was gone, that was that. We overcame this by going to the big cash and carry warehouses, buying what we were short of and selling them on. Although we didn't show a profit on these items, at least we kept our customers happy.

In the following weeks I got to know the customers better and they got to know me. Some of them took an interest in my musical pursuits, which worked well for me, as the more we talked the more I sold.

I'd been calling on one particular shop for weeks. It belonged to a baker who sold sweets and chocolate as well. He was always very pleasant and polite but he never placed an order. Nevertheless he was on my list so I continued to call on him; I didn't mind because I loved the smell of his baking. Anyway, one day I called just as he was placing a tray of freshly baked apple tarts in the window: they were topped with cream and looked delicious, and their aroma was exquisite.

'Hello there,' he said, clapping his flour-covered hands together as he turned to face me. I peered at him through the resulting haze. 'I don't think I want anything today, lad. How's your skiffle group going on?'

'OK,' I replied, gazing at the tarts in the window. 'They look great. I think I'll take a few home for the family. Can I have four, please?'

'No sooner said than done, lad,' he said, placing them into a cardboard tray. I handed him the money, and it was obvious by the smile on his face that he took great pride in his baking. They tasted even better than they looked – so good that they never even reached home!

A fortnight later I called in to see him and immediately ordered half a dozen. The shop was busy, so I paid him and started to leave. 'I can see you're busy, so I'll see you in a fortnight.'

'Hang on a minute, lad. I've got something for you.' He handed me a large sheet of paper. I looked at it and I was dumbstruck: it was a massive order.

'Thanks very much,' I spluttered. 'I'll see to this right away.'

'Do you know . . .' He broke off from serving a customer. '. . . I must have spent thousands of pounds with different firms over the years, and not one of them has ever bought as much as an Oxo from me. You're the first one to ever buy owt and it's much appreciated.'

He became one of our best customers, and after that I made a point of buying a little something from all our customers – and so did my boss.

In the months that followed the business began to show signs of recovering, and at the same time my confidence grew. Strange as it may seem, I've always had confidence in my ability but not always in myself. People find it hard to believe that I was basically a very shy person to begin with; I still am in many respects. This is something I've had to overcome. Once, when I was very young, I even peed my trousers because I was too shy to ask to use the toilet of a house we were visiting. It was only when I waddled out like a penguin that my mother realised what I'd done.

Being painfully shy even inhibited my very first public performance. It was at the St John's Ambulance Brigade Christmas party in the local Ambulance Hall in 1947. Each one of the brigade members' children had to sing a song, dance, recite a poem or do something in front of everybody. Well, short of peeing my pants, there was no way I was going to do anything. I was six years old and I flatly refused even to go onto the stage. Eventually a compromise was reached, and the microphone was brought to me in the stage dressing room, where I had sought sanctuary. I sang the song 'I Tawt I Taw a Puddy Tat' to the man holding the microphone, while the rest of the audience stared at the empty stage.

Shyness is a terrible obstacle to overcome, as anyone suffering from it will no doubt agree. But I've always subscribed to the theory that life is all about facing up to one's frailties and shortcomings – and being born shy, sensitive and later gaining an unfortunate limp gave me plenty to face up to! It didn't quite amount to being thrown in at the shallow end, did it? But as the saying goes, 'The Lord giveth and the Lord taketh away' – and with hindsight I can honestly say, as life has progressed that my initial cynicism has been overcome by a complete change of heart. Taking stock of all the suffering brought about by adversity, I realise I've been more than compensated by the modest talents I've been given, a wealth of true friends and the most wonderful daughter anyone could wish for.

So there I was, sailing through the late 1950s. By day I was strutting around looking all important with my briefcase, and by night I was trying to make a name for myself on the local club circuit with the group. During the summer months the demand for chocolate and such slowed down and I wasn't so busy, which left me time to pursue my favourite pastime – daydreaming. A hot sunny day was an invitation to find a nice grassy bank somewhere in the countryside, select a juicy stalk to chew on and lie in the sun. A few hours spent taking stock of my life interspersed with a modicum of speculation did wonders for my all-round well-being. It also set me up for a visit to one of my favourite couples.

They ran a little grocery store on the outskirts of town and they were a joy. He was one of life's true characters. Having lost one of his eyes while serving in the First World War, when he wasn't recounting the horrors of the Somme he had me in hysterics with his offbeat humour. She, by complete contrast, was quiet and homely, but they were perfect together. It was obvious to anyone that, despite their years, they were still very much in love with each other. If their recipe for happiness could be replicated throughout the world then we wouldn't be far short of paradise. I always looked forward to going there. Apart from the feel good factor, she made a great cup of coffee.

One particular day I called when they were trying to cope with a rush of customers. 'Go into the living room and make yourself at home, lad. I'll be with you in a minute,' she said, ushering me through to the cosy little room behind the shop. I went through and sat down in a big comfortable armchair and surveyed the scene. The room was in slight disarray – which was most unusual. The washing machine was chugging away amid piles of washing and things were generally chaotic. 'I'll make you a cup of coffee in a minute,' she called from the shop. 'We haven't had time to make your order out yet, but we shouldn't be long now.' Minutes later she dashed in, looking more than a little flustered. She took some mugs from a cupboard and placed them on the table alongside the sugar bowl. Then she poured some milk into a pan and placed it on the gas ring. 'Soon be ready,' she said, plunging one of the mugs into a large packet of soap powder. She poured most of it into the washing machine and placed it back on the table.

Then her husband came in from the shop. 'Mrs So-'n'-so wants some black cotton. Where is it?'

'Oh, I'll see to her.' She pushed past him. 'And while I'm doing that see to the coffee – and keep your eye on that milk pan!'

The pun wasn't lost on him. 'Are you being funny again?' he chuckled, making a pretence of smacking her. He turned back to me. 'Talking about being funny, have you heard this one?' He began to tell a joke as he spooned the coffee and sugar into the mugs.

She returned as he was pouring out the milk. 'Phew! That was a bit of a rush,' she sighed, sinking into a chair.

He handed out the coffees and we all took a sip. Mine tasted soapy. I knew straight away what had happened. Obviously he'd put the milk and coffee into the mug with the soap powder in it.

'Ah!' she sighed. 'I was ready for that.' She looked at me. 'Are you all right, lad?'

'Yes thanks,' I lied.

For the next half-hour I sat taking their order and forcing the coffee down. Why I didn't say anything at the time still mystifies me. Maybe it was for the same reason I peed my pants all those years ago – I was just trying to save someone's embarrassment. Strangely the resulting effect had certain similarities: whereas before I'd been left with a pair of soggy trousers, now I was beginning to feel as if I'd just consumed a pair – and the agony on the toilet afterwards was synonymous with trying to dispatch a pair. I don't know what came out, but I bet it was whiter than white. It had to be the first and only time I've left a toilet cleaner than I found it!

| Manager: LESLIE DARTFORT | **RAINBOW THEATRE**
 SOUTH PIER
 BLACKPOOL | Phone: 43096 |

THIS THEATRE HAS BEEN COMPLETELY MODERNISED, RE-SEATED AND ALL MODERN FACILITIES INCLUDED TO MAKE IT ONE OF BLACKPOOL'S MOST COMFORTABLE THEATRES

BERNARD HINCHCLIFFE LTD. proudly presents the

GRAND RE-OPENING
WITH THE

★★★★★★★★★★★★★★★★★★★★★★★
BIG WHIT SHOW
★★★★★★★★★★★★★★★★★★★★★★★

FOR NINE DAYS ONLY

WHIT. SAT. 1ST JUNE TO SUN. 9TH JUNE INCLUSIVE
TWICE NIGHTLY AT 6.15 & 8.30 (SUNDAYS AT 6.0 & 8.0)

BRITAIN'S GREATEST SINGING STAR
DANNY WILLIAMS

TV's "LITTLE MISS MUSIC" — GLAMOROUS
SHEILA BUXTON ★

THE VOICE OF THEM ALL
PETER CAVANAGH

BRITAIN'S FAVOURITE COMEDIAN
TED LUNE

NEWEST RECORDING STARS — DYNAMIC
VOLTAIRS WITH **SAMMY KING**

BBC's STAR COMPERE/SINGER
RAY PETERS
"HERE WE GO" etc.

HURRY — BOOK NOW 6/6, 5/6, 4/6 AT THEATRE BOX OFFICE

KING GEORGE'S HALL, BLACKBURN

BERNARD HINCHCLIFFE presents

SUNDAY, 19th JANUARY at 6-0 & 8-10 p.m.

Fabulous Recorder of "I'll Keep You Satisfied", "Bad To Me", etc.

BILLY J. KRAMER

Parlophone's Dynamic Recorders

THE DAKOTAS

Sensational Recorder of "I Only Want To Be With You"

DUSTY SPRINGFIELD

Decca's Star Group—Fabulous

THE BIG 3

Philip's Star Group—Pride of Lancashire

THE FOUR PENNIES

Voted Britain's Top New Group

SAMMY KING & THE VOLTAIRS

New Recording Stars	Compere—Teenage Idol
THE ECHOES	**GARTH CAWOOD**

BOOK NOW! STALLS 9/6, 8/6, 7/6, 4/6   BALCONY 8/6, 5/6
at Reidy's Penny Street, Blackburn. Phone: 7314

DEWSBURY'S TOP TEN

Dewsbury's top ten best-selling records this week according to J. W. Thornes' radio and record shop, Westgate, Dewsbury, are as follows:

1. You've lost that lovin' feelin'—The Righteous Brothers.
2. Cast your fate to the wind—Sounds Orchestral.
3. Tired of waiting for you—The Kinks.
4. Come tomorrow—Manfred Mann.
5. Go now—Moody Blues.
6. You've lost that lovin' feelin'—Cilla Black.
7. Only you—Sammy King and the Voltairs.
8. Ferry Cross the Mersey—Gerry and the Pacemakers.
9. Girl don't come—Sandie Shaw.
10. The game of love—Wayne Fontana and the Mindbenders.

The biggest surprise in this week's top ten is undoubtedly the appearance of local favourites, Sammy King and the Voltairs, at number seven with their latest ditty "Only you."

We made the Top 10 once! This was from my local newspaper in Dewsbury, West Yorkshire.

INTERNATIONAL SOCIETY

presents

International Rhythm Evening

with

The GAY "VOLTAIRS"

in attendance

Friday, 30th November, 1962

Admission
2/-

Social Room, Leeds University Union

from 7.00 p.m.

ON THE STAGE

GAUMONT-BRADFORD

General Manager
D. W. J. Willmott
Telephone 26716

SPECIAL PERFORMANCE — in aid of
'MEALS ON WHEELS' SERVICE

BRADFORD ROUND TABLE *PRESENTS* (by arrangement with Bernard Hinchcliffe)

SUNDAY, 8th. March 1964. at 6p.m. & 8-30

COLUMBIA'S SENSATIONAL

FREDDIE and the Dreamers

"You Were Made For Me" etc. etc.

GLAMOROUS RECORDING & T.V. STAR

KATHY KIRBY

"SECRET LOVE" etc.

FONTANA'S FABULOUS RECORDERS OF "I THINK OF YOU" etc. etc.

THE MERSEY BEATS

BRITAIN'S NEW TOP GROUP

SAMMY KING & THE VOLTAIRS

H.M.V. RECORDING STAR
MIKE SAGAR

THE DYNAMIC
RAY KENNON & The Quite 3

BRITAINS YOUNGEST STARS
The Walker Brothers

T.V.'s FOREMOST COMPERE
Roy Douglas

BOOK NOW ! Stalls: 9/6 7/6 6/- Circle 8/- Balcony: 5/6

CUT HERE

TO THE BOX OFFICE, GAUMONT BRADFORD
Please send me ___ Seats at ___ each for the 6 p.m. 8-30 p.m. performance

Poster makers and promoters almost invariably spelled our name incorrectly. It was supposed to be The Voltaires, with an 'e' - as in the French author and philosopher.

CITY HALL, HULL

TUESDAY, 15th OCTOBER
at 6-30 p.m. and 8-40 p.m.

Dynamic H.M.V. Recording and T.V. Star

JOHNNY KIDD
AND THE PIRATES
Hit Recorder of "I'll never get over you", etc.

Recorder of "Just like Eddie", etc.

HEINZ

THE ROLLING STONES
Decca's Stars of "Come on"

Decca's Star Group **SAINTS** "WIPE-OUT"	Sensational Group **PLUS FOUR**
Britain's Fabulous **SAMMY KING and the VOLTAIRS**	Your Compere **GARTH CAWOOD** "MR. SHAKE"

BOOK NOW at Paragon Music Stores, Paragon St., phone 32631
STALLS: 7/6, 6/- and 4/6. - - - - BALCONY: 5/6.
GALLERY: 3/6 - - - - - PLATFORM: 3/6

ST. GEORGE'S HALL, BRADFORD

WEDNESDAY, 16th OCTOBER
at 6-30 p.m. and 8-40 p.m.

International Film and Recording Star
JOHN LEYTON

Dynamic H.M.V. Recording and T.V. Star
JOHNNY KIDD
AND THE PIRATES
Hit Recorder of "I'll never get over you", etc.

Recorder of "Just like Eddie", etc.
HEINZ

Decca's Star Group **SAINTS** "WIPE-OUT"	Sensational Group **PLUS FOUR**
Britain's Fabulous **SAMMY KING and the VOLTAIRS**	Your Compere **GARTH CAWOOD** "MR. SHAKE"

BOOK NOW at St. George's Hall Box Office, phone 32513
STALLS: 7/6, 6/6 and 5/6. - - DRESS CIRCLE: 7/6 and 5/6.
UPPER CIRCLE: 6/6, 4/6 and 3/6 - - - PLATFORM: 3/-

KING GEORGE'S HALL
BLACKBURN
6-0 — SUNDAY, 5th APRIL — 8-10

BERNARD HINCHCLIFFE presents ANOTHER TOP-VALUE SHOW

COLUMBIA'S DYNAMIC RECORDING
T.V. & FILM STARS

FREDDIE
AND THE DREAMERS

FABULOUS RECORDERS OF "I THINK OF YOU" etc.

THE MERSEYBEATS

LIVERPOOL'S SENSATIONAL RECORDING & T.V. STARS

THE UNDERTAKERS

BRITAIN'S NEW H.M.V. RECORDING STARS

SAMMY KING & THE VOLTAIRS

H.M.V. RECORDING STAR	THE DYNAMIC
MIKE SAGAR	**RAY KENNON**
THE SWINGING	COMPERE — TEENAGE IDOL
QUIET 3	**GARTH CAWOOD**
LANCASHIRE'S MILL STAR GROUP	**THE WARRIORS**

BOOK NOW!
STALLS 9/6, 8/6, 7/6, 4/6   BALCONY 8/6, 5/6
at REIDY'S, PENNY STREET, BLACKBURN   Phone 7314

QUEEN'S HALL - LEEDS

BERNARD HINCHCLIFFE presents ANNUAL

MAMMOTH ALL-NITE BEAT BALL
FRIDAY, 26TH JUNE, 1964

10 p.m. to 7 a.m.

PHILIPS' DYNAMIC RECORDERS OF "JULIET," etc.

FOUR PENNIES

THE SENSATIONAL

MANFRED MANN

"5, 4, 3, 2, 1," "Hubble Bubble," etc.

H.M.V. RECORDERS OF "WHAT'S THE SECRET"
SAMMY KING & THE VOLTAIRS

HULL'S TOP PARLOPHONE GROUP
THE ACES

H.M.V. STARS
MIKE SAGAR - RAY KENNON - QUIET 3

SHEFFIELD'S FOREMOST R. & B. GROUP
THE CHEVRONS

FROM HUDDERSFIELD
GARY STEVENS & THE OVERLANDERS

NORTH'S TOP DISC JOCKEY — GARTH CAWOOD

LICENSED BAR UNTIL 1.30 a.m. (applied for)
BACON AND EGG BREAKFASTS (4/6 extra) from 4.0 a.m.

Tickets 10/6 until 19th June inclusive, then after 12/6
Admission at Door 15/-

Tickets from Queen's Hall, Lewis's and Vallances, Leeds; W. H. Smiths, Bradford; Music Centre, Huddersfield; Thornes, Dewsbury and Batley; Nicholl, Brown & Coyle, Halifax; Bill's Snack Bar, Brighouse.

To: Box Office, Queen's Hall, Sovereign Street, Leeds,
Please supply ...... tickets at .... for the All-Nite Ball on the 26th June at the Queen's Hall, Leeds. Enclosed P.O./Cheque ....
Name ....
Address ....

We appeared on the bill with Tommy Bruce or 'Mr Gravel Voice' as he was affectionately known. 'Ain't Misbehavin'' was his most popular song.

TEXTILE HALL BALLROOM, BRADFORD
FRIDAY, JANUARY 18th, 1963
Dancing 8 p.m. — 1 a.m.
Al St. George-Withall in association with Garth B. Cawood presents
COLUMBIA'S TOP RECORDING STAR

TOMMY BRUCE
AND HIS BRUISERS

PLUS
RADIO & T.V. STARS **THE VOLTAIRS**
PLUS
THE DYNAMIC **TORNADOES**

5/6   Nº 733   5/6

Chapter Eight
ROCK'N'ROLL DAYS

As business picked up my enterprise was rewarded with a few extra quid and I began to look around for a better drum kit. My old kit was beginning to look more old fashioned by the day: the trend by this time favoured a smaller, more compact drum. I managed to acquire a half-set, which proved to be not only more portable than the old kit but better sounding too.

The '50s were drawing to a close, and the skiffle craze began to recede as the electric guitar became more prominent. Most of the skiffle groups, including our own, folded or emerged as rock'n'roll bands, revelling in the fresh new sounds being imported from the USA. Stars like Elvis, Buddy Holly and Jerry Lee Lewis were being emulated by anyone who could twang a guitar or plonk a piano. The music industry was undergoing a complete renaissance, mainly because, for the first time, songs were being written *for* the young, *about* the young, *by* the young. All the frustrations of youth, interspersed with hope and expectation, poured from the speakers of every Dansette record player in every teenager's bedroom. Youth culture was changing. Young people began to rebel, demanding the right to dress or wear their hair in the same fashion as their heroes. The formality of ballroom dancing was cast aside in favour of the wild indiscipline of the 'bop'. All this was happening in the name of rock'n'roll – and I, like every other starry-eyed kid, was determined to be part of it.

By this time I'd begun to take more than just an interest in the guitar. At first I practised on my brother's while he was at work, and soon I'd learnt enough chords to accompany myself singing the popular songs of the day. Before long I had a guitar of my own and the drums began to play second fiddle, so to speak. Though the skiffle group had disbanded, my brother and I still continued to work the clubs as a duo, singing songs in the Everly Brothers style. We worked under the name the Twohig Brothers, and I always found it amusing when we arrived at a venue to find us billed as 'The Two Higg Brothers'!

Rock'n'roll seemed to revitalise everything. Previously defunct rooms and church halls were re-awakened by the pulsating beat of the new sound. The working men's clubs were subjected to a new level of volume, much to the chagrin of the older members who were more disposed to songs in the Bing Crosby style.

I earned as much on the clubs singing with my brother as I did at my day job, so I made sure all these earnings were spent upgrading my musical equipment – just in case the taxman took an interest.

We also increased the number in our act to three, joining forces with a young girl singer called Betty Gledhill. We met while taking part in a local talent show challenge contest. It was organised between the surrounding townships and was called Top Town. We were featured together in the show and decided to remain together, as the partnership had worked so well. At my mother's suggestion we decided to call ourselves the Three Lloyds, named after the bank we intended to keep all our money in!

We began to do well, and in the following months our Morris Minor Traveller was kept busy carrying us back and forth to venues throughout the West Riding. But while we were quite successful in our own small way, the likelihood of ever becoming famous was pretty remote. The initial requirement for stardom was to have a hit record broadcast over the airwaves, or to appear on television. Since all that kind of thing was controlled over two hundred miles away in London, the idea of being famous never entered our heads – until one day Betty's mother dropped in on one of our rehearsals excitedly brandishing a newspaper. 'They're holding auditions for the Carroll Levis Discoveries Show' in Leeds,' she enthused, 'and I think you three should enter. You never know, it could be your big chance!'

The Carroll Levis Show was a talent competition run throughout the country, which culminated in the winners of each area appearing in the televised final. The first prize included among other things a recording test. We entered, and eventually got through to the area final, staged at the Leeds Empire.

It was the first time I'd ever set foot on a theatre stage. It was magic! I was more excited than nervous and the atmosphere was tremendous. The lights were so bright that I couldn't see beyond the first few rows, but I could still sense the vastness of the auditorium. The now famous Jackie Collins presented the show. At that time she was an up and coming young actress struggling to make a name for herself in the shadow of her sister Joan. She looked absolutely stunning in a figure-hugging dress cut so low that at first I thought I was talking to two bald-headed men hiding in the top. But she looked gorgeous – more so, I thought, after she pinched my cheek and said I was 'cute'.

The talent in the show was of a very high standard, and while I felt we did well I knew we weren't going to win. But it was a tremendous experience, one I'll never forget. It must have made our parents very proud too.

While the votes were being counted it was left to Miss Collins to keep the audience amused, which delighted the male contingent no end. 'What shall I do?' she asked innocently. The audience stirred. No doubt there were plenty of chauvinistic suggestions suppressed by female elbows in the moments that followed. And it wasn't until she added, 'I can't sing,' and my brother cheekily chipped in with 'She don't have to!' that the tension was broken, and the audience started chuckling.

In the end a good mate of ours, Johnny Breslin, got the vote after wowing the audience with a first class rendition of Frankie Laine's 'In the Beginning'. We came away not too disappointed, and agreeing that it was probably for the best anyway. My brother had the makings of a good career in local government, Betty was in a steady relationship and I was quite happy just breezing along making up for lost time.

I began to spend more time practising my guitar, but I didn't discard the drums altogether. They were extremely good for getting rid of tension or aggression. Knocking hell out of them for an hour was very therapeutic – though I doubt if our next-door neighbours agreed! Strangely enough they never complained. I can only surmise either that they liked drum solos, were deaf or always out!

On occasion I managed to get a few extra jobs playing the drums. One particular gig took me to a local tennis club where, along with a pianist, I was booked to play for the New Year's Eve dance for the princely sum of two pounds – and all the beer I could sup. Arriving early, I set up next to the piano, which was situated in a corner of the L-shaped room out of sight of the bar. I got myself a pint and sat down. For the next half-hour I just sat there waiting for someone to arrive. Presently a group of people drifted in, one of them being the club secretary. He came over and shook my hand vigorously. 'You must be the drummer.' I was completely under whelmed by his observation. He looked at his watch. 'The pianist should be here any time. We book him every year and he's usually reliable. Anyway, when he arrives no doubt he'll make himself known to you.'

He hurried back to his chums and I sat down to await my fellow muso. More people began to filter in, and after maybe another half-hour a figure shambled across from the bar carrying a pint. He took a long swig of ale, sat down at the piano, plonked the glass on top of it and launched into a Charlie Kunz classic – the title of which escapes me. After four bars I thought it might be prudent to introduce myself, so I picked up my drumsticks and walked over to him. 'I'm your drummer this evening. Have you got a programme for me or what?'

'Just follow me lad, just follow me,' he said, without looking up. His left arm was in full swing by this time, as his hand grabbed more than an octave.

Well, I suppose I'd better join in, I thought, and sat down to accompany him.

We played fifteen-minute sets with a few minutes break in between, giving him time to go to the bar for his freebies. When he returned I was always met with, 'Just follow me, lad, just follow me.' In the end I christened him JFM.

During the evening Andy Coates, one of my old art school colleagues, came in and joined me. I was really pleased to see him as I was well pissed off by this time. JFM was starting to hit more cracks than notes, and his tempo was being influenced by Tetley's best bitter! My sanity was restored when Andy offered to take over the drums for the odd few numbers to give me a break. By this time nobody knew any different anyway – least of all JFM, who didn't even notice when we changed over midway through a number.

I was able to repay Andy by getting him free beer. Seeing as the drums were out of sight of the bar, the steward didn't know who was supping all the beer going round the corner. He didn't even notice that the drums were 'playing themselves' when I was at the bar ordering it. Later in the night, though, as I followed JFM to the bar for my umpteenth pint, he did remark, 'You musicians should all have gills. You sup like bloody fish!'

JFM was well gone coming up to midnight. One of his friends tried to wake him up during the break before the countdown into the New Year. As Big Ben began to chime from the radio behind the bar, he frantically shook his inebriated pal.

'TEN . . .'

'Come on, you drunken bugger, it's nearly midnight.'

'. . . NINE . . . EIGHT . . .'

'Wake up!' He shook him again. One eye seemed to open.

'. . . SEVEN . . . SIX . . .'

The other eye tried to join it.

'. . . FIVE . . . FOUR . . .'

His friend placed JFM's hands on the keys and sat him upright.

'. . . THREE . . . TWO . . .'

He began to stir.

'ONE. . . . HAPPY NEW YEAR!'

I crashed the cymbal and JFM joined in – purely by instinct. 'Should auld acquaintance be forgot . . .' he plonked away as the streamers were thrown and the balloons were burst and everybody began hugging each other. After that no one was in a fit state to care about anything. True to the song, old JFM was one acquaintance I never forgot. When the dance was over I packed up my drums and waited for my lift home, leaving him slumped over the piano fast asleep. I never did get to know his name.

Anyway, I left the tennis club feeling pretty pleased with myself – and why not? After all, I came out richer than I went in and I was able to enjoy a free night's drinking with a good friend. Needless to say they never asked me back. I guess that, after totting up the bar tabs, they realised it would have been cheaper to engage a quartet on a fixed fee!

For a while I drifted around the pubs and clubs watching and listening to the groups, paying particular attention to the guitarists. Occasionally I visited the Crown and Anchor in Wakefield to watch a group called The Dawnbreakers. They were a great band, and not

The Three Lloyds. Left to right: me, brother Brian and Betty Gledhill. We entered a competition at Leeds Empire called Carroll Levis Discovers.

Fellow competitors at a talent competition at Dewsbury Town Hall, 1956. Note Johnny Rock playing the bones!

opposed to letting the occasional punter get up and sing a song with them – so after a few beers I'd get up and sing the old Conway Twitty hit 'Mona Lisa'. Another band that regularly played at the same venue was Roy Mitchell and the Rhythm Makers. There seemed to be a surplus of good drummers too, like Colin Dack and Colin Marchant, a brilliant drummer who actually lived in the next street to me. It was after hearing the two Colins play that I decided to spend more time on the guitar!

There were a lot of good pubs around Wakefield at that time and one in particular became my favourite – the notorious Dolphin (featured in the Richard Harris film *This Sporting Life* in 1963). Run by the indestructible landlord Tommy Fisher, it boasted criminals, homosexuals, lesbians, bisexuals, misfits, drunkards – and that was just the staff. But I loved it. Apart from anything else, you could get a free pint if you got up and sang a song. So if money was tight at least you could have some sort of a night out. The resident band was a bunch of battle-hardened musicians who had seen and heard everything before. Just as well, perhaps, because all human life imaginable was paraded back and forth on that stage nightly. The whole scene was a mishmash of eccentricity interspersed with the odd comedian or stripper, all served up as good old-fashioned entertainment. It wasn't unusual to see the occasional celebrity rubbing shoulders with punters, such was the infamy of the place. It was there I first saw one of my heroes, and later great friend, 'Yogi Des' Francis performing. His handling of a rowdy group of rugby fans one evening was a joy to behold: professionalism at its best.

Above all it was a great testing ground for any aspiring entertainer. On any given night they could experience the very worst in crowd behaviour which, if nothing else, would teach them the value of a thick skin.

Progress

My quest for self-improvement, at least concerning my guitar-playing, took me to a pub in nearby Cleckheaton called the Royal. Bernard Lumb, an enterprising old mate from primary school, took me to see a lad he thought was a really good guitarist. The strains of Duane Eddy's hit 'Forty Miles of Bad Road' met my ears as we walked into the music room. Not just the playing but the guy himself impressed me. He was one of the nicest people you could ever wish to meet, and Eric Holroyd and I soon became the best of friends. Although he was a giant of a man, he was blessed with a gentleness which endeared him to anyone making his acquaintance. Already an accomplished trumpeter, he too was discovering the fascination of the electric guitar.

Before long I was commuting between my house and Eric's home in Bradford, which he shared with his wife Jean and their baby daughter. Some of my happiest memories are of the times we spent messing about with his old Grundig tape recorder. It would be fair to say that my recording career first began in that little house in Listerhills, Bradford.

I learnt a lot from Eric. He was great at working out things on the guitar. If he found out how to play a certain riff, instead of waiting till we met again he'd ring me up from the telephone box near his home and play it to me over the phone. God only knows what it must have looked like to anyone passing by. He had an insatiable enthusiasm for playing, and even did a few gigs with the Three Lloyds before we disbanded. His professionalism was exemplary and Bernard suggested that we should form a group under his management. So Eric and I began to put together a few numbers and Bernard went out scouting for other musicians to add to the band.

One night Bernard took me to a place in Dewsbury called the Cameo Club. He couldn't contain his excitement. 'You've got to hear this guy play,' he drooled. 'Much faster than anyone round here! He used to play with Ray Ellington and other London bands . . . He's called Jimmy Rogers.' We went into the small, dimly lit club just as Jimmy was finishing a solo. Bernard was right about him being fast. Jimmy's fingers were a blur as they sped up the neck of the guitar. When the band finished playing Bernard took me over to meet the guitarist. I shook Jimmy's hand and Bernard went into his spiel. 'We're getting a band together . . .'

When I got home I rang Eric and told him about Jimmy and that he was coming to the next rehearsal at Bernard's invitation. Eric, being a little older than me, was sceptical at first but agreed to meet him.

At the rehearsal Jimmy got up and sang 'China Doll', which was a plus seeing as it meant we had an extra vocalist too. He then launched into 'Guitar Boogie Shuffle', which featured his blistering solo. Eric was impressed, but not as enthusiastic as our manager-in-waiting. Bernard lost no time trying to convince him. 'Jimmy's played all over the country and is really well known. I think we ought to form the group around him and call it the Rogers Brothers.' Eric and I looked at one another. How we managed to keep a straight face I'll never know.

'Rogers *Brothers*?' Eric asked incredulously.

'Why not?' said Bernard, his mind obviously temporarily distracted by his enthusiasm. The fact that Jimmy was black had no doubt escaped his notice. This, coupled with the fact that the gigantic Eric and I only had our gender in common, made the statement even more amusing. But the story didn't end there.

We managed to fix an audition with the management of the Gaiety Ballroom in Bradford. Eric opened with 'Forty Miles of Bad Road', and then Jimmy sang 'China Doll' followed by his 'Guitar Boogie'. Once again his lightning fast solo wailed from his amplifier. I sang the next song and Jimmy played the solo in it. After a couple of bars I thought, wait a minute, I've heard this before. Eric and I looked at each other. It was the same solo that he'd played in the previous number. And so it went on. Song after song: the same solo. We'd only heard him play one solo before the audition, so we hadn't realised it was the only one he knew! We never learnt the outcome of the audition as we decided not to pursue the Rogers Brothers idea.

For all our musical differences, it has to be said that Jimmy was a lovely bloke and a perfect gentleman. I'll always be grateful to Bernard for introducing me to him.

Deflowered!

The year 1959 was to become very significant for me in many respects. I was on my way to being eighteen years old and was already well versed in the art of drinking, entertaining and dealing with the day-to-day eccentricities of the business world. The only activity I wasn't experienced in was the one my gender overwhelmingly considered being the most important – sex. Apart from the odd fumble up a jumper in the park or a snog in the back row of a cinema, my experience with the opposite sex was very limited. To be honest, the sum total of my participation in the art could be counted on the fingers of a fish. Most of my mates had been initiated ages ago, around the time I was in hospital. According to them, while I was experiencing 'proper' love with Nurse Elisabeth they were all at it like rabbits at the youth group. This might well have been true but as they say in France – '*Je ne regrette rien*'.

All this was about to change when I went to a local dance hall one evening to see a group from Bradford called The Dingos. Being very conscious of my disability I didn't dance and was just content to listen. This was also the main reason I never chatted up girls: the fear of being rebuffed would probably have shattered for ever the fragile confidence I'd worked so hard to build up.

The band had just finished one of their numbers when my attention was drawn to a tall and shapely girl walking towards me. She moved with the poise and confidence of a mannequin pacing a catwalk. Her smouldering eyes fixed me with the same unwavering stare that a predator adopts before pouncing on its helpless prey. Wow! I thought. I wonder what she wants with me. I quickly glanced to each side of me, to reassure myself that it really was me who was the focus of her attention. My hopes were confirmed – I was sitting alone.

'Mind if I sit down?' she purred.

'Help yourself,' I replied, offering her the seat next to me. She ignored it and settled her curvaceous form into my lap.

Stroking the back of my neck she went on. 'I've just been telling my friend that I think you're really fanciable, and she said I should come over and tell you.'

'I'm glad she did,' I croaked.

She wriggled about in my lap and my 'temperature' began to rise.

'I know you fancy me,' she giggled. 'I can feel it!' She wriggled some more, and my 'temperature' began to get harder.

The band began their next number, which intensified the situation. To continue the conversation she moved her head closer, causing her lips to brush gently against my left ear as she spoke. Deep joy! Without knowing it, she had tapped directly into one of my many erogenous zones.

In the fifteen minutes that followed our tête-à-tête was filled with an exuberance of erotic verbal foreplay, and somehow I knew that before the night was out I was going to be initiated. The sheer sexuality she was exuding was already prompting the little tadpoles in my reproductive system to pack their suitcases in readiness for their trip to Disneyland.

She took my hand and we headed for the exit. I draped my jacket over my free arm and held it in front of me to hide my 'temperature', which by now had reached its uppermost and was pointing the way out. We descended the steps casually – three at a time. 'The car's round the corner,' I said.

'You're in a car?' she exclaimed. 'Ooh, it gets better! We can go somewhere private.'

As we walked towards the car she began to play 'round and round the garden' with her forefinger in the palm of my hand. The tadpoles were starting to board the plane!

We drove to a quiet spot and, after stopping the car, I joined her in the passenger seat. She thrust her thighs against my 'temperature' and whispered in my ear, 'I made up my mind weeks ago that I was going to have you.'

'Weeks ago?' I croaked. My mouth was beginning to go dry in anticipation.

'Yes. I've been plucking up courage to tell you for ages,' she said, peeling back the lower half of her dress to reveal perfect thighs. She lay back trapping my arm against the seat and pulled me towards her.

'Hang on a minute, I'll just get a condom,' I insisted.

'Oh don't bother with that – I'm safe,' she replied.

The tadpoles were half-way across the Atlantic and I was losing the battle to 'slow the plane down'. I frantically unzipped my trousers and tried to pull them down.

'Oh hell,' I cursed. I'd forgotten to undo my braces. It was the trend to wear clip-on braces at the time. They were very fashionable, but not very practical when it came to de-bagging in the front seat of a small car — and especially when I only had one hand free. I couldn't even slip them off my shoulders without removing my jacket and tank top first. Anyway, time was running short; the tadpoles were all for bailing out. The clips holding the back of my trousers were clamped on like the jaws of an alligator, and I couldn't shift them. So I unclipped the front ones, leaving the braces to slide over my shoulders as I pulled my trousers down. It worked for the first few inches, then the adjusters on the braces snagged. She began to get more frustrated, moaning at me to hurry up as I struggled. The tadpoles were getting impatient too, and it took a great amount of willpower to stop them entering the 'Magic Kingdom' before the plane had landed. I somehow got around the problem by wedging my trousers between my knee and the car seat to stop them springing back up.

At last, I thought, I'm about to be initiated!

She moaned in a different way as my aeroplane entered Florida airspace. Again she thrust her hips against me — jerking my knee from the car seat. Boiing! Up came my trousers.

'Oh no.' I groaned, again pulling them down and wedging them against the seat. She thrust again. Boiing! Up they came again. It happened a third time and things were becoming impossible. Apart from anything else, I was having difficulty keeping the tadpoles under control — and I tried to think of all kinds of silly distractions to savour my long-awaited initiation. The following moments saw us trying to make love while my trousers continued to bungee jump. It was useless; I couldn't contain myself any longer. As I withdrew the tadpoles began to bale out.

Geronimo! Oh, the feeling! My God. It was wonderful. I had finally 'come' to Disneyland! Unfortunately the same couldn't be said for my partner d'amour. Judging by the look of disappointment on her face, I'd say her libido had only got as far as the check-in.

We tried again a week later, and while my performance wasn't a complete disaster it would be fair to say that her ardour was more in keeping with Blackpool than Disneyland.

Chapter Nine
THE DINGOS

I've always been proud of the fact that I was born in Batley – the same little West Yorkshire town that produced the great rock star Robert Palmer (though he was always reluctant to admit to it), the 'Gallant Youths' (Batley Rugby League football team) and Fox's Biscuits. But my alter ego Sammy was actually born ten miles away.

At that time the group scene in Bradford was the best for miles. By a strange coincidence I was drawn back to the place where fate – having robbed me of one kind of life – was about to offer me another in return. A phone call from my old mate Eric Holroyd set the ball rolling. He told me that one of The Dingos – Malcolm Clarke – had left the group and they were looking to replace him with another singer, plus a guitarist. Eric was going to audition for the guitarist's job and suggested I should go for the singer's. I was a bit apprehensive at first because Malcolm was a brilliant singer and in my opinion was irreplaceable. But I agreed to go with Eric anyway, to give him some moral support if nothing else. We made our way to the Tudor Café in Bradford, where The Dingos rehearsed. Eric and I sat down to watch a couple of others who were already auditioning. I couldn't believe what was happening and I sat there mesmerised, attempting to take it all in. Just to think that I, not very long ago, was sitting watching them in our local dance hall. And, although they didn't know it, these lads (in a roundabout way) were instrumental in helping me get laid for the first time. After all, it was when they started playing that she'd had to lean close to me to whisper in my ear . . .

All kinds of stuff kept going through my mind as I struggled to suppress my nervousness. Eventually Eric got up to do his bit and as I expected it was flawless. He was really good, and I fully expected them to take him on there and then. When he'd finished playing the lads had a confab, and then their attention turned to me. Garth Cawood, who seemed to act as the spokesman, asked if I'd like to sing a song for them. I agreed with a certain amount of reluctance and, feeling very nervous, suggested doing my pet song at that time – Conway Twitty's version of 'Mona Lisa'. Most of the group had heard it but had never played it, so Eric lent me his guitar to quickly run through the chords with them. 'Oh, so you can play the guitar as well as sing?' somebody remarked.

'And he can play the drums too,' Eric chipped in. This was typical of him, backing me to the hilt, but it might have served him better to have kept mum that evening: he was helping to talk himself out of a job!

I began to run through the chords of the song. Ken Fowler, the lead guitarist, was pleased that it was in the key of E – which meant he wouldn't have to use his capo (a playing aid for the guitar). 'Smudge' Smith didn't need to know, being the drummer, and cheerfully rattled round his drums, while Stuart Ellis, the bass player, stood quietly aloof. Spike O'Brien, who was sitting quietly at his piano wearing a pork pie hat, muttered, 'I don't suppose you can play the piano as well, can yer?'

'Well, as a matter of fact . . . '

He turned round to face his instrument before grunting, 'He's a proper little Sammy Davis Jr, isn't he?'

We swung into the song. It sounded great, and afterwards the lads went into a huddle at one end of the room while we hopefuls sat in anticipation at the other. After a short meeting Garth popped his head up from the huddle and said, 'Hey, Sammy!' They didn't know my name. 'Will you come here a minute?' I was offered the job and Eric, being the person he was, said I'd be mad not to take it. And, as he pointed out, he was already playing in an established group (Dal Stevens and the Four Dukes), so he wouldn't be left high and dry.

So that's when Sammy was born – in the Tudor Café, at the top of Dudley Hill in Bradford, in 1959. From that moment on I was Sammy to the band, and it stuck.

Joining The Dingos was a whole new experience. It was the first time I'd been involved with a group that had a recognised following. I was really excited at the prospect of being part of the raw and earthy sound that the group was noted for: they were one of the few groups that people preferred to watch and listen to rather than dance to.

Malcolm, the lad I was replacing, was a terrific ballad singer, and there was no way I could reproduce what he did, so I introduced Elvis Presley and Eddie Cochrane songs into the programme. This proved to be a success, as I was judged in my own right and, more importantly, the music seemed well fitted to The Dingos' style. They were the first Rhythm and Blues band I'd heard – years ahead of their time. The thing I liked best about them was that while every other group was trying to emulate Cliff Richard and the Shadows, they stuck to their own style. Many years later, when I was leading my own group, we supported an exciting new band called the Rolling Stones. I really enjoyed listening to them but it was nothing new to me. They did exactly what we were doing years before – even down to using maracas and a tambourine. I know millions will probably take me to task, but I still think The Dingos did it better!

Having a different sound worked to our advantage. From time to time we got prestige gigs supporting 'name' bands, because we didn't clash with them. One of my favourite bands was Screaming Lord Sutch's outfit, The Savages. Dave Sutch was the showman supreme and he never failed to impress me. I was always in awe of his backing group. His lead guitarist at that time was Richie Blackmore who, heavy metal fans will know, went on to take the world by storm with Deep Purple and later Rainbow. What a talent! I think hearing him play finally convinced me to concentrate on singing. Another group we were chosen to support, Johnny Kidd and the Pirates, had just had a massive number one hit with a song called 'Shakin' All Over'. (By a strange coincidence their recording manager, Wally Ridley, became my recording manager a few years later. I made four records for HMV and Wally produced them all.) As a gimmick Johnny wore an eye-patch during his show, and after one show he gave it to Garth as a keepsake. After that 'Shakin' All Over' became a feature of our show – with Garth wearing the genuine patch. During the next few years it probably caused more impact than any other

The Dingos round the piano.

The Dingos reunion, 2004. Left to right: Spike O'Brien, Ken Fowler, Garth Cawood, Dave Butterfield, me and Irvin 'Smudge' Smith.

The Dingos' string section

The original Dingos, before I joined.

A nineteen-year-old Eric Holroyd.

A recent picture of me and Eric Holroyd. I took Eric to the audition for the Dingos with no intention of joining, but ended up as singer and guitarist after Eric suggested I did an audition.

song. Wherever we went people loved it – but usually for the wrong reasons. Garth really put himself about during the song and invariably, purely by accident of course, something would get damaged. Tables, chairs, curtains, microphones, fluorescent lights and, more often than not, pianos. Garth, being the ultimate showman, was game for anything and Spike encouraged him, so most of the action usually took place around the piano. To begin with, most of the pianos we came across were not used much and usually a bit dilapidated, so if Garth leapt onto them you could say it was only half his fault if they came apart – which they often did.

There was never a dull moment with The Dingos. They were a great bunch of lads and generally we got on pretty well together. Only occasionally was there a clash of personalities. Any mischief that arose usually involved Spike or Smudge. Garth came in for most of the wind-ups, but he always handled them with great dignity – apart from one occasion when Smudge unscrewed the tops of his maracas leaving them barely held together. Half-way through our performance, when Garth gave them a good shake, the tops came off and there were dried peas everywhere. No one owned up to the misdemeanour – but we were instructed to put things right before the next spot. Someone went to a shop to buy a packet of dried peas during the interval, and proceeded to fill the maracas – right to the top. When Garth came in to try them he could hardly lift them, and in a fit of pique threw them at us – again demanding that they be put right. He went off to the pub to calm himself with a pint, leaving us to remove the peas from the maracas. We took them all out, leaving a solitary pea in each one, before placing them on the stage next to his tambourine. We were already into our first number when he returned from the pub. Without a word he strode onto the stage, picked up the maracas and discovered that the peas rolled around inside like a motorbike on the wall of death. Garth's face was like thunder. He slung the maracas away, picked up the tambourine and started bashing it. And when the little cymbals on the tambourine began falling off that was the last straw. He threw it away, stormed off and didn't return. The funny thing was – no one had tampered with the tambourine.

To his credit Garth never carried grudges and he soon got over it. He always had a great capacity to shrug off these agitations without effort, and I dare say he sees the funny side of this episode when he looks back on it now. It was one of the many things I came to admire about him during our association. One other thing that I admired was his taste in women: he married five very beautiful women – separately of course!

Spike, on the other hand, never seemed to bother with a steady girlfriend. He was a free spirit and tended to play the field. Before he joined The Dingos he hung around with the local hard men and frequently got into trouble. In fact it was his unrestrained lifestyle that eventually led him to join the group. The police chased him into a dancehall where the lads were playing one night, and to hide from them he leapt onto the stage and began playing the piano. It was a masterstroke. The cops only checked the audience and left – never thinking to check the band So that night The Dingos inherited a new pianist – bloodstains and all. He eventually moved down south and played with a few top London bands.

Our drummer Smudge – his real name was Irvin Smith – was a really likeable, happy-go-lucky type. He was born under the sign of Libra like me, and in consequence we shared many traits. Technically Smudge was a good drummer, but sometimes the fast numbers had a tendency to slow down. I like to think that this was because he worked so hard during the day; he must have been completely exhausted by the time we got to the gig!

Ken, the lead guitarist, was the quiet, studious one. He was so laid back that he only moved at one speed – and that was 'stop'. Like me he'd studied art at school, but he was so talented that he had no problem making a living from it. He was also a great guitarist, and it has to be said that his style was largely responsible for giving The Dingos their distinctive sound.

The only one who never really seemed to fit in was Stuart, the bass player, and after a while he left and was replaced by Dave Butterfield. Dave slotted in straight away and his permanent smile and his personality gave the band's presentation one hell of a boost. He loved playing with the band as it gave him a welcome break from his studies. I never found out what he was studying but it must have been worthwhile. He's now very wealthy – and owns his own yacht!

The only downside to the change in personnel was that when Stuart left so did half our transport. Transport was always a problem in those days. It was expensive, and the band tended to travel long distances, in all weathers, returning at all hours in the morning. Because of this it was with a certain amount of reluctance that my mother gave me permission to use our Morris Minor Traveller. Though I felt competent enough in her eyes I was still very young –

and inexperienced. Unfortunately her fears were well founded. When we were returning from a gig in Nelson, Lancashire, I lost control when the car hit a patch of black ice, and ended up ploughing into a lamppost in the early hours. Smudge and I were taken to Burnley Victoria Hospital, but fortunately the head wounds we suffered weren't too serious. We were discharged the next morning after being stitched up – much to the relief of our respective families. Ken, the other band member travelling with us, hurt his back – but only slightly; he seemed more concerned about the state of his amplifier. He was amazed that it still worked having survived such an impact.

Later the police informed me that they wouldn't be pressing charges. On their way to investigate the smash their patrol car had hit the same patch of ice and had only missed the same lamppost by inches. But having escaped death and prosecution by the skin of my teeth, I still didn't get away from it all scot-free. Apart from the physical and mental scars, it has since cost me dearly in terms of insurance.

I was with The Dingos for three years, and apart from the prang I enjoyed every minute. Not long after I joined them I met and fell in love with Susan – a dark-eyed young beauty who became my first serious girlfriend. We were inseparable, and our relationship lasted for most of the three years. I have to admit to feeling heartbroken when she called time on our relationship, because she felt she wanted to live a little before settling down. We were both very young, and although I knew her reasons were justifiable I still found it very hard to come to terms with.

What does a heartbroken, lovesick teenager do to purge his inner torment? He gets stoned or he writes a poem or a song. I chose the latter. Susan's sister Jean sent it off to John Schroeder at Oriole Records in London – probably hoping the distraction would ease my suffering. It didn't work, only adding to it when the rejection letter arrived by return of post. I still have it – and sent him a copy after we met at a book launch recently. He was slightly embarrassed, but I told him he needn't be: it was a crap song, and if anybody should be embarrassed it was me!

Not long afterwards Susan decided that the world outside our relationship wasn't that much greener, and wanted to come back to me. Though I still thought the world of her, I'm ashamed to say that the old foolish pride got in the way of common sense and I decided to go my own way. I feel sure that had we met later in life the outcome would have been so different. We were ideally suited, and I'm certain we would have been happy together. Call me cynical, but once again it seemed as if some unknown force had taken a hand in making me completely disregard my natural instincts in order to pursue my destiny.

In many ways this period was a watershed for the group in more ways than one. Ken and his girlfriend Mona parted company in similar circumstances to me and Susan, as did Smudge and his girlfriend Linda. It seemed such a pity, for I liked the two girls very much. This went back to my first days with the band. On my first appearance with them I was feeling a bit lost during the interval: I didn't really know anyone, and just hung about on my own like a spare part waiting for the next set. Linda seemed to sense that I was shy and self-conscious, and she immediately invited me to sit with her and Mona. I never forgot her act of kindness and, though we didn't know it at the time, our paths would cross many times in the future.

I really loved my time with the band. It opened up a new world to me, and in many ways helped to build the confidence I'd need to get me through whatever lay ahead. When I eventually left The Dingos the whole episode was tinged with a great deal of sadness. The tragedy of it all was that it was because of a misunderstanding, which turned out to be something and nothing.

Thirty years later we re-formed the band for one night to play a gig for charity. I was amazed to see many of our old fans in the audience – even more surprised that I could still recognise some of them. What a night that turned out to be. I hadn't even seen some of the band for thirty years. It was like welcoming back long-lost brothers. At the rehearsal in the afternoon we all creaked onto the stage, someone counted in and when we launched into the first number it was as if we'd never been apart. It was amazing.

And the evening was even better. Some of them brought their families with them, and between us we made it one of the most memorable nights of my life. So successful was the gig that we decided to do it every year, and as the word got round more and more old friends were reunited – even Susan came one year, with her American husband. She lives in California now, and happened to be in Bradford visiting her father when she heard about the reunion. I gave her a hug and we talked for a while. Her husband seemed to be a very nice guy (the swine) but seriously, I was really glad that she was happy. She asked after Soaks – her pet name for my dad, whom she adored, and was genuinely upset to hear that he'd died a few years before. It was really good to see her again, but alas, the old feelings were no longer there.

House!

For a while I wandered about like a lost soul. Bradford had been my second home for the past three years, as I'd spent most of my time there with Susan and the band. I missed Susan and all the new friends I'd made in the town, and I missed playing the popular venues like the Gaumont, the Students Club, the Kings and Queens and the one I liked best, the Majestic. (Believe it or not, I've only just realised that it had the same name as Mum and Dad's ballroom! Another coincidence?) We used to play there once a month on a Monday night, and I got to know many of the regulars.

I was feeling completely isolated, and didn't know what to do about it. I couldn't just drop back into my old life, as most of my old acquaintances had either got married or moved on. The old haunts around Batley and Dewsbury that I used to frequent were still there – but the people there were all strangers.

By chance I happened to bump into Neil Dixon, one of the lads who played with a local group called The Voltaires. I'd done him a favour a few months before when I'd rescued his amplifier from another group. We (The Dingos) had been playing at the Doncaster Corn Exchange along with another group, who shall remain nameless. The Voltaires came to do an audition for the dance promoter the same evening. Unfortunately they didn't make any impression on him. They were a show group really, more suited to the social clubs, and a bit too lightweight for the dance hall circuit. So after doing a short spot they didn't hang around and headed straight back for Dewsbury, leaving a brand new Hofner Truvoice guitar amplifier behind.

The other group claimed the amp on a 'finder's keepers' basis, so I stepped in. I told them that I knew the lad who owned it and would return it. They thought I was trying to pull a fast one and refused to part with it. At this point Harry Smith, the big ex-wrestler who drove us about, sensed a free-for-all and suggested we toss a coin for it. The others took one look at him and reluctantly agreed. Fortunately God was on our side, we won the toss and the Voltaires got their amp back. I asked Harry what he'd have done if we'd lost the toss and his reply was simple. 'We didn't, so what does it matter?'

That was Harry – a lovely man with a simple, and sensible, philosophy!

Anyway, I mentioned to Neil that I'd left The Dingos and was at a bit of a loose end. He suggested I should come and see the lads sometime – so I did. I even filled in on the drums when their drummer was unavailable for a gig at the Leeds United Supporters Club. I appreciated the cash – more so as I was a Huddersfield Town supporter!

I was still doing my repping job of course, but my heart really wasn't in it. On a scale of one to ten my enthusiasm was barely nudging two. I missed the buzz of the group scene. To break the monotony I even thought about starting my own band, but soon gave up on the idea. There just didn't seem to be anyone available.

So I mooched about for a while trying to pick up the threads of what was left of my previous social life. I also began to spend more time helping Mum on the market stall. Before long I began to spot one or two familiar faces among the customers. Alex Camponi was one. I'd worked with Alex on the club circuit, before he went on to become a very successful businessman. He came to buy a packet of cigarettes, and naturally asked me how I was getting on. Before I could finish my tale of woe he came up with the solution to all my problems. 'Come for a game of bingo!' he said.

I was faintly amused. 'You've got to be joking!'

'Listen,' he went on, 'I've turned the Vale cinema in Mirfield into a bingo hall and it gets packed. Come along and see for yourself. You don't have to play bingo – you can watch the acts that I put on between the sessions. Anyway, the offer's there, and if you've got nothing better to do you might as well.'

So that night I slipped into the Vale with my collar pulled up to hide my face, trying to appear inconspicuous. This was of course very naïve of me, because my limp was as well known as the town hall clock. I popped into the office, where Alex was surprised to see me.

'What time does the act come on?' I asked sheepishly.

'Not until after the first session. Here, take this book of tickets, and if you win anything we'll share it.' He handed me a book of bingo tickets and instructed one of his girls to find a marker pen for me to use. He seemed to find my embarrassment highly amusing. 'Go upstairs and sit in the balcony – no one will see you there,' he chuckled.

I crept into the upper circle and sat on the back row. It wasn't as full as downstairs but there were still a lot of people around. Oh God, I thought, if any of the lads see me now I'll die of shame.'

The auditorium hushed as Alex went onto the stage and called 'Eyes down for the first house.'

The first two houses were reeled off in no time and I began to relax a little. But on the third house I began to mark numbers off like mad. Oh no, I thought; it can't happen. But it did. 'House!' I called half-heartedly, secretly hoping it would go unnoticed. I liked the thought of winning a few quid but there were certain limits . . .

'House in the circle!' one of the staff called out. 'Hold your card up, please!'

I swear the whole of the cinema turned round to look at me. I couldn't tell for sure, because by this time I'd slithered down into my seat – leaving my arm visible holding the card aloft. When the ticket had been checked and confirmed as a winner, two old ladies in headscarves glared at me – so I decided I'd had enough, and went downstairs until the end of the session to talk to some of the girls who worked for Alex. He was delighted that I'd won, and gleefully shared the spoils – he always was a lucky so-and-so.

'Who's the act tonight?' I asked casually.

'Oh, you might know them. Local group called The Voltaires – the punters love 'em.' Oh great, I thought. It isn't going to be a bad night after all. I just hope they didn't see me playing bingo.

I enjoyed their spot – but I noticed that one of the singers was missing. Normally they had two vocalists who took turns singing; tonight there was only one. When they'd finished I continued to natter with the staff, making it clear to all and sundry that I was there to see the show. But I don't think the punters gave a toss either way: when 'eyes down' was called I could have committed hara-kiri and they wouldn't have noticed. Anyway, Bernard Fenton, who managed The Voltaires, came looking for me. Alex had told him I was in – and that I'd won a game of bingo . . .

Evidently the group had had a bit of a fall-out. One of the singers hadn't bothered to turn up, and the other one had walked out after the first spot. This left them in a bit of a predicament, and Bernard wondered if I could help them out by singing a few songs with them. Well, being the kind-hearted, affable, wonderfully obliging person that I am, how could I refuse?

Anything was better than 'legs eleven', 'clickety click' and all that crap. So I did a couple of songs with them, and they went so well that I was invited to join the group permanently. I graciously accepted the offer – and so began my long and eventful association with The Voltaires*.

* This is the correct spelling, though bill posters and promoters often omitted the 'e' from the band's name.

Chapter Ten
THE VOLTAIRES

I never liked the name Voltaires. Whenever I heard the name the first thing that sprang to mind was 'electricity' – and I always thought it would have been better suited to a firm of electrical contractors. But apparently it was conceived when the trend was to dress groups according to their names – so Nero and the Gladiators wore Roman costume, Johnny Kidd and the Pirates wore pirate gear and The Spotnicks wore spacesuits. The group was supposed to dress like the great French philosopher Voltaire, hoping to catch the eye of some TV producer or entrepreneur. I'm certainly glad they never got round to it: there's no way I'd have ever set foot on a stage in South Yorkshire dolled up like the Scarlet Pimpernel.

I don't know who dreamt the name up. It was probably Bernard Fenton, the manager. (Why were there so many managers called Bernard at that time?) I liked him: it was he who suggested that I add King to my nickname and make Sammy King my stage name. Bernard had a wonderfully creative mind and also a wicked sense of humour. He was one of those guys who could put his hand to anything, and do it well. The only problem was that he did everything at his own pace – which was best described as leisurely. His wife Doreen was a diamond and also very gifted artistically. Paul, his eldest son, was taking drum lessons at the time and Bernard had hopes of him joining our band. Unfortunately consensus among the lads was that he lacked experience, and we had to turn him down. Though disappointed at the time he need not have worried, as he went on to be a very successful drummer, playing with Marc Bolan and the group Christie of 'Yellow River' fame in the '70s. The combined potential of the family was extraordinary.

Bernard put his heart and soul into The Voltaires and sadly got very little in return. There was already a degree of unrest in the band when I agreed to join. Chuck, the bass player, was on the point of leaving, while Teddy, the extremely talented guitarist, wasn't getting on well with Johnny, the saxophonist. It was left to Bernard to sort everything out. Eventually Chuck left and was replaced by 'Mack' Oates, whose brother had played alongside me in the old skiffle group. Later Pete Kelly, who'd also played in the skiffle group, replaced him. For a while the group seemed to settle into a routine, and was very successful around the clubs and local venues. But despite playing to packed houses and rave reviews in the club magazines we still weren't going anywhere. Bernard felt we had to try for better things, so in order to further our career he approached a local impresario, Bernard Hinchcliffe. Yes – another Bernard!

We auditioned for him at a night-club in Huddersfield. He was promoting a tour at that time and in the audience were two American stars of the show – Brian Hyland, who was in the charts with a song called 'Sealed with a Kiss' and Little Eva, who was at number one with 'The Locomotion'. We featured 'The Locomotion' in our show, and Little Eva thought it was great. I was invited to her table and she sat on my knee for the rest of the night. She was quite taken with me and wanted to take me back to the States with her! Brian Hyland, on the other hand, didn't have his own backing group and wanted to take the whole group back with him.

BH (Bernard Hinchcliffe) must have spotted some potential in us, and decided to take us under his wing. Soon we were doing more prestigious gigs and everything began to get more and more exciting. We began to work alongside stars we had only seen on television or heard on radio. I got quite a buzz out of being on first-name terms with people I'd admired for years.

We even went to work in Blackpool over the Whitsuntide holidays. Danny Williams was enjoying a massive hit record – 'Moon River' – and we were booked to support him on the South Pier. The weather was gorgeous, too good really, because no one wanted to sit in a dark theatre when the sun was shining. BH had a brainwave: we set up on the roof of the pier entrance and began to play. In no time people stopped to watch. The younger end started dancing, and before long the crowd spread from the pier across the tramlines and over the road until it completely blocked the promenade. Traffic came to a standstill, trams were backed up and the whole place was in chaos. Eventually the police came and put an end to our venture, but not before we had caused quite a stir. It was even reported back home in the newspapers under the headline – 'Local Group Stops Traffic In Blackpool'. It was a marvellous publicity stunt, but unfortunately the sun still shone and people still didn't come in to see the show. BH can't have been a very happy chappy, but you would never have known it to look at him. His disposition could be best described as unflappable. He was one of the most laid-back people I've ever known; a complete one-off. Always well groomed and immaculately dressed, BH's quiet charm and silvery tongue constantly worked wonders, ensuring that we were given every opportunity to further our careers. On top of featuring us on his own promotions, he lined up TV auditions and occasionally brought influential people to see us. Dialogue was his true forte, persistence his greatest asset. He was also completely impervious to abuse. I've seen him on the receiving end of some of the most blistering verbal assaults – after which he simply smiled and invited his aggressor to join in him a nice cup of tea to sort it all out! It was useless trying to get mad with him – you just couldn't. Personally I think Bernard missed his way: his attributes would have been better suited to politics.

 But whatever I or anyone else thought was of no consequence to BH. His convictions were well and truly focused on making money from showbiz. One of his greatest coups was booking the Beatles for virtually nothing. Originally they were intended to support the Acker Bilk Band along with us. But by the time the show came around they'd taken the country by storm and the show was a complete sell-out. (My own contribution to that show is documented in the preface!)

 Just before that show we did a short tour that featured the American rock legend Gene Vincent. Also on the bill were ex-Shadows Jet Harris and Tony Meehan, along with actor singer John Leyton. It was a tremendous show. We came off to an incredible ovation and were still up in the clouds for hours afterwards. The two

Bernards seemed pleased for different reasons – sheer pride and sheer profit. You'll probably be able to work out which was which for yourself. The audience screamed themselves hoarse throughout the rest of the show, and it was the same for the rest of the tour.

In Sunderland I was mobbed as I walked out of the stage door. Thinking that only the big stars would come in for that treatment, I foolishly tried to board the tour bus and was immediately grabbed. One of the minders rescued me and pulled me back in. There was a unit of police present, but as the crowd began to grow in number outside the stage door it became obvious that they'd soon be struggling to cope. So they sent for reinforcements, and it wasn't until the dog handlers arrived that the crowd was brought under control. But even this didn't stop two fans sneaking aboard the tour bus and stowing away to our next gig in Nottingham.

The Nottingham crowd was just as noisy but fortunately not as persistent, just as well really because we performed on an open stage and were completely surrounded. When we moved on to Blackburn pandemonium was restored – plus interest. Nottingham must have given me a false sense of security, because after I'd finished my spot I decided to nip out to the pub for a quick pint with one of my friends, Tommy Mitchell. Tommy, who'd done a bit of bouncing in the past, had been assigned to mind us by the tour management. We were ambling down a side corridor when I heard a female voice behind me shout, 'It's HIM!' I looked round, and about twenty young girls raced towards me. Tommy couldn't do anything to help as they completely surrounded me and slammed me against a wall. I was helpless as they demanded kisses and autographs. Tommy stood there laughing, and even lent them a pen.

'I haven't got any paper to sign on,' I pleaded.

'Never mind the paper,' said one of them, 'Sign this . . .' She unbuttoned her blouse, exposing one of her large boobs, and thrust it in under my nose. Tommy dined out on that story. But when he told it he always said that I kept spelling my name wrong and had to rub it out three times! The truth, of course, is that I did sign it – once – and I even dotted the 'i'. I wonder if Engelbert Humperdinck had all this fuss! For obvious reasons I don't remember her face, but I must confess that my mind's occasionally wandered back to that event – usually when I've been given a receipt by a buxom young sales lady in a shop or a bank accompanied by the request, 'Would you sign this, please?'

Eventually I was saved by the announcement that John Leyton was about to appear. They released me and ran off to watch his show. But that wasn't the last I saw of them: they were waiting, along with a hundred others, behind the police cordon outside the stage door. As we left, the crowd pushed through the police line, cutting us off from the tour bus. The others managed to get to the coach, but not being as fleet-of-foot as the rest I got caught. Now you may think that this sounds like a lot of fun, but I have to say that it frightened me to death. More than a dozen pairs of hands were pulling at me from every direction. They tore my clothes; every button popped from my shirt; they clung to my boots and trousers. I was scratched in the process – and lost great chunks of my hair. I was terrified, but just when I really thought I was about to be torn to pieces a great big police sergeant waded in, picked me up like a rag doll and literally threw me into the coach.

And who was already sitting there grinning from ear to ear recounting the boob signing episode to everyone? Only my 'minder' Tommy!

'The times they are a-changing'

After the rock'n'roll tour it was back to the real world of clubs and dance halls, but working with the top groups had been a tremendous experience and we'd learnt a lot from them. We'd also been made very aware of our shortcomings. The group still lacked guts somehow, and everyone had different ideas on why this was. Teddy and Johnny clashed on a regular basis, and morale in the band was low – even though we were enjoying celebrity status at home. Something needed to change, and before long it did.

I was giving Teddy a lift home one night after we'd been rehearsing. He was very quiet, and when we pulled up outside his home I found out why. A group that was about to make a record and appear on TV had approached him, and only his loyalty to Bernard and the rest of the lads had prevented him from accepting their offer. He asked for my advice. I knew he wasn't happy with the Voltaires, that his mind had already been made up and he just wanted me to tell him to accept the offer – so I did. I told him he'd be a fool not to. Any one of the others would have jumped at the chance!

So Teddy left. The other group didn't take the country by storm, but it gave him a leg up, because he later broadcast with the Arthur Greenslade Orchestra and eventually joined Freddie Starr.

So now we were left without a lead guitarist. Remembering how my old mate Ken Fowler managed to sing and play lead with The Dingos, I thought now would be a good time for me to learn to do the same. It took a bit of getting used to, but after taking a leaf out of Ken's book and introducing a bit of 'raw earth', the group suddenly acquired guts!

During the following months quite a few things changed. We decided to dispense with Pete, our bass player, who'd become very unreliable, and replaced him with Tony 'Petal' Lockwood. Bernard Fenton didn't really care for the new-look Voltaires and I could understand his reasons. After all, they were his group to begin with, and now all his ideas were being overridden in an attempt to bring the band up to date. His child was outgrowing him and about to become independent. He lost all interest in the band and basically washed his hands of us. I'm happy to say, though, that we remained great friends.

Now only Neil remained from the original group. He was smart, intelligent, clean cut and a really nice lad to boot. And that, as it happened, posed a bit of a problem. His disposition wasn't really conducive to the earthy new image we were trying to promote. And he also played rhythm guitar: round that time rhythm guitarists were becoming extinct.

We were playing at the Cavern Club in Manchester one night with a group from Birmingham. Their drummer seemed surprised that we still had a rhythm guitarist, and he told Johnny, our sax player, that they'd got rid of theirs months ago. They'd locked him in the toilet before they went on stage one night; he took the hint and left. Just before we took the stage for our second spot I heard a lot of scuffling behind me: Neil was vainly trying to stop our much heavier sax player from dumping him in a cupboard. There was never much love lost between them.

Eventually Neil did leave, and in all honesty it was probably for the best. He was studying hard at technical college by day and traipsing round the country with us by night. In the end he collapsed in the dressing room of a local club and was taken to hospital with breathing difficulties; later he was diagnosed as having a perforated lung. Fortunately he made a full recovery, and eventually got married and settled down.

Bernard Hinchcliffe now assumed full control over the band, and the talk was about turning professional. By this time my old boss had sold his business, and in between my activities with the band I was doing a bit of repping for my mum, who was now wholesaling. She didn't need to do it; I think she just went into it to give me something to do. Anyway, she didn't kick up or even seem surprised when I told her about our plans. There were mixed feelings about the idea in the band. Basically we were all for it, but two of the lads – Colin the drummer and 'Petal' the bass player – were married with young families to support, and naturally they had reservations. This left Johnny, me and Joe Kenyon, who by this time had joined us as transport manager cum roadie. Joe turned out to be indispensable. His genius kept the band mobile and plugged in over the next few years. And he could drive through fog better than anyone I've ever known: he must have had an in-built radar system.

Eventually we all decided to give it a try. At first it didn't seem much different, as we were working regular bookings to begin with. The South Yorkshire club circuit was thriving, and that kept us going nicely. Colin was even able to keep his other job for a while. But to keep our book full we had to do the occasional long distance journey, and some of these were killing.

One that immediately springs to mind is the King's Hall, Aberystwyth, in Wales. It seemed to take a lifetime to get as far as Welshpool, and there was still a hell of a long way to go. I remember someone looking at the map and saying, 'Look, if we cut across here it'll be a lot quicker' - famous last words. For the next few hours we were going up and down mountains, opening and closing farm gates . . . we even had to seek out people who spoke English, as all the signposts were in Welsh and in general the people we came across didn't (or wouldn't) speak our native tongue. Somehow we arrived at the King's Hall with minutes to spare. It was fortunate that the dance had had a late start. We didn't take the place by storm and, to be truthful, it was a bit of a struggle to begin with – not made any better by Colin. He loved to leave his drums during the show to come to the front and grab the microphone, usually to poke fun at one of the band. But on this occasion he grabbed the mike and chided the subdued audience with, 'Come on then, get up and dance. What's up with yer? Have you all got wooden legs or something?' I groaned – for in sight of the band, but not to Colin, was a young lass sitting directly underneath the front of the stage, with her artificial leg sticking out! Well, that was our last gig in those parts for sure. But the worst of it was we still had another set to play – and after that we

Paul Fenton with Marc Bolan of T Rex. I include this picture because we turned Paul down as drummer with the Voltairs, despite it being Paul's father who founded the band. This was because he was more of a rock drummer and we were a cabaret band. He later went on to greater things as drummer for Christie and T Rex.

The Voltairs.

Cilla Black.

Lulu.

had the journey home to look forward to! So at the interval we went to the pub and downed a few. The dance finished about one o'clock in the morning. At half past we were walking on the beach drinking bottles of beer. I still have memories of us falling about on the sand in fits of laughter as Johnny peed into the Irish Sea. He'd thought that it looked a bit low and needed topping up!

I don't remember much about the journey home – and neither did anyone else apart from Joe, who was the only one who remained sober. I awoke ten hours later as our group van pulled up outside a club in Doncaster. We'd been booked for a lunchtime show and the club officials were yelling at us to hurry as the club was full and the audience was waiting. My head was banging and my mouth tasted as if I'd been poisoned. I was tired, unkempt, unwashed and feeling absolutely crap. I more or less stumbled into the club to be met by a sarcastic voice saying, 'It must be nice to be able to start work at dinnertime!' If I'd had any strength left I'd have punched the bastard.

We were making a living with the band but we were far from making a fortune out of it. What we needed was a hit record. We'd made a few demo tapes of pop classics and sent them off to companies, but without success. Then Bernard came back from London with a bit of good news. He'd been doing a few promotions featuring Ronnie Hilton – who'd had a smash number one hit in the '50s with 'No Other Love' and was currently having success with a song called 'Windmill in Old Amsterdam'. Ronnie's manager, Wally Ridley, was also the head of HMV Records – part of the EMI group and well respected by his peers in the music industry. Wally was the man responsible for getting Elvis Presley's 'Heartbreak Hotel' released in Britain. When the record was first offered to the company the men in suits didn't like it and weren't prepared to release it. Wally put his job on the line and released it anyway – and the rest is history: it was a smash hit! Bernard had played Wally our tape. He quite liked the group, but he needed to hear us play something original. So we had to find an new song.

I had made a few attempts at writing songs when I split with Susan, but that was mainly to purge my broken heart and could hardly be classed as chart material – more like music to slit your wrists by. Anyway the onus fell upon me to come up with something, so I began to tinkle about on the guitar and piano. For a while nothing was forthcoming. Then I saw an advert on TV for Camay soap. It featured a woman rubbing soap onto her face, with someone off camera asking her, 'What's the secret of your soft skin?' This was followed by a jingle that the whole nation started singing: 'You'll look a little lovelier each day with fabulous pink Camay!' It was a marvellous advertising campaign. Everywhere you went people were singing the jingle, and every other hoarding had a poster that read 'WHAT'S THE SECRET of soft skin?' You just couldn't get away from it. In fact I was sitting on the loo one morning reading the paper and when I turned the page over there it was again – 'WHAT'S THE SECRET?' At the same time I was humming a little tune to myself and the phrase seemed to fit perfectly. 'Oo, oo, oo, What's the secret? Oo oo oo, What's the secret? What makes me love you like I do?' And that was it. Before the day was out I finished the song and called the guys together to see what they thought of it. After we'd rehearsed it a bit it started to sound OK, so we went into Matt's, a well-known studio in Huddersfield, and made a demo.

It was duly sent off to HMV and wonder of wonders – they liked it! What's more, we were invited to come down to the famous Abbey Road studios in London. It was like a dream come true: I kept pinching myself on the way down there, just to make sure I wasn't dreaming. We were all in really high spirits as our battered old van rattled through the opulent suburbia of St John's Wood. When we swung into Abbey Road and reached the studios I have to say that my excitement was tempered with a certain amount of disappointment: the building wasn't half as imposing as I expected it to be. But that was soon forgotten when Colin spotted one of his idols unloading some drums. It was Johnny Dankworth's drummer, Kenny Clare, probably the finest drummer this country's ever produced. Colin went over to talk to him and was overwhelmed by his friendliness. Joe unloaded our battle-scarred equipment and took it through one of the side doors into the studio. There was a stark contrast between the gear being taken in and a stack of gear waiting to be taken out. It was brand spanking new and belonged to The Shadows, who'd been recording there the previous day.

I just couldn't believe it was all happening. I made sure I savoured every second of the experience. This was the place where so many great records had been made. And in all probability I was about to sing in a mike that could have been used by Shirley Bassey, the Beatles or even Cliff Richard. There was so much about this legendary place that intrigued me and I just couldn't take it all in.

The engineer on our session was Norman Smith, who later got

to number one in the charts in his own right. He sang a song called 'Don't Let it Die' under the pseudonym Hurricane Smith. His young assistant also went on to make a name for himself when he was chosen to engineer the classic Beatles album *Sergeant Pepper*. And considering that Wally Ridley was responsible for introducing 'double-tracking', it's no wonder that I felt more than a little overwhelmed to be in such illustrious company. Wally's charm and Norman's wit soon put us at ease. It was easy to see why these people were so successful. It soon became apparent that recording was a whole new ball game. Mistakes couldn't be covered up by visual distractions as they could in live performances: in a recording studio every sound came under scrutiny. After thirty takes we were still no nearer getting the song right, and we were beginning to get a little bit downhearted: the latest playback was still full of mistakes. What didn't make things better was Paul McCartney calling into the control room – just out of curiosity apparently – as we struggled away. He didn't stay long, probably because nobody screamed! The only ones who didn't seem too bothered were Wally and his team. The young assistant came out to adjust one of the mikes and I apologised to him for our failure to get things right.

'Oh don't worry,' he said. 'It took Ken Dodd over seventy takes before they were satisfied with '"Tears"!'

Wally sensed our mood and suggested that we should go to the pub, get something to eat and relax for a while. We had something to eat – and we also had something to drink. We weren't too impressed by the southern beer, but it must have had something in it as we came back completely relaxed and finished the song in no time. Not only that – we did the B side in one take!

Bernard spoke to Wally as we packed up ready to leave. Wally seemed pleased with the result, and on the journey back Bernard told us there was every possibility that we could have a record released by April. We were all in a celebratory mood as we drove north up the A1. Johnny celebrated in his usual way by quaffing beer and breaking wind, prompting the strait-laced Bernard to utter the immortal phrase, 'John, you really must stop all this nasty pooping!' From then on, every time Johnny broke wind it was greeted by the phrase from the rest of the band, in a posh voice and in unison.

We got back home in the early hours of the morning, and I was so excited that I woke my mum to tell her we'd made a record. She was still half-asleep when she replied. 'Oh that's nice, son. We'll have to buy a record player to play it on, won't we?' I had to smile when I realised that she was right. My old Philips 'Disc Jockey' had long since expired . . .

During the next few weeks we were all in a bit of a daze. The press came to interview us and we had photographs taken for publicity. Our record release date was confirmed and Bernard put us on one of his promotional tours. This time we were billed as 'HMV Recording stars'.

Now things were going to be different! Now was the time for leather jackets, long hair – and corns. Yes, corns. Cuban-heeled boots were the fashion, and I particularly welcomed them as they made me a little bit taller – but corns were the price I had to pay for those extra inches. Oh, the suffering I went through in the name of vanity. It was bad enough having a limp – but corns as well!

We were booked to tour with Freddie and the Dreamers, the Four Pennies and two Liverpool bands – the Big Three and The Undertakers. At the last minute, apart from doing our own spot, we were roped in to back a young girl singer called Cilla Black. We didn't really hit it off. To begin with she seemed a bit miffed that it wasn't a Liverpool band that was chosen to back her. She also didn't know what key she sang her songs in – and expected us to know. Nothing seemed to be right for her, and it was left to her boyfriend Bobby – who later became her husband – to sort things out. I wasn't very impressed with her show and she probably wasn't impressed with us. A few weeks later she sat on the panel of the TV programme *Jukebox Jury* and voted our record a miss. Unfortunately she was right – it did turn out to be a miss. But we still got a buzz when we heard it on the show and later on radio stations, and I derived a certain amount of satisfaction from knowing that it was also released in other parts of the world. A girl I took out on a few occasions heard it in New York when she went to work out there; she even rang me up to tell me she'd bought it. And although we didn't sell a great number of records, it was amazing to me *where* they were sold. Our first royalty statement informed us we'd actually sold one in the United Arab Emirates. Who the hell bought that one only Allah knows! It appealed to my sense of humour: I like to imagine a po-faced Arab climbing down from his camel in the desert, winding up one of those old phonographs and playing our record until the desert sun sank slowly in the west behind a far distant oasis . . .

Getting back to reality, I got a great thrill when I received my first fan letter. It came from a young girl called Dorothy Fear who lived in Weston-super-Mare. I sent her a signed photo and thanked her for buying our record, and we corresponded for years. I never got to meet her but I got to know all about her. She eventually married her boyfriend and became Mrs Dorothy Harvey. I'd love to know what she's doing now.

Meanwhile we continued to work with many top recording artists, including the Rolling Stones and the Walker Brothers. The Stones were a friendly enough bunch, but I couldn't get over how thin they all were. I really enjoyed their show – but my lasting memory of them will always involve Mick Jagger and a biscuit tin. I was talking to him in the dressing room before the show and he had a streaming cold. His eyes and nose were running to the extent that he was 'snooking' after every sentence. On the table was a biscuit tin that was full of harmonicas, and by the time I'd finished talking to him he must have picked up and blown every one of them. I remember thinking that there must have been enough germs in that tin to put a small country out of action for a month. What made it even worse was that Brian Jones walked in minutes later – and he started sucking and blowing them too. Yuck!

The Walker Brothers were a complete contrast. They were very quiet, very private and very American. I really enjoyed working with them, primarily because it gave me the opportunity to listen to what I considered to be one of the best male voices in the world, that of Scott Engel, the lead singer. I never got to say more than 'hello' to him as he kept himself very much to himself backstage, so I didn't impose myself upon him out of respect. But he did become very friendly with a girl I used to go out with: it was nice to know we had something in common!

I went out with quite a few girls at that time – too many for my own good. Like sailors, we groups had girlfriends in every port. It was OK, so long as they never met. Unfortunately for me four of them came to the Walker Brothers concert. I spotted them all in the audience, and the memory of Blackburn – and what a group of women were capable of doing – prompted me to go to ground after I'd finished my spot. I knew they wouldn't be allowed to go backstage, so I'm ashamed to say I hid in the dressing room for the rest of the evening. It wasn't as if I'd been bonking them or anything: I was never one of the one night stand 'love 'em and leave 'em' brigade. I just enjoyed the company of the opposite sex and a good snog, and over a period of time I acquired a large circle of female friends. It all seemed very harmless to me, but unfortunately they didn't see it that way – which resulted in me getting into a bit of bother from time to time.

Mind you, I've always had a talent for getting into bother unintentionally. I once got a bollocking from Dusty Springfield for singing the song 'Twenty Four Hours from Tulsa'. It was another big show, also featuring the Merseybeats, Sounds Incorporated and Dave Berry (who I thought was brilliant). She informed me, in no uncertain terms, that I had no right to sing 'her' song. I told her that if it anybody's it was Gene Pitney's, but she pulled rank and we had to drop it from our set. We substituted the old Platters song 'Only You', and it pulled the place in. She did us a favour. I even recorded it later on in my career, and it got to number one in the bestseller's chart – even if it was in the local record shop in Dewsbury! Even though I didn't exactly see eye to eye with Miss Springfield, I have to concede that she had a great voice – and a great act.

Though I didn't work with many female pop stars, the one who impressed me most was a wee young lassie from north of the border. The first time I saw Lulu she was sitting in the corner of a dressing room in Sheffield University. We'd been booked to support her band for a students' union dance. I couldn't get over how quiet and shy she was. She seemed so small and frail, and I just couldn't believe that such a powerful voice could originate from such a tiny frame. But when that tiny frame stepped onto the stage and that voice came into action, I witnessed one of the most dynamic performances I'd ever seen. She was tremendous. Lulu had a great feel for music and was one of the best movers in the business.

It was a wonderful experience working alongside these great artistes; there was so much to learn from them. But the late nights and constant travel began to take their toll. Expenses started to increase, and after they'd been deducted from the money we earned there was hardly enough left to pay our way – which put a strain on the two lads with families. This brought about the usual bickering and falling out, and the prospects began to look gloomy. Then we had some more bad luck, when we were involved in a smash with a car on the way home from a gig. The car – a Ford Zephyr Zodiac – lost control and ploughed into our van, peeling the side off and leaving us looking like a freshly opened tin of sardines. Johnny Robb, a friend of mine who'd gone along for the ride, was still asleep after the impact, and when the ensuing panic eventually woke him up he thought the van was on fire. The reason for this was that the little gutter where the roof of the van met the side was always used as an ashtray by the band. So when the car hit us the huge cloud of ash that had accumulated over the years was released into the atmosphere. But although it wasn't on fire, the accident still heralded the sad demise of our battered old Bedford. And to make matters even worse the driver of the Zodiac wasn't insured.

Everything seemed to be going sour. HMV weren't happy about the image that the band presented, and suggested that changes should be made. Initially I was the only one who'd signed a contract with them: they didn't think it was necessary to sign the rest of the band. Understandably this didn't go down well with the lads, and when I was summoned to make another record – without the group – things went from bad to worse. The upshot of it all was that we parted company.

I wasn't happy about the record company not wanting the group, but I'd signed a contract and they were calling the shots. Joe, our roadie, stayed on of course. He always had a mind of his own and he enjoyed the showbiz life. So now I had to find a new group. There were quite a few floating about, including one called the Quiet Three. I'd worked with them on quite a few occasions so I knew them pretty well. Bill and Barry had recording experience working for Joe Meek with the band Jamie Lee and the Atlantics, but Harry, the drummer, had not. Anyway, I talked Wally into letting the lads play on the B side of the record, and so they – apart from Harry – went down to London with me. My second record was a cover version of the hit song 'Rag Doll'. The Four Seasons were currently at number one in the United States with it, and as there were no plans to release it in the UK, HMV thought it would be a good opportunity to jump in with a version. This time I wasn't only feeling nervous, I was also feeling ill. I'd been under the weather for a week or so and my throat was really sore. I told Bernard that I wasn't up to it and he didn't seem to be worried at all. In fact nobody did – so I did the worrying for everybody!

The musical director was Ivor Raymonde, who arranged all the Walker Brothers and Dusty Springfield hits. Oh no, I thought. Just when my throat's bad I get a top arranger. I felt even worse when I saw John Paul Jones of Led Zeppelin sitting at the organ in the orchestra and Dougie Wright from the John Barry Seven on the drums. I needn't have worried, though. Ivor, in between borrowing fags off everyone, was a hoot, and the guys in the orchestra were really understanding and supportive. After they'd put the initial track down, John Paul Jones stayed behind and provided some input, while Dougie played drums with the new Voltaires on the B-side.

Although I personally thought my own performance was under par, HMV were happy with the result and set a release date. Unfortunately for us, though, the Four Seasons record was released two weeks earlier than ours – and they grabbed all the spoils. We still sold a lot more than we had of 'What's the Secret', and we also doubled the fan mail.

I made two more records with HMV – 'Only You' and 'If You Can Find Someone to Love You' – neither of which took the country by storm, and the company didn't renew my contract. But Wally told me to keep on writing songs and to call in to see him whenever I was in the neighbourhood, which I did. It was nice to pop into the EMI offices in Manchester Square from time to time and be welcomed by the staff. They were like one big happy family at that time – which probably contributed to the great success the company enjoyed.

Chapter Eleven
BACK ON THE ROAD AGAIN

By now the rock scene was beginning to look a bit of a no-no. Without a record to promote, we joined the many thousand groups doing the dance hall circuits in the '60s. But there was another option. Apart from the lucrative working men's clubs, there was also a thriving casino and night-club scene. The casinos were paying good money for show-groups and top artistes to bring the punters in, and there were rich pickings to be had by anyone coming up with the right formula for a suitable act. So with the accent more on variety and comedy, we set about putting a new act together. I even did a mime routine based on the P.J. Proby record 'Somewhere'. It went down great with the audience and I got quite a buzz from making the audience laugh. The only time we came a cropper was at a club in Retford. The tape recorder, which we used for the mime, broke down, leaving me out on a limb. Joe, who was feverishly tinkering with it, yelled at me, 'Tell 'em a joke while I'm fixing it!' So I bumbled through, muttering anything that came into my head until we got organised. As an introduction to stand-up comedy my performance left a lot to be desired. But it was the start of what was to come. Afterwards I kept slipping an odd joke into the act, and eventually started stringing a few together into short routines. We began to get a nice little act together and things were going quite well. But Harry, our drummer, wasn't comfortable with what we were doing and decided to leave. Our previous drummer Colin, who by this time had split with his wife, was keen to rejoin, but he wasn't happy about the way the band was being managed. This view was shared by the rest of the lads. Although we were earning good money, Bernard Hinchcliffe – our second manager – was taking quite a chunk, which left us struggling to make ends meet. We were bemoaning this to the young concert chairman of a local Liberal club when he came up with an offer we couldn't refuse: he offered to manage us for nothing. On the face of things he had the right credentials: he was astute, ambitious, had good connections and best of all was free! So Derek Smith became our new manager, and we parted company with Bernard who, quite understandably, wasn't too pleased.

The first thing Derek did was sign us up to the top Leeds agency ATS (Artistes Theatrical Agency), which was based at the famous City Varieties Theatre. It was customary for every newly signed act to do a week at the theatre (including two matinées) for 'expenses' – which amounted to a few quid. The fee was so meagre that we didn't even bother to cash the cheque: we kept it as a reminder of the experience. And what an experience! The show was a variety of sorts interspersed with a couple of strippers. As one of them took her gear off we rolled ours on behind the curtains. And when the curtains opened there was an audience of maybe twenty or more blokes, in dirty raincoats, who sat in stony silence through our act. That week felt like a year, and when it ended I began to understand the reasoning behind this obligatory booking. It served to remind us that if we got too big for our boots we'd probably end up doing another week there. For the rest of our association with the agency this venue hung like the sword of Damocles over our heads. Fortunately we did OK, and in no time we were enjoying the long-awaited pleasure of a few bob in our pockets. The work was regular and we began to get better class gigs, which also meant better pay. We started to do 'doubles' – two clubs a night – usually a social club first and a nightclub afterwards. I really worked hard, and on average soaked through three shirts a night. At one time I owned twenty-one white shirts – most of which were Rael-Brook poplins (the shirt you don't iron!).

This was 1965 and businesses were booming (especially the shirt industry!). People were beginning to cast aside the old tradition of putting a bit by and saving for a rainy day. It was a case of enjoy yourself while you can. After all, we were all living under the threat of the atom bomb – so what the hell.

Most of the nightclubs we worked had gaming licences, and in essence were really casinos with cabaret. We were employed to put the punters in a good mood before they transferred their attention – and their money – to the tables. If they were skint when they left, at least they'd had something for their money – us! Basically we did the same act as the one we did in the social clubs – but the presentation had to be slicker, more polished, and most importantly not too loud. We soon learnt the ropes after a disastrous appearance at the Ace of Clubs in Leeds. We played a bit of rock'n'roll, and while the crowd loved it the club proprietor didn't. He thought the music lowered the tone of his precious establishment, and told us in no uncertain terms that we'd be on our way if we didn't cut it out. Mind you, the same proprietor didn't like a young singer called Gerry Dorsey and wanted to sack him after his first spot. Having a young wife and family to support, the singer begged to be allowed to finish his week's engagement. It was only through the intercession of the owner's wife that he was allowed to do so: she felt sorry for him because he was so upset. Gerry Dorsey went on to become Engelbert Humperdinck, of course, so the night-club boss obviously had an eye for talent!

We were allowed to finish our week's engagement, provided that we didn't play rock'n'roll. Some of the regular punters in the crowd, and in particular one group who'd been really enthusiastic, noted this. I was invited to their table to explain why we'd dropped the rock. They turned out to be a group of actors and film crew working for the BBC; they'd been filming in the area and had come into the club after work to unwind. The group included such notable actors as Peter Vaughan, Jimmy Devlin and Jack Smethurst of *Love Thy Neighbour* fame – a top TV comedy in the '60s. Dame Thora Hird was also there, and she was a joy. She sat me down, pushed a drink under my nose and proceeded to give me a lot of very good advice. Things like 'you only get one chance to make a first impression, so make sure it's a good one' and 'make sure you know what you're going to say before you go on' and 'when you *do* say it – *mean* it'. She gave me lots of other little tips aimed at improving our show, which I immediately took on board. After all this was a true professional giving me advice – priceless advice – and it wasn't costing me a penny! Meeting her is something I'll never forget.

So with all that in mind, along with a nice mixture of music and comedy, we began to put together a successful little cabaret act, and before long we were making a name for ourselves on the local circuit.

Later, after a glowing review in *The Stage*, we began to get offers of work from further a-field. This pleased me no end, and I was quite looking forward to going on the road again. Only this time things were going to be different, so very different – and it didn't take me long to find out just how much. The first, and most important, lessons I was to learn was that comedy didn't travel very well. Different parts of the country laughed at different things. A sense of humour could disappear in less than a hundred yards! In the north-east, for instance, what brought belly laughs on one side of the road would be met with stony silence in a club on the other side, and vice versa. As far as comedy is concerned 'Geordieland' was – and still remains – a complete mystery to me.

I enjoyed travelling around; I found it the most stimulating part of the job. I was eager to see, and learn about first hand, all the places I'd only ever heard about. An unfamiliar accent was music to my ears, and exploring the streets of a new town or city kept my inquisitive mind busy when I wasn't working. Most people in my line of work were happy enough to stay out late and spend most of the following day in bed recuperating – but not me! After breakfast I was up and out of the digs to go exploring. I particularly liked hanging round markets and cafés: these were the places where the true character of the places shone through. Listening to the banter and gossip gave me a first-hand insight into the local culture. It's an activity I still indulge in to this very day. Often, when the mood takes me, I set off and visit a place I've never been to before just to say I've been there. Maybe there's a little bit of gypsy in me somewhere – inherited from my mysterious Grandpa perhaps?

Occasionally the whole group went out together during the day – usually to the cinema. Being members of Equity meant we could get into any cinema in Britain free of charge, and over quite a short period we more than recouped our yearly subscriptions. But I never felt comfortable in a group. Doing what everyone else wanted to do never really appealed, as I suppose I had an independent spirit that dated back to my hospital days. On top of that I needed time on my own to psyche myself up for the evening show.

The responsibility of carrying a show, especially a comedy orientated one, weighed heavily upon my shoulders. I always felt confident about the musical side of things; it was the comedy side that gave me the sleepless nights. After all, it was comedy that enabled us to command higher fees. Making people laugh is a serious business. Unless you've actually stood in front of an audience and done it, you'll never begin to understand the meaning of the word 'isolation'. It's like being pushed to the front of a minefield and being told to go first. If you get through everyone's happy; if you don't, it can leave you in bits. I don't think the rest of the band understood the true significance of the task that confronted me each night. The never-ending struggle to prise laughter out of a very demanding, and often very fickle, public was daunting at the best of times. Oh, I could be as witty as the next one after a few drinks in the pub with my mates, but facing a room full of strangers when you have never considered yourself to be a natural comedian is another matter. Everything I did was put together painstakingly in the hope that it would be acceptable to the unknown audience waiting on the other side of the footlights. Comedy has always meant hard work to me, work I've never really looked forward to; but I have to own up to experiencing a certain amount of self-satisfaction, having turned more than a few cold and unresponsive audiences into giggling masses on more than one occasion.

I'm certain that show business would have been much more acceptable to me had I *not* been required to go down the comedy trail. If I'd just been called upon to stand and sing to an audience, maybe I could have loved performing enough to be fully committed to it. But in retrospect I feel that once again the forces of fate were back in force. I'd managed to overcome the physical setbacks that had steered me towards my destiny, and now I was about to meet the mental challenges that ensured it would be fulfilled. And another factor was about to enter the equation: travel. Travelling long distances between gigs could be both boring and tiresome, while shorter distances could be even worse – especially when there was a deadline to meet. This usually happened when I had a 'double'. If this was a nightclub and a social club it was usually OK, as more often than not they were in the same town, but when the double involved two nightclubs it usually meant dashing between towns – and that's when the problems really started. More often than not the towns were miles apart, and the time we had to get from one venue to the other was less than adequate, to say the least; sometimes it was darn near impossible. No allowances were made for setting up equipment or dismantling it, or for loading and unloading – not to mention being kept back for an encore if we'd gone down well. Most of the night-club doubles we did were in Lancashire, and the Lancastrians were appreciative audiences, which meant we were victims of our own success. The better the act was received, the later we reached the next venue, which eventually resulted in an unwelcome addition to our group – stress.

I hated rushing. It usually resulted in things going wrong, and, being the front man, I had to fill in.

The only other person who came under more pressure was Joe, our roadie, who was mechanic, electrician, gopher, packhorse and Formula One driver rolled into one, expected nightly to get us from somewhere like St Helens to Preston in less than ten minutes! One week we even did a 'treble'. It was a killer – three different casinos in three different towns every night for a week – and we only did it once. In just a week Joe collected enough endorsements on his licence to paper a bedroom with, and lost his licence. We agreed to share the driving until his ban was over. We couldn't afford to lose him: he was an integral part of the band, an unsung hero. No one realised how much responsibility rested upon his shoulders. Stopping for a red light could mean the difference between a backslapping and a bollocking from a club manager. Facing an impatient audience was bad enough for us, but when it came to being late for a gig the buck was invariably passed down the line and laid firmly at his feet. This helped to take the pressure and, more importantly, the management off our back. Fortunately there was no one better equipped for this than he was. His blank stare and a complete show of indifference met any amount of ranting and raving from an irate club manager – or anyone else, for that matter! This ability to remain detached and impassive, we assumed, stemmed from Joe's background.

Born in Germany, he came to live in Britain just after the war with his German mother and English stepfather. He was justifiably proud of his origin, and this, together with his British upbringing, resulted in a persona capable of handling any situation, whether verbal or physical. But behind the cool unruffled exterior lurked a great sense of humour. In the band everyone came in for a bit of piss-taking, and Joe was no exception. Even though he got more than his fair share, especially from Colin the drummer, he took it all in good fun.

Colin – when he wasn't being a pain in the arse – reduced us all to tears with his references to Joe and the Second World War. In a mock-German accent he taunted him if he thought he was driving too fast, with remarks like "Slow down, Josef! You're not in der

Luftwaffe now! Zis is a Bedford not ein Messerschmitt!' Or he commentated on Joe's marriage: 'And der bride, Hildegarde, wearing a vedding gown in battleship grey decked with swastikas, vill be transported to ein bunker in ein Tiger tank flanked by Field Marshal Rommel's third panzer division, where she vill be met by der twenty one-gun salute as she is received by der Führer himself. He personally vill conduct der ceremony saying, "Do you, Hildegarde, take Yosef to be your lawful vedded husband – coss if you don't – vee haf ways of making you!" After der ceremony der happy couple vill don their jackboots and goose-step down der aisle to der tune of "I was Kaiser Bill's Batman".' And on it went.

There was always banter flying back and forth. It's the same in any group of guys living and working together. I suppose it's a way of letting off steam, counteracting the nerves and easing the tension.

The fear of the unknown always got to me. If I'd worked a venue before I knew what to expect, and could prepare myself accordingly. But new venues were a different matter and I always likened them to parachuting in the dark. You could land on your feet, fall flat on your face – or just float into oblivion.

So when we were booked for a week's appearance at the Cleopatra's Club in Cardiff it's true to say that I was more than a little apprehensive. To begin with, we couldn't have picked a worse time to go. It was at the time of the crisis in the Middle East when the Egyptians were at war with the Israelis. The owner of the club, Annis Abrahams, just happened to be an Egyptian, while the club was situated in the docklands – which accommodated a fair-sized Jewish community. You didn't have to be an Oxford undergraduate to realise that we weren't exactly going into Enid Blyton country. The club had been targeted on more than one occasion – our original booking being postponed when it was set on fire! So you can imagine how I felt walking into a club that was done out like a Pharaoh's tomb surrounded by an alleged mob of Jewish pyromaniacs: I wanted my mummy!

The club compère filled us in with what was expected of us. Apart from the warring factions, it seemed that the owner had never paid such a large fee to an unknown act before: he'd read our glowing revue in *The Stage* and was expecting great things. We fell silent: nothing could be heard but the sound of knocking knees – mine! Everyone in the business, including us, knew that a write up in *The Stage* carried about as much clout as a fairy's fart. He also told us that Mr Abrahams, a huge man, would be sitting at the front table with his wife, who at one time had been in show business. If we didn't meet with her approval we wouldn't get past Tuesday night. We were also informed that we had to use the club's microphone system, which would be controlled exclusively by the owner himself. By this time my knees had stopped knocking; I was concentrating all my efforts on stopping my bowels emptying. All I needed now was for someone to tell me that it would be an all Welsh-speaking audience. Had this been so, I could have popped round the corner and jumped into the famous Tiger Bay. Fortunately for me they weren't. But one night I wasn't sure.

We opened with an up-tempo rendition of the Latin-American song 'Brazil', which was met with a fairly lukewarm reception. Then we hit them with a spectacular guitar instrumental followed by a version of the classic 'I Only Have Eyes For You' in the Ray Conniff style, which was popular at the time. By this time the audience was beginning to warm to us a little. Now was the time to hit them with a few gags, I thought . . . but not a titter. Oh well, maybe they'll go for a big ballad. So I powered out a big bellowy ballad – and there was great applause. Now for the high spot: the P.J. Proby routine. The audience loved it – belly laughs, cheering, clapping. Ah, deep joy. Surely my gags won't fail now . . . so I gave them my best political jokes. Stony silence! Back to the songs . . . great! We left the stage to thunderous applause but I was puzzled: perhaps they were all Welsh-speaking after all. Actually, I wasn't that far off – they turned out to be Norwegian!

A Norwegian fishing fleet had put in to port and the crews had completely taken over the club. Many of them could speak English (a few of them spoke to me afterwards), but I guess their sense of humour didn't tally with mine: they said they didn't understand my jokes. Even so, they came back to see us two nights running and the act – minus my gags – went down really well. I suppose their appreciation ensured that we could finish off our week's engagement. When they sailed I was sorry to see them go, and the night that followed saw the club strangely subdued and much less busy. Maintaining the momentum of the previous two nights was difficult: it was virtually impossible to get the smaller audience going. But help was at hand in the form of an old friend of ours: Norman Collier.

Norman was working at another club across town and popped in to see us. The one thing you can say about Norman is that he really enjoys a chuckle. It didn't take much to start him laughing and when he did it spread right through the audience. He ended up sliding under the table, and a woman who'd been sitting stony-faced throughout the act finally cracked and couldn't contain herself. He really made the night for us, and in gratitude we went to see him and reciprocate his support. The only trouble was, when we went to his club we were the only ones in the audience. One of the downsides of night-club gigs was the quiet nights. At the weekend you could more or less guarantee a full club, but during the week they were sometimes completely empty. I hated these nights as the management still expected us to go on and perform. We argued that, being on an Equity contract, we couldn't be expected to perform to less than five people. This didn't wash with some of our employers, and they invariably found ways of getting around it.

Like the time we found ourselves facing a small audience in Widnes. It was actually made up of a solitary man sitting alone at a table at the back of the club. After waving our contract under the nose of the manager and pointing to the five-person clause, he proceeded to sit four of his bar staff at the front table and we were ordered to perform. This we did reluctantly, and when it came to the point in the act where I had to tell my jokes I just pulled up a seat to their table and said, 'Have you heard this one?' They saw the funny side of it, but the lone member of the audience appeared not to. Throughout the act he sat at the back of the room with his head in his hands.

The following evening there wasn't a soul in the club – even our solitary friend wasn't there. I remarked on this to one of the waitresses.

'Oh!' she replied seriously. 'You won't have heard, will you?'

'Heard what?'

'Well, last night after he left the club he went home and hanged himself.'

Without thinking I blurted out, 'The act wasn't that bad, was it?' After I'd said it I hated myself for being so insensitive. But that's what the business does to you. Wit and cynicism tend to become part of your make-up in the constant battle to preserve your sanity. I had good reason to remonstrate with myself: it turned out the poor bloke's wife had left him.

While I've never been keen on performing in nightclubs, I welcomed the opportunity to get to know the people who frequented them. Behind the majority of part-time punters there was always a slightly dodgier element – but I never really looked upon them as villains. Being wet behind the ears, I tended to think that all the *really* bad people were in London and living in Soho. I dismissed the common assumption that evil lurked around every corner. So when I occasionally rubbed shoulders with people best described as 'slightly dubious', was initially oblivious – believing that crime and deception wouldn't come into my life unless they were invited. And there really was a Santa Claus . . . And it don't rain in Indianapolis in the summertime . . . I was as naïve as a turkey looking forward to Christmas!

I remember one particular occasion. The scene was an exclusive night-spot in the north-east. It was a real classy place frequented by lots of beautiful women. After I'd finished my spot one evening I went to get a drink. Seated at the end of the bar was an absolutely stunning young lady; she wouldn't have been out of place on the front page of *Vogue*. When she smiled and beckoned me to sit on the stool next to her I casually flew to her side. She began to tell me how much she'd enjoyed my act and how I'd made her laugh. After a while I began to realise that she was coming on to me. I was flabbergasted; I couldn't believe such a beautiful woman would be interested in me. All right, I had my winning smile and I could sing a bit, but even so . . . Anyway, I wasn't complaining. She asked me where I was staying, and after I told her she suggested that I should stay with her: she had a large flat all to herself. I couldn't believe my luck. Here she was touching my cheek and stroking my hair – I haven't always been bald!

Just then Colin came over and said he wanted to talk to me.

'Go ahead,' I said.

'No. I want a word in private.' He was strangely firm and unsmiling, which was unusual for Col.

'Give us a few minutes,' I told him. 'I'm a bit busy right now.' Just then the doorman, Big G, came over to join Colin. He grabbed my arm, Colin grabbed the other and between then they lifted me off the stool and carried me into the dressing room kicking and protesting. They locked the door and explained to me the reason for their actions. Evidently the beauty I was making cow eyes at was the girlfriend of the local mobster, who was out of town. Now, according to Big G this guy wasn't averse to sending people paddling in the Tyne – complete with concrete boots. So Big G told Colin to go and rescue me – and while we were arguing he spotted the boyfriend's car drawing up outside the club. Obviously his girlfriend was unaware that he was back in town. The big doorman's swift action probably saved my life! It goes without saying that for the remainder of the week I never came out of my dressing room.

I suppose that episode was largely responsible for transporting me from the land of Fern Gully into the Real World. I began to cultivate a seventh sense – self-preservation. For the first time I began to question people's motives – especially women's. On encountering a pair of fluttering eyelashes, instead of going all starry-eyed I asked myself, 'Is she after stealing my heart – or my wallet?' The cocoon surrounding my dream gradually began to crumble, and the shock of encountering the more sinister side of showbiz chipped away at my confidence. Those rose-tinted glasses I'd been looking through for so long were suddenly tinged with the cold grey light of reality. I began to realise that as long as I remained in this business, life would never be a bowl of cherries. I made up my mind to make the best of it – even though things didn't get any easier.

We were working in a seedy night-club in the Midlands. I was in a frivolous mood and cheekily taking a rise out of three big guys sitting at one of the front tables. The one in the middle seemed to be enjoying the show but the others remained completely unmoved. As one of them leaned forward to pick up his drink his jacket opened slightly, just enough to reveal a shoulder holster with the butt of a gun sticking out. Needless to say, within seconds my line of patter went from caustic to gibberish. The second time I saw a gun, it was produced and brandished by a drunk in a club in the north-east. I've never seen a room clear so fast. People dived through doors and windows that weren't even there. And there was I, thinking all the bad lads were in Soho!

But this sudden awareness, and my determined efforts to make the best of it, didn't mean that I'd accepted it. Subconsciously it only added to the pressures I was battling every night. Because of this I felt an even greater need for solitude. It wasn't always possible, and the rest of the lads began to feel I was being a bit antisocial. This wasn't true at all – it was just my way of dealing with things. Nevertheless a void began to open up between me and the rest of the band. It was a pity because usually we got on really well, and we enjoyed some great times together – especially when we went to places like Wales. My happiest memories revolve around our trips to the social clubs of the Rhondda and the surrounding valleys.

The land of song, laughter and heartbreak

Long before Cleopatra's club in Cardiff, my only impression of Wales had been based upon that disastrous trek to the King's Hall in Aberystwyth. Memories of the total lack of help and indifference we encountered still rankled. So when we set off on our first trip to South Wales I wasn't looking forward to it one bit. If the rest of Wales turned out to be the same as we'd already sampled, I'd be catching the next train back. To my great relief my fears were totally unfounded. I found the people of South Wales warm and very welcoming: it was like a home from home. There were more than a few similarities between their way of life and our own back in Yorkshire: the rows of terraced houses, the pits and the close-knit communities to name just a few. Over the next few years not only did I learn to love the place, but I also grew to admire and respect the resourcefulness of the people – particularly the folk in the valleys. They received us into their clubs and homes like long-lost sons and we revelled in our common love of comedy and music. There was always a simple and straightforward approach to life and of course many unforgettable memories.

One of the first things I noticed when we got there was the vast number of sheep. They seemed to be everywhere, not just in the fields but roaming round the towns and villages as well. Whenever we reached a club there were always a few waiting for us – and always in front of the door where we had to take our equipment in. It was uncanny: we didn't have to ask where to unload – we just drove to where a flock of woolly groupies had gathered! We got so used to moving them out of the way that later in life I seriously thought of adding 'part-time shepherd' to my CV.

Some of the clubs we visited were in the remotest places. I remember one in particular – a large nissen hut at the end of a cart track, on top of a mountain in the middle of nowhere. When we arrived the sheep were at the front entrance, so we nosed the van through them, pulled up and got out. The doorman, a wizened old chap wearing a massive flat cap, greeted us: he was so thin and the cap was so wide that he reminded me of a toadstool. He gave us a sinister smile and led us into the lobby, where he pointed to a picture of a well-known guitarist of the '60s, Bert Weedon. 'We paid him off last week,' he remarked casually. He paused as if to seek a reaction from us. He didn't get one. Undeterred, he shuffled along, pointing to the photographs of other famous people as he went. 'And we paid him off, and him . . .'

Have they ever liked anyone here? I thought. By the time we got into the concert room I was in no doubt that this toadstool was of the poisonous variety. He continued to narrate his tales of gloom as we were setting up.

'We had a group here the other week. Their first spot didn't go down well at all.' He shook his head sadly before continuing in his lilting Welsh accent. 'Do you know, when the curtains opened for their second spot, the stage was completely empty. Rather than face the audience another time they'd buggered off through the dressing room window – drums and all!' I couldn't help smiling – at the same time noting a possible escape route.

While our confidence was being boosted by the Funereal Fungus, our fellow artiste arrived – a young girl saxophonist from Manchester. My heart went out to her as the Toadstool transferred his attention to her. He began to reel off all the great female artistes who'd gone before her and died the death. The poor girl's confidence was visibly crumbling when the organist and the drummer, who also doubled as compère, arrived. We all went into the dressing room to discuss the running order, and at the same time escape from the Mushroom of Doom.

Soon I heard the audience arriving. The scraping of tables and chairs being moved was interspersed with the sound of knives being sharpened. I had visions of shrouds being made-ready and cement being poured into the drinks. The organist, a blonde lady, smoked continuously. The rest of us smoked nervously too and before long visibility in the dressing room was down to nil. 'Which way to the stage?' someone asked.

'Switch your fog lights on and follow the cat's eyes!' was the reply.

The young girl was told to go on first, so she started to go through her music with the organist – who just lit another fag and appeared to show only a slight interest in what the girl was saying. The drummer-cum-compère didn't even bother to listen: he just stood talking to us. What followed I just couldn't believe.

The compère went on stage and announced the girl. The organist immediately started to play – without waiting for him to get back to his drums. But what really made us sit up was that the organist was only playing with one hand, using the other to hold the ever-present cigarette. We watched in disbelief as she even stopped playing to turn the pages of her music: instead of using the hand her fag was in she used the other one, which meant the girl playing the saxophone, was on her own until the page was turned. The saxophonist's act was turned into a complete shambles. The drummer even got up from his drums midway through the last number and walked into the wings in readiness to bring her off in his capacity as compère! She had to finish her final number with half her accompaniment gone. When the compère walked out to lead the applause, which was conspicuous by its absence, he grabbed the microphone and beckoned to the girl, who by this time had left the stage, totally demoralised, to come back on stage and take a bow. 'I know she's died the death,' he boomed into the mike, 'but give her a big hand anyway.'

By this time I had one leg out of the dressing-room window. The poor girl was in bits and I didn't fancy our prospects at all. To make matters worse, Paul Minchella (our drummer at the time) bought a card for the bingo game, which took place before our spot. Needless to say he was crossing out numbers right and left and my heart sunk when he crowed, 'Hey, I only need one number!' I could feel the hairs on the back of my neck begin to rise. Without looking round, I knew all eyes would be directed towards our table and the vibes would be anything but genial.

Being the one in the front line about to face this formidable audience, I pleaded frantically with our excited percussionist. 'For God's sake don't shout if you win. We'll never get out alive!'

No sooner had he told me in no uncertain terms to fuck off when the worst happened. 'House!' he shouted with glee.

His cry was followed by an earth-shattering silence. The only audible sound was the thud of my jaw hitting the floor. How am I going to make this lot laugh and be happy? I thought. In their eyes, not only were we about to make off with their prize money, we were being paid to do it! If ever I needed help from above this was the time. Well, my prayers must have been answered for, by some miracle, we managed to come through our ordeal unscathed – much to the chagrin of the Toadstool, I bet!

That particular club, I'm happy to say, was a one-off and not typical of the vast majority. On the whole the audiences were marvellous and very appreciative. The clubs were run in a very efficient and democratic manner; being on the committee was a great fillip to anyone who was chosen to serve, and they took great pride in their duties. For a fortunate few it was also a great opportunity to sample the perks . . .

Many of the clubs booked a stripper for the Sunday lunchtime shows, and the committee of one particular club we went to got more than a show! Every so often they booked a certain stripper who wasn't very popular with the audience – but very popular with the committee. After she'd done her bit for the lads on stage, she went on to the committee room and did a bit extra for the committee; they received their 'commission' in the form of a hand job. On this particular day we were in conversation with an ex-committee man, who told us it was the first visit of the stripper since the election of the new committee. And for one new member – the concert chairman – it was going to be the culmination of a whole year's canvassing and junketing: four feet ten inches of pulsating Welsh testosterone had worked his balls off all year to get elected and sample the perks. It was obvious to everyone that he was feeling as frisky as a rabbit in spring. He was up for it all right – best suit, aftershave, - the lot. We followed the whole episode with interest on the advice of the ex-committeeman; he'd been tipped the wink that something was going to happen.

So after the stripper had done her bit on the stage, the randy little chairman followed her and the committee into the committee room. He was really chomping at the bit. When one of the others told him that it was customary for the newly elected member to buy the drinks, he dashed off to the bar. When he returned with a large tray of drinks he found the committee room door had been locked. 'Let me in you bastards,' he yelled, thumping on the door. 'Let me in, you rotten sods!' They didn't let him in, and we couldn't stop laughing. A little later, when we went outside to our van, we found him jumping up and down outside the committee room window shouting abuse at the others, who no doubt had everything in hand.

But not only did we share their laughter; we also had cause to share their unforgettable sorrow. It was our second trip down there – the week after the terrible disaster at the village of Aberfan. I was moved to tears when I witnessed first hand the indescribable heartbreak those poor people had to endure. When that mountain of slag swept down on the village, engulfing the school and its children, the whole world was stunned. It was a tragedy beyond words, and sadly unforgettable. The South Wales mining community has had to cope with many disasters, but never one quite like this. It involved children, was above ground, and was delivered in such a way that many, like myself, began to call into question our most fervent religious beliefs. The plight of the people of Aberfan made my own problems seem pathetic and insignificant. I vowed never to moan again but, being a mere mortal, I regret to say that I did.

While everyone was getting caught up in the drama and passion of the catastrophe Joe, his usual pragmatic self, pointed out that one of the clubs we were booked at in the next few weeks was actually in Aberfan. I couldn't believe that the gig hadn't been pulled. When we questioned this with the agency they insisted, after consultation with the club, that the booking should be honoured.

When we arrived I hadn't a clue how I was going to approach things. I didn't feel like telling jokes. How could I go on stage looking as if I didn't have a care in the world in the light of what had happened just down the road? I discussed my fears and apprehension with the concert chairman – a quiet and dignified chap who immediately put me at ease. He put his arm round my shoulder reassuringly. 'Don't worry, young man,' he said. 'Just go on and do your show. I'm sure everyone will appreciate what you do.'

'But I don't feel I should be telling jokes,' I moaned.

'Listen,' he said quietly but firmly. 'We need laughter in our lives more than ever right now – and you can help.' I agreed with him – but with a great deal of reluctance. 'Off you go then,' he said. 'You go and get ready and I'll introduce you.'

He went back and took his place in the concert room and I joined the lads in the dressing room. I think they were feeling the same as I was, but no one said anything.

The chairman gave us a wonderful introduction, adding that he felt sure the audience would enjoy our show, and off we went. We swung into our usual opener – an up-tempo song called 'Do What You Do Do Well.' We hadn't played two bars of the introduction before the rest of the band turned to me with a look of horror. They had realised that the first line of the song was 'He couldn't move a mountain' – as had I. What am I going to do? I thought. My brain went into overdrive – talk about thinking on your feet! I don't know how or why, but I blurted out, 'He couldn't climb a mountain or pull down a big oak tree . . .' The sigh of relief from the rest of the band was probably picked up the far side of Swansea. Perhaps that's what settled us down, for after that we went from strength to strength and made sure that the audience enjoyed a good night.

More than one person came up to thank me afterwards and I happened to mention to one lady the misgivings I'd had before the show, and how the chairman had put paid to them.

'Well,' she said with a sigh, 'there was no one better qualified to do so – he lost both his children.'

I have to say that as we drove away from the club that night I was filled with admiration for that man: it was probably the greatest show of courage I've ever seen. And it wasn't until I was blessed with a child of my own in later years that I could ever begin to understand how he and his wife must have felt.

I've been granted the good fortune to be able to watch my daughter grow up and go out into the world to make her own way. I thank God for that – but I'll never come to terms with or understand why such a terrible thing had to happen to those lovely people in Aberfan.

Chapter Twelve
CORRIDORS OF POWER

For the next few years, our van got to know its own way down the M5. South Wales was awash with money and the clubs were booming; but the fact that we had to travel all the way down from the north meant that we had to increase our fees considerably – which didn't go unnoticed by some of the more price conscious committees. I remember standing behind the curtains waiting to start our show at one particular club when the president climbed onto the front of the stage to tell the audience, 'These boys have come all the way down from Yorkshire and I hope you enjoy them – because, Christ, they've bloody well cost enough! Now here they are . . .' It might not have been the introduction we'd been expecting – but it was inspired, because after that we worked our socks off to justify our fee and we ended up having a really good night. And as we received a tremendous ovation the president climbed back onto the stage to share in the glory. Our big fee had been justified and he was in his element! After all, wasn't it he who told the concert secretary to book us? – Of course it was – he told us so in his closing speech. Yes, he had never been in any doubt that we would be well received. And, being the modest chap that he was, he invited the concert secretary and the agent (who happened to be in the club) to join him on stage to share in the plaudit. Yes, there's no business like show business and he loved every moment of it. As it was customary to sing the Welsh national anthem at the end of the night, he grabbed the microphone and launched into it in his native tongue. The audience rose to its feet and joined him in song, and he put his arm round my shoulder and clung to me like a brother. Caught up in the emotion, I began to mime the words – big mistake! Thinking I knew them, he thrust the mike into my hand and invited me to lead the singing. I gave it back while suddenly developing a cough – which I had to keep up throughout the anthem.

We made quite a name for ourselves around South Wales, and in so doing got to know many of the committee members. This gave us an insight into the running of the clubs. It was fascinating – even frightening – to contemplate the sheer potential of these places. They were thriving businesses turning over great sums of money – but run by people who were not, for the most part, businessmen. The opportunity was there for the guy who swept the factory floor during the day to be elected president of his club, and enjoy the same executive status as the factory's managing director. Of course there were always those who betrayed this trust put in them, but there were many more, I'm pleased to say, who didn't. I learned to respect and admire certain members of this elite body of clubmen, who were just as capable of running a business as their counterparts in the world of commerce.

One club we went to had a different organ each time we visited. 'How can your club afford a new organ for the club every year?' I asked one of the committeemen.

'We can't,' came the answer.

'So how come there's a different one every time we come?'

'What we do is ring up a music shop and get one on trial for six months. We send it back after the trial period and ring up another shop.'

'But what'll happen when you've run out of shops?' I asked.

'We won't. We haven't even used all of them round here yet! And when we have done there's always Bristol, Birmingham, Manchester . . .' I didn't need to hear any more.

There always seemed to be a wonderfully optimistic outlook down there, which is one reason I always looked forward to going. The local club was seen as the centre of the community, and was looked upon with great pride. In many ways it was similar to the club-life in Lancashire but not, dare I say, in the greater part of Yorkshire and the north-east, where, for some reason, members seemed to take the clubs for granted. Perhaps this was because the clubs, particularly in South Yorkshire, were more numerous and in closer proximity, so tended to compete with one another. This tended to divide the local communities.

In an attempt to steal members away, some of the larger clubs put on shows to rival any West End revue, featuring many top names in the world of entertainment – like Bob Monkhouse, Adam Faith, and Val Doonican. Some of the supporting acts have gone on to be very successful in their own right as well: Freddie Starr, Charlie Williams and Little and Large, for instance.

Freddie was – and still is – a complete nut case. He was adept at ruining people's acts! It didn't matter who was performing, but if he was in the room he was driven by a strange compulsion to create havoc. He'd walk across the stage without his trousers on, or begin serving tea to the band while someone was singing a meaningful ballad. Oh yes, he was a real laugh – but he was also a pain in the arse! Little and Large, on the other hand, were brilliant in every respect, completely down to earth and as much fun off stage as they were on it. We came across them quite a lot on our travels and their attitude never altered: even when they hit the big time they were as approachable as the day we first met them. I even got to write a song for them to perform on the old BBC kids' programme *Crackerjack*: it was called 'Rock Steady'. I watched their career with great interest, and when I saw them driving around in a plush limousine I remember thinking back to the digs in Sunderland when we had to push-start their old Morris 1100. The battery was flat and they couldn't afford a new one. When they got to a club they had to find a place to park which had a slope – so they could start the car off after the show. Sometimes the nearest slope was miles from the venue.

And talking about cars in Sunderland . . . The first car I ever owned was stolen up there. It was my pride and joy and I was gutted; so was the car for that matter. The police came to take the details. 'It's a Mini,' I told them.

They began to shake their heads – there were thousands of them about. But when I told them it was sprayed metallic purple they seemed a lot more optimistic – and so they should have been: as far as I knew, it was the only one of that colour anywhere in the country. A friend of mine had done the paint job especially for me. Not surprisingly they found it the next day – but minus the radio, and the dashboard was ripped out.

This was the start of a love-hate relationship with 'Geordieland'. I always found the north-east to be a place of extremes. It was a place with very little compromise as far as I was concerned, which left me constantly exasperated: they seemed to be so set in their ways that no one was prepared to meet you half-way. You even ended up talking like them!

As I mentioned earlier, you could have two clubs on opposite sides of the road that were totally different in character. As an example, the first club I ever did up there wouldn't have been out of place in Dodge City. We arrived on the Sunday lunchtime to find the concert room completely devoid of furniture: it had been smashed to pieces in a fight the night before. So we carried our equipment into the club alongside committeemen who in turn were lugging benches and trestles that they'd borrowed from the canteen of a local factory. According to one source this was a regular occurrence – which led me to speculate that the local canteen was on a retainer! It really was a rough venue – and yet across the road there was another club that was the complete opposite. Lovely people, tasteful decor – a different world. And that's how it was with audiences too. You either went down a bomb or you died a death.

Despite all this I developed a grudging respect for the Geordies. I think it was the unceremonious way in which they spoke their mind that appealed to me. One bloke told me that my act was crap – but in a way that I didn't leave me feeling offended. He was also buying me a drink at the time, which added to my confusion! And I never did get to grips with their sense of humour. It was lucky for us that we had more than one string to our bow – so if the comedy wasn't going well we could fall back on our musical talents. Looking back I think that of all the club audiences we faced the Geordies were the most critical. If the chairman didn't think you were up to it sometimes you didn't get past the first spot. There was one club, which was at the side of a busy dual carriageway. The concert chairman, who was considered to be a bit of a martinet, came into the dressing room before we went on and told us what he intended to do. 'When you start playing I'll go out of the club and I'll go across the road to the other side. And when I get there I'll be listening.' He paused and fixed us with a stare. 'And if I can't hear any applause you needn't bother going on for your second spot.' With that he went back into the concert room, announced us – and left the room. Well, we did our second spot – which is more than a colleague of ours managed.

Whilst *he* was doing his first spot the chairman got knocked down crossing the road. When our friend went looking for him – after he'd finished his spot – a committee member told him the chairman had been taken to hospital in an ambulance. The singer replied, 'Oh, really . . . I don't suppose he happened to mention anything about me doing another spot before he went, did he?' You might think that this was a tad insensitive on his part but, as the saying goes, 'He who lives by the sword . . .'

The one thing you couldn't say about the north-east was that it was dull. There was always something going on – car theft, stabbings, murder! And this was quite apart from the numerous acts that died on stage every night.

Our first week was quite an experience. As our first club was devoid of furniture, our second was devoid of people. There was hardly anyone in. I didn't know what to make of it all, and by the third night I was ready for home. When we reached the club, which was down in the dock area of Sunderland, and pulled up by the emergency exit, the first thing I noticed was a large bloodstain. Someone had been stabbed there the previous night. As we set up I noticed the bar staff half-filling pint glasses with beer and placing them all along the bar – which stretched half the length of the room. I'd never seen this practice before and I wondered what was going on. When the doors opened I found out. The crowd came in like whirling dervishes and descended on the bar like a plague of locusts. The bar staff could hardly keep up with demands. Seeing all this, I began to anticipate a good night, thinking that if they carried on drinking like that they'd be in a good mood by the time we got on. I was wrong. The audience completely blanked us. No laughs, no applause – nothing. To make things worse, we were booked to appear there two days later. We contacted the agent the following day, fully expecting to be informed that our services wouldn't be required. Wrong again. 'No, they want you back,' he said.

'But why?' I asked – reminding him that we'd completely died on our arse.

'Oh, don't worry about that – they do that to every act new to the club. It's a kind of a weighing-up process. They like to make their mind up about you before they commit themselves. Just wait and see. If they liked you they'll be completely different. Just do the same act and don't worry.'

He was dead right too. The same people who'd sat stony-faced

Billy Daniels was a massive star in the 1950s, singing classics such as 'That Old Black Magic'. When we appeared with him we were on first and the audience didn't really want a change of mood, so when Billy came on he was booed. After a few minutes he wowed the crowd and they loved him! He signed this for me when we were working together in down-town Newton Aycliffe in the north-east of England.

SAMMY

The Sammy King Five. Left to right: Paul Minchell

NG FIVE

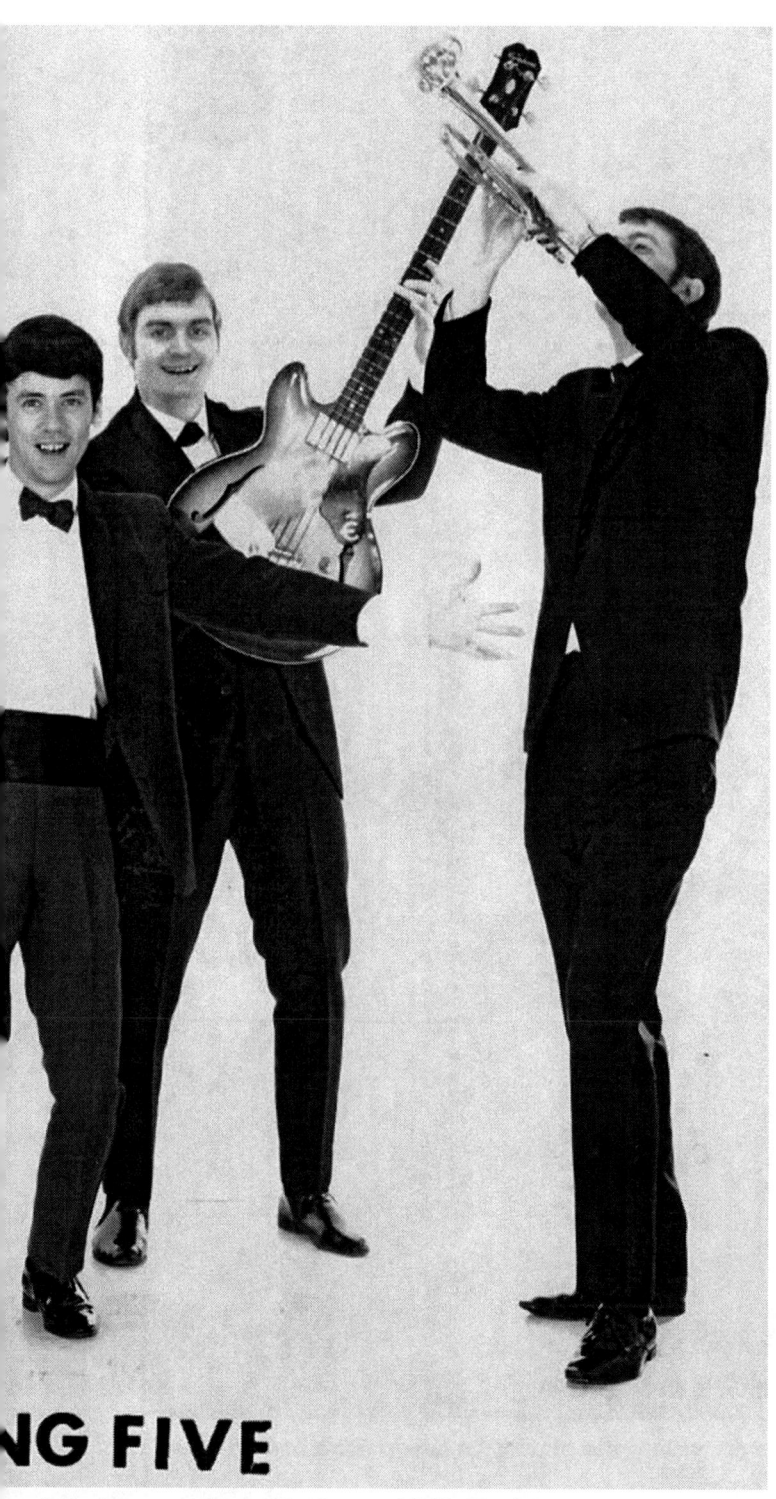

erek Smith, me, Barry Taylor and Bill Clarke.

Here's a very young me playing at Cleopatra's in Cardiff.

through our show went through a complete transformation. I was getting belly laughs at jokes that had met with total indifference two nights before.

Yes, the only thing you could be certain of up there was uncertainty. But one thing I appreciated was that, regardless of everything else, you were always given a chance. And sometimes the audience could be won over – even against all the odds.

Indirectly I had a hand in one of the most impressive performances by an artiste I've ever witnessed. It was an evening in Newton Aycliffe, near Durham, and we were booked to support an American singing star – Billy Daniels. He was well known for popularising the classic song 'That Old Black Magic' and had played top venues all over the world, but, like many other stars of that era, his popularity had begun to wane because of the changing fashions in music – chiefly brought about by the rock'n'roll explosion. For a man of his calibre, who'd headlined in Las Vegas and London, it would be fair to say that this gig was a bit of a come down. The place was heaving when we opened the show. Without being conceited, we absolutely tore the bollocks off them for the next hour. We went down so well that we had to do several encores, and I had to admit feeling quite pleased with myself as we trudged off the stage soaked in sweat.

Billy Daniels was standing in the wings resplendent in full evening dress, and as we passed him he muttered something complimentary like 'Great show, boys'. I acknowledged him, but at the same time I remember smugly thinking, follow that! I didn't fancy his chances at all. The odds were really stacked against him. To begin with, he was about to face an audience that had been milked dry for over an hour. On top of that he had to rely on accompaniment from just a piano and drums – no orchestra. And, to cap it all, he was about to be scrutinised by some of the most critical people in clubland. Undaunted, Billy set about his work with the same professional approach that I remember seeing when he'd topped *Sunday Night at the Palladium* on TV.

I didn't go into the dressing room to change; I stood in the wings, dripping wet and still clutching my guitar, curious to see how he'd be received. As I expected, it wasn't too well. It came as no surprise when they talked all the way through his first song and most of his second one. Billy carried on with great panache, undeterred. It was easy to see why he'd enjoyed such success in his heyday.

Although his style of singing wasn't really to my taste, I knew I was watching something special. I couldn't take my eyes off him, and I was really incensed when someone in the audience shouted, 'Get off home, you has-been' midway through his second song. Obviously the idiot who shouted hadn't enough sense to realise he was witnessing professionalism at its highest level. It didn't seem to worry the great man, and he carried on singing and smiling. He began to exchange pleasantries with some of the crowd who – little by little – were beginning to listen and take note of what he was doing. Sheer talent gradually subdued the baying horde. It was as if they'd all been put under a spell. Yes, he certainly wove his 'old black magic' on them and in no time he had them eating out of his hand. By the time he began to sing 'Sunrise Sunset' from *Fiddler on the Roof* you could have heard a pin drop. The punters were mesmerised.

If I hadn't seen it, I'd never have believed it. I'd never been so impressed by a performance, and haven't been since for that matter. When he finished his spot the whole room stood in tribute and applauded him. They wouldn't let him go, and my earlier crass thoughts of 'follow that' were blown into oblivion, where they well and truly belonged. I was taught a very valuable lesson that night, not just in professionalism but also in humility. It also prompted me to do something I'd never done before. I raced into the foyer and tore his photograph from the board advertising the show, then took it backstage to be autographed by him. As he wrote he chatted away to the rest of the band who, like me, had been drawn towards him by that magnetism only true stars seem to possess. Quite apart from his musical talent, he displayed a refreshing sincerity that was a welcome change in the backstabbing world of show business.

It might seem strange to many people, but that was one of the high spots of my career, and also a watershed. The stark realisation that I could never possess whatever it was that made this man such a wonderful performer led me to reassess my own talents. As far as I was concerned, he was born to perform; somehow I knew I wasn't. But I soon cheered up when I began to count my own blessings. I'll bet he can't play the guitar as well as I can, I thought. And I bet he doesn't write his own songs either!

So from then on I decided to concentrate more on the things that came naturally to me.

Bread and butter – and bingo!

We began to work regular stints in the north-east but I was never happy about it; I was always glad to escape back to the sanctuary of South Yorkshire – which is where we earned our bread and butter. The audiences could be tough, but at least I knew what to expect. Most of the clubs were large, well established, well run, but, like everywhere else, preoccupied with the dreaded bingo! I hated the game. To me it was the ultimate crowd killer, the club artiste's arthritis: it was something you couldn't do anything about but had to learn to live with. To make matters worse, it was treated like a religion. To speak while a game was in progress came close to being sacrilegious. It was considered by many of the punters to be the main event of the evening, and was the only attraction that could guarantee complete silence while it was in progress.

At one particular club in Sheffield, only minutes before a game was about to start, one of our speakers – which we'd hung up on one side of the stage – proved to be too heavy for the hook. It crashed down, and smashed the bingo machine below it to smithereens. The deathly hush that descended on the room was only interrupted by the sound of liberated ping-pong balls coming to rest. The audience was in complete shock, the committee mortified. Somehow we got the feeling that the magnitude of the situation was on a par with desecrating the high altar in Westminster Abbey. Apart from the damage, we'd unwittingly knackered the Sunday lunchtime routine. Evidently the bingo had to start at a particular time to co-ordinate with another club a hundred yards away, whose bingo was timed to start shortly after the first session finished; they even took into consideration the time it took the punters to walk between the two clubs. And there was a third club waiting at the end of the chain! The falling speaker had really thrown a spanner into the works. This left the audience on the horns of a dilemma. Should they wait to see if a replacement bingo machine could be found quickly, or risk missing two more sessions? No contest. When the curtains opened up for our first spot we were greeted by wall to wall furniture. No bingo – no audience.

Yes, the old 'housey-housey' was a serious business – after all, there was some serious money to be won. But woe betides any artiste who dared to win any – especially a jackpot game. One of the worst things I ever did was win a jackpot house. I got the money all right, but that was all I got. I didn't get another clap or laugh that evening –

I was totally ignored. From that day forward I decided to have nothing more to do with the game: if I didn't play I couldn't upset the audience, or so I thought. On one occasion I recall arriving at a small village club on the outskirts of Leeds to be met by a flustered committeeman. The rest of the committee had walked out after an argument, leaving him to run the club by himself. He pleaded with me to help him with the bingo: there was only one game and he had no one to call it. So I agreed, thinking I might earn a few brownie points with the audience. I should have known better. I called it, and who won? My roadie! I was lucky to get out of there alive.

It never ceased to amaze me how much power was wielded by a wooden box, ninety ping-pong balls and the equivalent of a hair drier blowing up a tube. Such was bingo's influence over the massed members of the working men's clubs that many an artiste found him or herself sympathetic to the Luddites – which resulted in the poor old bingo machine coming in for a bit of the same treatment as the loom on occasions. Most of the machines were the type that blew ping-pong balls up a tube, and some disgruntled acts sabotaged them after a bad night. One of the commonest practices was to remove the retaining spring at the top of the tube, so when the machine was switched on the balls came out of the tube like bullets from a gun and shot all over the place. Sometimes the wiring was tampered with, making the blower suck – leaving the bingo-caller wondering why the balls weren't coming up the tube. I also heard of one group, who after a really bad night removed a large number of balls from one machine. And later, when a game was in progress, the bingo-caller shouted, 'Anybody sweating?' Everyone shook their heads – leaving the poor caller slightly puzzled. 'Well, there bloody well should be,' he said, staring at the solitary ball pinging about inside the machine.

Chapter Thirteen
COUNTDOWN TO A BREAKDOWN

As the '60s drew to a close the storm clouds began to gather. On the surface things seemed to be going well for me. I had plenty of work and my bank balance was healthy enough, but I was far from being content. Demanding audiences were putting more of a strain on me than I realised, and continual travelling and performing left me no time to pursue any other interests. Life was a treadmill from which there seemed to be no escape. Our heavy workload prevented me from striking up any kind of relationship with the opposite sex, and being away from home left me short of a much-needed sympathetic ear.

Although I didn't realise it at the time, I was beginning to display signs of an impending breakdown. Trying to get to sleep became nigh on impossible. Apart from hearing garbled voices and strange music whenever I closed my eyes, I was subjected to what I can only describe as huge electric shocks as I was about to fall asleep. It was really frightening, more so because I didn't know what was causing it all. I couldn't get through the day – or the night – without experiencing weird sensations. There was one occasion when I felt my head was about to explode; another time I thought I was having a heart attack. We were on our way to a gig one evening when for some reason I felt as if my whole body was being squeezed in an invisible vice. It left me gasping for breath and very frightened. The gig was a disaster. I spent most of the time flat on my back in the dressing room, leaving the rest of the lads to struggle through on their own. It frightened me so much that I called at the local hospital on the way home. After a brief examination I was assured that my heart was fine. But I was still advised to see my own doctor. The next day he gave me a thorough check-up, and I was pronounced to be as fit as a fiddle. He told me that it might help to take things a little bit easier, but being in show business that was easier said than done! I tried not to worry but for the next few days I was walking on eggshells. Being reassured by the doctor helped a little, I suppose, but I still knew there was something terribly wrong. Adrenalin rushes made my whole body tremble for no apparent reason. Other things happened too, which I wouldn't know how to describe. No, in order to understand what I was going through you'd have to experience it first hand – and I wouldn't wish that on my worst enemy.

With the symptoms getting worse and no one able to help me, the whole situation came to a head one Sunday lunchtime. Returning from a lunchtime booking, I'd elected to drive. It helped to keep my mind occupied and suppressed the terrible feelings of despair I was experiencing on a regular basis. We were crossing the bridge above the M1 motorway at junction 40 when the vice-like grip took hold of me again, only this time it came with a vengeance. It wouldn't let go, and I was seized by panic. It was as if life was being squeezed out from me, and I couldn't do anything about it. There was a tremendous pressure between my shoulder blades, as if someone had plunged a knife into my back – causing me to push my chest forward involuntarily. I couldn't breathe and I really thought I was going to die.

I steered the van into the side of the road and one of the lads asked me what was wrong. I couldn't tell him – I couldn't even speak. I wanted to scream, but couldn't. Such was the intensity of my panic and frustration that I began to sob uncontrollably. The floodgates opened and years of frustration and tribulation poured forth in a deluge of tears. At first the rest of the lads were stunned and didn't know what to do. Then someone said, 'We'd better get him home!' I couldn't stop bawling my head off – it was beyond my control.

Naturally my folks were concerned when we reached home. My

mother took charge straight away and rang the doctor. Strangely it was my father who sat me down and cuddled me. Although he was a very loving man he'd never held me close like this before, but I think he sensed that this was more than a show of emotion. He rocked me back and forth like a baby. The lads hung around for a while, but left when they realised there was nothing more they could do. I was still sobbing uncontrollably when the doctor arrived – being the weekend it was a locum. After a short consultation with my mother he pulled a hypodermic syringe from his bag and stuck it in my thigh. In a matter of seconds I lost consciousness. I awoke twenty-four hours later.

It's hard to describe how I felt; I wasn't sure I felt anything. It was if I was existing rather than living. I must have lain awake for more than an hour, staring at a mark on the ceiling. Tears began to roll down my face. My mother came into the bedroom. 'You awake, son?' she asked – with that look of concern I'd seen too many times before. I couldn't reply – or didn't know what to say; I was in limbo. 'I'll bring you a cup of tea, love – that'll make you feel better.'

She returned with my tea, and a little later Dr Hinchcliffe called. I don't remember much about what was said. He left a prescription and promised to call back the next day.

Later that night the anxiety attacks returned. I felt as if I was being squeezed to death again, and only when I started to cry did the pressure subside. I was given some tablets, which sent me off to sleep. The following evening it was the same. Then the tightness lessened slightly, to be replaced by a depth of depression I'd never encountered before. It felt as if I'd been plunged into a different dimension. I descended to depths I never knew existed. No one could get a word out of me. My mind was more or less redundant: thoughts neither came in nor went out, and my whole consciousness seemed to be shutting down. I couldn't be bothered to dress, and spent the whole day sitting in an armchair in my dressing gown. Eventually the doctor decided I was beyond any help he could give me, and a psychiatrist was sent for. After a brief examination the shrink wasted no time in suggesting that I should be taken away for a 'rest'. He informed my mother that a place would be found for me at St Luke's psychiatric hospital in Huddersfield. He hadn't finished speaking before that 'Here we go again' expression appeared again on my mother's face.

A few days later I was picked up by a man in a Renault Dauphine who whisked me off in the direction of Huddersfield. I couldn't have cared less. As far as I was concerned we might just as well have been heading for the moon. It wasn't me any more – it was what was left of me. The last flicker of spirit had been extinguished days ago. I was completely devoid of emotion. Everything seemed to have been drained away by the endless bouts of sobbing, which by now had become second nature. I was an empty shell existing in a vacuum. This isn't a part of my life that I wish to remember, but it's one I can't choose to forget, unfortunately.

One limped into the cuckoo's nest
In less than thirty minutes the little car pulled up in front of St Luke's. The driver opened my door, and I eventually got out and followed him through the glass doors into the reception area. Some visitors recognised me; actually I found out much later that it wasn't me they recognised, it was my limp! But for my distinctive gait they wouldn't have known it was me, such was the state I was in. The driver handed me over to a nurse who led me down a long corridor: I followed her like a lost sheep. We eventually reached another small reception area. 'Take a chair,' said the nurse.

Strangely enough, I remember replying, 'Where to?' – probably because they were the first words I'd spoken for days.

Presently a more senior member of staff came in. She began filling forms in and asking me questions. 'Are you taking any medication?' 'Have you ever contemplated taking your own life?' I responded with either a shake of my head or a shrug of my shoulders.

After she'd finished filling in the forms I was told to wait until someone else came for me, so I wandered over to a window and stared out. Almost immediately the top of a ladder clattered against the windowsill. It began to shake as someone below began to climb it. Then the window cleaner's face peered through at me. He must have been put off by what he saw because he went straight back down the ladder before his wash-leather had even touched the glass! I suppose coming eyeball to eyeball with someone who looked like Uncle Fester of the Addams family would have been enough to unnerve anyone – let alone a poor bloke trying to do his job.

I continued to stare out of the window until a young male nurse gently touched me on the shoulder to bring me out of my trance. His name was Leonard and he was of West Indian origin. For some reason I felt more at ease with him than the rest – possibly because he sang and clicked his fingers as we walked to where he was taking me. He also talked to me as if I was 'normal', which made a somewhat refreshing change.

We reached the ward I was assigned to, and the first thing I noticed was the set-up. I'd been in many hospital wards before – but never one like this: it was laid out in the shape of a cross. We entered via a small reception area, which eventually became a corridor containing various treatment rooms and a padded cell. It was bisected by the main part of the ward, which, to the left, was a dining cum television area and to the right a series of cubicles. Each of these contained four beds and the top half of the cubicle was completely panelled with glass: the patients were observed at all times.

I was shown to my bed and left to unpack my case. I sat on my bed for ages just staring around me. Most of the other inmates were walking about in a trance. Talk about not being a full shilling – the collective mental state of the whole ward couldn't have amounted to more than two pence at the most. For no apparent reason a well-dressed middle-aged man went into the next cubicle, threw himself onto one of the beds and began to cry. It seemed a strange – even pathetic – sight but it had no effect on me. I remained completely detached. I walked to a window and stared out again. The whole scenario was like a dream, but I knew that it wasn't – I never limp in my dreams.

Leonard came in to see if I'd unpacked. I hadn't so he helped me. Afterwards he told me that I could walk around for a while if I wanted to – so I wandered down the ward. I stood by the entrance to the dining area and looked in. For some reason I began to feel slightly agitated. Three of the patients were watching television. Music was blaring from the set, and when it began to annoy me I immediately strode in, switched the set off and strode out again. I remained by the door to see what happened. Nothing. The eyes of the three viewers remained glued to the set. They continued to stare at the blank screen for the next few minutes until it gradually dawned on them that something had happened. Then they began to create, shouting and bawling until one of the staff turned the TV back on. But as soon as the nurse had left the room I went back in and turned it off again. For some reason I'd developed an aversion to music. For the rest of the day I went round switching off radios and televisions.

I was billeted with two young lads, which left the fourth bed in the cubicle unoccupied. I knew one of these lads slightly: he came from Batley, and was having emotional problems brought upon by marital difficulties. The other lad seemed perfectly normal on the surface, until he asked, 'Do you want to come with us?'

'Where to?'

'To the morgue!' he replied. 'Come on, I'm going to look at some dead bodies. They keep them in big drawers which you can pull out.'

Normally I'd have been disgusted; instead I just shook my head.

'It's OK,' he reassured me. 'The bloke in charge won't mind. There are new ones coming in all the time. Some of them are really funny . . .' He prattled on, describing in graphic detail the things he'd seen on his many visits. I just switched off.

That first evening I couldn't sleep. I was given a measure of the drug largactil but it had no effect on me. An hour later I was trudging down the ward asking for more. It was like a scene from *Oliver Twist* . . . 'Please, nurse – can I have some more?'

I was given another measure but it didn't have any effect. Four times I returned, and in the end the nurse scolded, 'I can't give you any more. I've already given you enough to knock out the whole ward!'

Even that didn't make me sleep. I remember dawn breaking and the day staff arriving to take up their duties. We were all told to get up, wash ourselves and make our own beds. Reluctantly I did what I was told, filling the wash-basin with water, bending over it and washing my face. But as I lifted my head to reach for the towel I caught sight of myself in the mirror behind the basin. It frightened me to death: staring back at me was a complete stranger. I honestly couldn't identify with the face in the mirror – it really was like looking at someone else. The rest of the ward went into the dining room for breakfast. I didn't bother; instead I lay on my bed wondering what the hell had happened to me. It's a terrible feeling knowing that you might be losing your marbles. Perhaps the realisation of this put the brakes on the downward spiral. It's hard to say where the slide stopped and the point of recovery started, but I'm nearly certain that the catalyst had something to do with that unknown face staring back at me from the mirror.

The doctor came in to see me later that morning. He decided to try me on certain drugs, to see how I reacted to them. The first batch didn't agree with me at all and I just flipped. Fortunately the right cocktail was found and I was given three tablets three times a day.

These drugs didn't seem to take effect straight away, and in the meantime I continued to act a bit eccentrically. The strange part about all this was that I was aware of what I was doing – yet I couldn't seem to do anything about it. My antisocial behaviour affected my family when they came to visit me. I remember telling my mum and sister-in-law June that I didn't want to talk to them and that they should go, reducing them both to tears. I was completely impervious to their feelings, which was very much out of character. Fortunately this behaviour didn't last long. The drugs kicked in and, with the help of the staff and my family, I gradually began to emerge from my 'cocoon of doom'. For brief spells I began to show a semblance of normality – but I was still a long way from being normal. I was still prone to involuntary bouts of crying and moods of deep depression. Evidently this was commonplace for someone in my condition.

As time went by I began to open up a little, and entered into the odd conversation with members of staff. Everything I said and did was taken note of and presented to the psychiatrist to be studied. By all accounts a patient's problem could sometimes be pinpointed this way, and if the cause of the problem could be identified it could sometimes reduce the recovery time by half.

In the meantime a few of my fellow eccentrics began to display patterns of behaviour far beyond the norm. Most of the patients looked pretty normal, but some left you in no doubt why they were in there. Unfortunately for these poor souls their predicament wasn't just a temporary setback; their long-term outlook was pretty bleak. However, comedy and tragedy go hand in hand in places like these, in many cases applying to the same situation. Having experienced life on both sides of the fence, I feel I'm well qualified to chronicle certain goings-on without fear of being branded callous.

I was having breakfast when I came into contact with my first 'character'. A rather effeminate young lad minced over to my table, walking with the same camp elegance as a male ballet dancer. His short blond hair was brushed forward in classic Greek style, a demeanour he immediately complemented by adopting a pose reminiscent of 'The Thinker' on the chair opposite. He would probably have felt more at home in the temple of Apollo. Perhaps he thought he was. Apparently he was a brilliant music student who'd 'gone over the top' while studying the piano. Having learned from someone that I was involved in music, he was curious to know more about me. He began to ask questions, but I wasn't very forthcoming and the conversation didn't last very long. At the mention of rock'n'roll he registered a pained expression, swept over to the nearby piano and began to play, calling over his shoulder as he did so, 'THIS is the only kind of music . . .' He began to play a very complicated classical piece, which brought howls of derision from most of the others in the room. In a fit of pique he slammed down the piano lid and stormed out, pouring scorn on his critics as he left. After he'd gone, one of the blokes on the table next to me said, 'You'll have to watch him, you know. He'll try to swap teapots with you.'

'What?'

'He'll try to swap his teapot with you.'

Seeing my puzzled expression, one of the others explained to me what he meant. We were all given individual teapots at mealtimes. The one given to the pianist also contained bromide, to discourage him from having sex by himself, which he frequently indulged in. It was a well-known ploy for him to distract someone in order to switch teapots. The way I was feeling at that time it wouldn't have mattered if he had, because the only thing that rose for me in the morning was the sun!

But the Bromide Kid was a brilliant pianist. The trouble was that no one was in a fit state of mind to appreciate him. More than once I heard someone complaining, 'He gets up in the middle of the night, he does – stark naked – and he starts playing that Walsall Concerto thing, or whatever they call it!'

At mealtimes the young pianist took his place at the same table as a senile vicar and an ex-rugby league player, who suffered from seizures. I don't know what the vicar suffered from, but he always reminded me of a turtle. He had that kind of expression on his face, his long thin neck seemed to snake out of the mass of shawls or scarves that were loosely wrapped around his neck, and his every movement was conducted in slow motion. He was also confined to a wheelchair, which he insisted on propelling by himself – one wheel at a time. Any attempt to help him was met with the most un-vicarlike abuse – and in consequence it took an age for him to get from A to B. If he went for a pee he'd probably have had one by the time he arrived. The ex-rugby player, however, was a really nice bloke. He was a huge man who'd played at top level for a leading Yorkshire club, and but for his fits he was completely normal. Most of the others avoided him and he sat alone watching the telly. I'd seen him play on a few occasions so I was eager to make his acquaintance. He was very quietly spoken for a big man and I took to him straight away. We got on very well and I spent a lot of time sitting next to him watching TV. He occasionally spoke about his condition, which could be held in check by drugs most of the time. There was still a lot the doctors didn't know about epilepsy – like many other things.

I'd only ever seen one person have a fit before – when I was a young lad. A young man in the local fish and chip shop fell to the floor shaking violently and foaming at the mouth. The proprietor, to his credit, got him through the crisis. But after he'd been acclaimed by all his customers, the shop immediately cleared because of their sudden loss of appetite.

One evening when I was watching TV with the big rugby lad, he seemed to go a bit quiet. I was just about to ask if he was all right when he flung his arms sideways with such force that me and my seat were sent tumbling backwards. In no time at all the entire nursing staff came running in, as chairs and tables were sent flying all over the place. The poor chap was taken into a side ward and placed in a special bed under restraint. For the next hour he strained at the straps that held him down. I watched through a small window in the door as they ministered to him, and I felt really sad. It was the only spark of emotion I'd felt for ages. Could it be that I was getting better?

After a week or so he was allowed up again, and he seemed to be over his crisis. I wasn't put off and continued to socialise with him – though I did keep a watchful eye open. For a while he seemed to be OK, until one morning at breakfast. I was just thinking what odd dining companions he, the vicar and the pianist made, when suddenly his face took on a strange expression and he started to slide back into his chair. Oh shit, I thought. Within seconds he let out a roar and the table went up in the air. The pianist leapt out of his seat like Nureyev and the vicar looked towards the heavens as cutlery and crockery – bromide and all – rained down on him. Everything was knocked for six. The poor old clergyman – who by this time looked utterly ridiculous, being covered in beans and tomatoes – made no protest when a nurse wheeled him out at great speed. It was like something out of a silent movie. Food was flying everywhere, people shooting in all directions in panic – it was a real mess, but soon things got back to normal. Half an hour later it was as if nothing had happened.

I must pay tribute to the wonderful staff too. It was only after

I'd completely recovered that I could fully appreciate how special they were. At that time psychiatric nurses were the lowest paid of all nursing staff, but never once did I hear one complain. Anyway it wasn't about money, it was about caring. They were saints, the lot of them. And when I see governments bestowing honours on 'personalities' who aren't fit to lace the boots of these angels, then I feel it's the MPs and not the patients who need their heads testing from time to time.

Haven or hell
The poor old rugby player was moved to another hospital, Storthes Hall (which has now closed). Although it was a much older place than St Luke's, it was better equipped to deal with his condition. Built in the 1920s, it had all the features you expect of a 'loony bin'. But despite its foreboding presence it still provided a good and necessary service.

I visited the place in the '80s when my father was taken there. The advanced stages of Alzheimer's disease had finally made it impossible for us to give him the special care he needed, so we reluctantly decided he should be admitted. I visited him regularly, and although it was nothing like St Luke's, there were many aspects of the place, which brought back to me a certain feeling of *déjà vu*.

On my third or fourth visit I found he'd been moved from his original ward, so I went to the main desk to discover his whereabouts. The chap behind the big reception desk was a picture of sartorial elegance – which more than added to the high regard I already had for the staff. He had a neatly trimmed moustache, and sported a dark blue blazer that more than complemented the immaculate white shirt and striped tie underneath. He spoke very 'posh'.

'Can I help you sir?' he beamed.

'Yes, I'm looking for my father, Edmond Twohig. Can you tell me which ward he's on, please?'

'Just one moment, sir.'

He ran his finger down a list in front of him and moments later gave me the ward number. In the meantime a scruffy looking individual shuffled through the door behind him and spoke.

'What are you doing, Willie?'

'I'm just helping this young . . .'

The scruffy guy didn't let him finish. 'I've told you before, you're not allowed behind this desk! Now bugger off and get back to your ward!' He shooed the immaculate figure from behind the desk, in so doing revealing the lower half of Willie's attire. Needless to say it didn't come up to the standard of the top half. His shabby trousers barely reached beyond his knees, and a pair of football socks and plimsolls finished off his outfit. I had to smile as the scruffy receptionist apologised for Willie – but strangely enough he'd given me the right information. And not only that, he showed me the way to my father's ward. It wasn't always easy to tell the difference between the patients and the staff...

On another occasion I was involved in a conversation – bordering on the intellectual – with a person I assumed to be one of the nurses. I was nearly convinced by the political argument he was putting forward until an orchestral piece began to play on a nearby radio. He stopped mid-sentence, frowned and walked out of the room. He returned with a baton, stood in front of the radio and began to conduct with great verve. I left him to it, and as I passed him by he muttered with a smile, 'No one buys me nuts at Christmas – we've got enough in this place!' I still don't know to this day whether he was having me on or not.

Dad degenerated quickly, but thank God he didn't suffer – we all did that for him. He wasn't aware of anything towards the end, and when I went to visit him I'd sit with him for ages – but he didn't know who I was. Even so, he seemed to like me holding his hand. He had lovely soft hands: even though he'd worked hard the whole of his life they never felt hard. Perhaps it was because his touch was so very gentle.

One day the senior nurse suggested that I should put Dad in a wheelchair and take him for a ride down to the shops in another part of the hospital. I did, and it felt good to get out of the depressing ward. Dad seemed to enjoy the change too. When we arrived at the shops I bought us both a cup of tea, parked Dad's chair next to a bench on the main thoroughfare and sat down. Presently a scruffy individual sat down at the other end of the bench. He began to glare at people, and there was no doubting his mental state. Everyone who passed him by was subjected to a foul look and a verbal attack of filthy language. Even a clergyman and his wife were told to fuck off. No one escaped his obscenities, and he went through every swear word known to man. But although his tongue was vicious he was never a physical threat. Nevertheless I didn't relish the prospect of running the gauntlet of verbals when the time came for us to go.

Eventually the time came when I had to return Dad to his ward. I steeled myself in readiness for the inevitable onslaught, and as expected he shouted at me as we passed. 'Hey you!'

I tried to pacify him with a smile as I passed by. 'What are you pissing looking at?' he snapped.

'Hello', I thought, 'I've got off lightly'.

Then as I walked away he added, 'Cunt!'

It wasn't until a few years later that I realised I'd encountered a condition now recognised as Tourette's syndrome.

The bed now arriving on platform 4 . . .
But getting back to my time in St Luke's. After the incident in the dining room, things soon got back to normal – well, normal by our standards. I began to respond a little better to treatment after attending group therapy. This involved about ten of us – male and female – sitting in a circle and being given a topic of conversation. It could be anything – football, shopping, you name it. We were invited to express our opinions, which we eventually did. And sometimes one of us would start talking about his or her problems. This could have a knock-on effect, prompting others to do the same – which was the whole object of the exercise.

It's amazing what could bring about people's psychiatric problems. As well as the more obvious causes like stress and overwork, there were lots more – many of which came to light in those group sessions.

Occasionally I sat next to an alcoholic. He came from Scotland originally, and after explaining to me how he'd drifted into alcoholism he went on to describe the treatment he was receiving. He slept by himself in a room that always smelt faintly of beer. This was done deliberately: every so often he was given something to make him sick, so that whenever he came into contact with beer the smell of it would make him feel ill. It worked too – even passing the door of a pub would upset him. But unfortunately the effect wore off after a time and he had to be re-admitted.

Some of the cases in there were very sad. There was a young man, maybe in his thirties, who couldn't come to terms with the loss of his mother – and this drove him to suffer terrible fits of depression. Most of the time medication kept him on an even keel, but there were other times when even drugs couldn't compensate. I remember being awakened by terrible cries of anguish one night. He was staggering down the ward stripped to his waist, blood dripping from a large cross he'd carved into his chest with a razor. His arms were held aloft, like a child reaching for its mother. The staff tried unsuccessfully to pacify him, and in the end could only sedate him to bring peace to his troubled mind.

The brain is a very complicated part of our anatomy and it's said that we only use a fraction of it. There's also a school of thought that our physical capabilities are much greater than we realise. Reports of people lifting cars to release victims trapped underneath have added weight to the theory. I subscribe to both of these ideas – and especially the latter. I have a vivid recollection of a young girl, who couldn't have been more than fifteen years old, throwing male and female nurses all over the place. She'd totally flipped, and the strength she displayed can only be described as phenomenal. The padded cell on the female ward was already occupied and when they tried to put her into the vacant cell on our ward it was like a scene from a tag-wrestling match. The odds were four to one in favour of the staff, but they weren't winning! The door on the cell opened outwards, and every time they got her inside she pushed it back open before they could lock it. She must have been in and out half a dozen times before the door was secured, and it took two big male nurses and the two burly female nurses escorting her to do it. I was intrigued by the whole situation, and couldn't resist glancing through the window in the cell door a little later. The poor kid was totally out of it: she clung to the wall of the cell, screaming her head off like a trapped animal.

Concern for the young girl seemed to spread throughout the ward. Maybe the shock of seeing her tragic predicament helped us to forget – and later even re-evaluate – our own. The only one who seemed to find it amusing was my young roommate – the one with the fascination for corpses. I can't remember his name – and I don't know why, because he was responsible for all the roguery in the ward. In order to record his exploits I'll refer to him as Mort – seeing as he spent quite a lot of time visiting the mortuary. Anyway, Mort was forever peering in at the cell window and giving progress reports on the girl's condition. This upset her, of course, and he was prevented from going anywhere near her. But this didn't stop him from getting up to other mischief: he was always on the lookout for it. As another example: when some of the patients went for ECT (Electroconvulsive Therapy, which involved passing an electric charge through their brain, temporarily erasing their memory and giving them a brief respite from their troubles), they walked back from the treatment room like zombies. Mort would hang about and walk back with them. For some reason their blank facial expressions were a huge source of amusement to him, and sent him into hysterics. The situation was really bizarre.

Mort was a typical teenager, slightly built with unkempt hair. His pale thin face made his dark piercing eyes seem wider apart. Although his interests seemed a bit morbid, he always had an impish grin on his face. He was a bit of a loner and disappeared from time to time, returning with tales and gossip from other parts of the hospital. Nothing escaped his attention. He seemed to know about everyone's problems, but for some reason no one ever got to know about his. In fact there were times when I wondered why he was in there at all. Perhaps he wasn't supposed to be – or perhaps he'd been put there on purpose – as part of the cure. Somehow I don't think so, because he had this knack of getting people to do things that they weren't supposed to do. Like when it was my birthday . . .

Seeing all my cards, Mort informed me that he'd have a surprise for me later. That evening, after my visitors had gone, I was just settling down after taking my medication when he came and told me to get dressed – because he was taking me to the hospital canteen. I did as he asked, and he led me down a maze of corridors. Eventually he opened a door that led outside. 'Where are you taking me?' I asked suspiciously. With his track record we could have been on our way to look round a cemetery.

'Come on. You'll soon see,' he said, beckoning me on. We walked across the road and into the Craven Heifer! 'Two pints, landlord,' he chirped. 'It's my mate's birthday.'

What a cheek! He wasn't even old enough to drink. But the landlord seemed to know him and we got our two pints.

After two pints I began to feel a bit strange. I couldn't believe what I was doing! I was also feeling a bit panicky, so I decided to get back to the ward. Mort moaned as I made for the door. 'You're not going are you?' he protested. 'It's not closing time yet!' He reluctantly followed me out, complaining as we made our way back.

Fortunately no one had missed us when we got back. I changed into my pyjamas and plonked myself in front of the telly. No sooner had I sat down when the fun and games started. As I stared at the TV the screen appeared to get wider. It stretched and stretched until it eventually divided, and I found myself looking at two identical sets. Then as one of the sets began to rise the other one started to sink. It was as if my eyes were working independently. I didn't know what the hell was happening, so I gripped the seat and held on. Then the room began to go out of focus. The wishy-washy picture on the televisions suddenly burst into colours of an intensity I didn't know existed. Somehow I managed to get back to my bed, but not before staggering all over the place on the way. I saw things that night that I'd never seen before – and have never seen since. I don't even know whether I went to sleep or not: it was just a blur – but even that was in Technicolor! Yes, medication is medication and beer is beer – but I tell you now, ladies and gentlemen, never, ever, should the twain meet. Needless to say Mort thought the whole episode was a hoot. 'I told you it would be a surprise,' he chuckled.

What a character he was. It was never dull when he was around, but occasionally he took things too far and earned a good ticking off – after which he'd sulk. He was soon back on form, though; not a lot seemed to bother him. The only thing that really upset him was having his sleep disturbed. We only realised this when a young lad was brought in to occupy the vacant bed in our cubicle. His arrival put an end to the peace and tranquillity of our little room – and to Mort's slumber.

He was the typical spoilt kid. About twelve or thirteen, he was still very childlike: the type of kid who's just made for school bullies to torment, with a squeaky voice, ginger hair and large round specs balanced on a snub nose, which gave him that 'I'm brainier than you' look. You'll find one in every school – and now we had one in our cubicle. When he first came in Mort wasn't sure what to make of him and gave him a wide berth. But Mort being Mort he eventually gave him the third degree. The lad didn't want to know – which didn't go down well with Mort, of course.

Presently the lad's parents arrived, and he began to throw a tantrum. They seemed to be very nice people and it was obvious that they doted on their son. He was very unhappy about it all and made it clear that he had no intention of staying. As he was already in his pyjamas, the attending nurse suggested that his street clothes should be taken home to prevent him escaping. But it was all to no avail. Later that evening, when no one was looking, he got out of bed and walked out. He went down to the bus stop and caught a bus home – in his pyjamas! They brought him back the next day, but it was very much under duress. He continued to throw a peeve, and that night he kept us all awake by keeping the staff going back and forth with his demands. When he finally did get off to sleep he began to snore – loudly. Weren't we blessed? We certainly were – but the best was yet to come.

The following day Mort came back with the low down on the new arrival. I could tell by the grin on his face that he'd got some gen. 'Guess what he's in for,' he smirked.

Me and Al (the third member of our trio) shook our heads.

'Trains.'

'Trains? What sort of trains?'

'Steam trains.' Mort went on.' He's a fanatical train spotter!'

'So?'

Mort couldn't contain himself. 'It turns out he only likes steam engines. He lives for them. And now they're replacing them with diesels he's gone bonkers. He's been out of control, going down to the station chucking bricks at the diesels, and they can't do anything with him.'

Then Mort went over to talk to the lad, and must have upset him because he came away grinning in his usual fashion. 'I've just been asking him about trains,' he smirked.

That night the young lad was given something to make him sleep. We were all pleasantly surprised when he didn't snore and began to sleep soundly. But just as I was dropping off to sleep I heard a strange sound. 'Chuff chuff chuff chuff . . .' It seemed to be coming from the lad's bed. I looked across and his blankets were going up and down – in time with the chuffs. He was obviously dreaming about a steam engine, and his arms were pumping away like piston rods. 'Chuff Chuff CHUFF CHUFF,' he went on – getting louder all the time, and continuing until eventually he let out a piercing 'Wooo – Wooooooo'!

Mort sat bolt upright in bed. 'What the fuckin' 'ell's that?' he cried. He looked at the pistons cranking away opposite and groaned. 'Oh, I don't believe this.' Opening the door to our cubicle, he shouted down the ward, 'Nurse! Can you come and do something about this?'

'What's the matter?' I could hear her voice in the distance.

'I can't sleep for this racket.'

'What racket?'

'Come here and have a listen . . .' The lad was still chuffing and wooing away. By this time he was getting up a real head of steam.

'I'm busy. Go back to sleep,' the nurse replied.

Mort shouted back, 'How the hell can I? It's like King's Cross station in here. You try getting to sleep with the bloody Flying Scotsman coming through every five minutes!' He returned to his bed and buried his head under his pillow. I had to smile because I'd never seen him so wound up before. Al found it amusing too, and after a while we tried to get back to sleep, leaving the Flying Scotsman to continue on its journey. Mort continued to mutter, and a few minutes later I heard the sound of blankets being cast off his bed.

'Oh, *bollocks* to this!' I heard him say, and the next thing I heard was the sound of wheels turning. I opened one eye and as I did so I caught sight of the 'Flying Scotsman' actually moving past my bed! 'Chuff chuff chuff,' it went – its pistons going up and down. It chuffed out of the door and disappeared up the ward.

A few moments later I heard the nurse shouting, 'Where are you going with that bed?'

In between the faint 'chuffing' I heard Mort say, 'I'm just shunting this bugger into a siding so I can get some sleep!'

Whether he knew it or not, Mort, in his way, inadvertently dragged a few of us back towards normality. Through him I seemed to rediscover the ability to smile. And apart from reintroducing me to drink, he also found a way of getting me free cigarettes after the psychiatrist encouraged me to start smoking again (which of course would be unheard of today). There was a large common room at the disposal of both the male and the female patients. There were facilities for playing cards, table tennis or just sitting around; and every so often they played a few games of bingo. The prizes usually consisted of a bar of chocolate for a line and a packet of cigarettes for the full house. A nurse would usually start calling the numbers out, but more often than not she'd get called away to do another job. Mort, who on the surface was the only one with faculties anything near intact, always volunteered his services in the role of caller. He then proceeded to fix the games in favour of his friends, which after a few weeks made certain people a tad suspicious. Eventually several disgruntled ladies confronted one of the senior staff. 'Why is it that when he calls the numbers his mates win all the cigs and we're lucky if we get a milky bar?' Needless to say

Mort was sacked – but not before we'd had free smokes for a few weeks!

Back on track
The big hall had quite a nice atmosphere. As I began to improve I spent more time there, and it was a nicer place to receive my family and friends when they came to visit me.

In the next few weeks Al went home and the 'Flying Scotsman' was put back on the rails, leaving just me and Mort in the cubicle. As the days went by I began to notice a slight change in his attitude. He began to go off on his own more, and his mischievous grin wasn't always in evidence. I think he was beginning to realise that he would soon be the only young person left on the ward. I'd already sensed that he felt a bit left out when friends began to visit me regularly.

It surprised me who came to visit. Apart from my close friends there were some who in the past I'd hardly been on more than nodding terms with. But their reasons for visiting became apparent when I learned that they too had been in similar circumstances, and had come to offer their support. It gave me a tremendous lift to talk to people who truly understood what I was going through.

There was one young girl who I hadn't seen for quite a while who came to visit me. I'd known her in years gone by and we'd gone out together on occasions, but there was never anything serious between us. I first met Dorothy, or Dot as she preferred to be called, in the local coffee bar. I'd just returned from the Gene Vincent/John Leyton tour and was chatting to some friends. She was sitting at the next table and – catching the gist of our conversation – asked me if I'd ever met Billy Fury. I said that I hadn't and she lost interest straight away. It was obvious to anyone that she was totally besotted with the Liverpool pop singer. The mere mention of his name caused her eyes to cloud over, and a look of longing graced her pretty young features. She was a few years younger than I was, and apart from my sneaking regard for Billy Fury we had nothing much in common, but I liked her. Her long blonde hair and disposition put me in mind of Twinkle – a young girl pop singer who sang the hit song 'Tommy' in the '60s. I also admired her individuality. She dressed to suit herself and wasn't drawn into the trendy trap. Over the next few years I bumped into her occasionally in the pub and sometimes gave her a lift home. After that I didn't see or hear from her for ages – until she came to visit me one day in St Luke's. I was both surprised and delighted to see her. We went down to the little snack bar in the hospital where I bought her a coffee, which she hardly touched. I later found out that she didn't drink tea or coffee – but she was too polite to refuse.

She'd changed a bit since I last saw her – more grown up – and she'd put a little bit more weight on, but she was still very attractive. She told that she'd been working in Great Yarmouth. On her return a mutual friend had told her about my nervous breakdown, and, as she hadn't started a new job yet, she decided to come and see me. We got on really well, and she promised to come and see me again. When it was time for her to go I walked her to the hospital entrance. It was a fine day, and under normal circumstances I'd have walked down to the bus stop with her. But for some reason I found it impossible to set foot outside the hospital. It was a scene I'd often seen acted out on the cinema screen. You know the one – where a person, usually in a trauma, finds it impossible to walk through an open door. To tell the truth I thought it was a load of nonsense. I used to think to myself, it's just a matter of putting one foot in front of the other – and going through! But now I knew exactly how it felt. As soon as I reached the hospital entrance my body completely shut down. It was as if the lines of communication between my brain and the rest of me had been severed. As hard as I tried I couldn't get my legs to move; they'd been set in marble. Nothing responded to my will. It was one of the most frightening experiences I'd ever witnessed. It couldn't have come at a worse time: I'd just begun to think I was on the mend, and the medication was making me feel better. But obviously the effect of the drugs didn't extend to walking through force-fields!

Fortunately the phobia didn't stay with me very long, but it really scared the pants off me. I persevered with my efforts to venture outside, and when I eventually did the relief was indescribable. But after the initial euphoria I was back to square one. It began to dawn on me that I'd exchanged one weird situation for another, for almost immediately I began to feel as if I was enclosed in an invisible cocoon: my senses were dulled to the extent that I couldn't feel the wind on my face. I mentioned it to the psychiatrist when I went for my next assessment, but he seemed unconcerned and decided it was high time that I faced the outside world again.

Chapter Fourteen
A SPARE PART IN A ZEPPELIN FACTORY

When I was discharged from St Luke's I left with the minimum amount of fuss. By the time I reached home I was beginning to feel a bit edgy. Being surrounded by normal people as opposed to those who 'understood' seemed a bit unnerving for some reason. For the first few weeks I was reluctant to leave the house. When I eventually did it was to go for a drive in my car. But before I'd gone half a mile I had to turn back home: I'd lost all my confidence. My parents and the rest of my family – God bless 'em – did their best to help me cope with my bouts of unpredictable behaviour, but despite all their efforts I was beginning to feel that I might need to return to St Luke's. Things were beginning to get on top of me.

And that's when the cavalry arrived – in the form of my friends. You know, I've always believed that a man's real wealth is his friends. Even though you can't 'spend' a friend, a true friendship can sometimes pay dividends. Between them they rescued me, by literally dragging me back into the real world. George – my great friend and fellow explorer of childhood days – came to take me out for a walk in the Yorkshire Dales one day. I wasn't sure at first: I hadn't been out of hospital all that long, and it had been snowing. I hadn't any suitable gear to go tramping about in the snow, but he'd taken care of that by borrowing his wife's cagoule and walking boots for me. We set off to drive up the slushy road to Bradford and beyond. We didn't talk much on the way; we didn't have to. That's the way we've always been, just happy to be in each other's company. And when we reached our destination the scene was simply breathtaking. I'd never before witnessed the unique splendour of the Yorkshire Dales in wintertime.

It was one of those days you never forget, most probably because you'll never experience one like it again. The sky was clear and a brilliant blue and the sun shone. There was no wind, but the air was so crisp and clean that it made me gasp, as did the view that stretched before me. The whole landscape was a sea of virgin snow, only interrupted by the dark lines of dry stone walls. Fingers of icicles hung everywhere, glistening in the sun, and waterfalls hung motionless, frozen in time. We crunched through the snow, and every step seemed to re-awaken a part of me I thought I had lost for ever. The brilliance of nature began to supersede the uncertainty that had clouded my mind that day. It served to remind me that I'd not yet lost sight of the many things I so loved about life. Once again I was back to being a young kid, out with his best mate and exploring. Only this time we'd moved on from the jungles and prairies of Batley Carr to take on the might of the Dales – or was it Antarctica?

That day was yet another watershed in my life. It inspired me, and the motivation to write words and music seemed to stir within me again. Without realising it, George had chosen the perfect spot – and it couldn't have been at a better time. I'd already come to terms with the fact that the group was no longer an option. The Voltaires had disbanded, and I had no desire to charge up and down the country night after night. The only thing I was comfortable with was my own company and writing music.

Gradually I managed to pluck up enough courage to start venturing out on my own again, usually for a drive out somewhere that I could muse or draw inspiration and ideas for songs. But one evening, in stark contrast, I ended up going to a pub in Dewsbury called the Little Saddle. It was one of the 'in' places. Dot and her friends went there a lot, so I knew there'd be someone to talk to. Being on medication meant that I couldn't drink much – which was just as well, for by this time all my savings had gone and I was relying on sickness benefit – aptly named, because the pittance I received was enough to make anyone sick! But it was difficult being there: I felt like a fish out of water, and I wanted to escape to the security of my family home. Just as I was about to make a run for it one of the guys who'd been standing at the bar came over to me. Whether he'd sensed my distress, or there was some other reason, I'll never know, but he began to chat to me. He said that someone had told him I was in the music business and that I'd been ill. After I'd owned up on both counts he asked me if I liked jazz. For some reason this put a brake on my planned retreat, which surprised me more than anyone. Before this I'd refused to have anything to do with music, and walked away rather than talk about it.

'Do you like Jimmy Smith?' he asked.

I said I'd never heard of him.

'I think he's brilliant. If you're in tomorrow I'll bring you an EP of him.' To my surprise I didn't decline. He kept me talking for a while: there was something in his demeanour that commanded attention. His manner was forthright, and he was smartly dressed in a well-cut dark blue suit, which led me to assume he was probably connected to the business world – yet his stocky build and tanned complexion suggested he might ply his trade in the open air. I was right: his name was Alan Senior, and I later learned that he was a civil engineer who worked around the world building bridges and other structures. Though he was well known locally, it would be true to say he wasn't the most popular person around: Alan put a lot of noses out of place by telling it as it was. But I liked him straight away, and we soon built up a rapport. Neither of us was really into small talk at the 'in' pub, and before long he dragged me out to other places to listen to and talk about music again. The next thing I knew was that he'd left for Brazil to build a bridge, and I didn't see him again for thirty years! He – like others – dropped into my life, steered me through a rough patch and left when I was back on my feet. Once again it endorsed my belief that the Lord does indeed move in mysterious ways.

After Alan got me going out again things began to improve. He helped me to re-engage with people again. Sometimes a new avenue of conversation triggered off a new idea – and I was hungry for those. For a while I was happy enough traipsing around Dewsbury with the 'set', but soon the fickle finger of fate began to tap me on the shoulder, and a voice inside began to remind me of a few home truths.

'Er . . . just hold on a moment, Sam. This isn't really you, you know, floating from pub to pub every night. Haven't we been here before? Mark my words, when the conversation runs out you'll begin to realise that you've just substituted one treadmill for another. Didn't the spell in the nuthouse teach you anything? Obviously not – at least the other treadmill paid well.'

The old fickle finger was right, of course: I was constantly aware of it. But what was I meant to do? Where did my destiny lie? I was constantly at odds with myself. Maybe the fact that I was trying to wean myself off medication had some bearing on all this. I wasn't finding it easy: the medical profession hadn't realised that the drugs I was being given were addictive, and there were times when I lapsed into brief fits of depression if I didn't take them. Shortage of money didn't help either, and I didn't want to start borrowing off my folks as they were letting me live at home rent-free. So how could I earn a bob or two? The answer came by accident . . .

I ventured into Leeds one day for a look round. And a look round was all it was, because I was just about skint. Anyway, I wandered into a small warehouse behind the Corn Exchange that I remembered someone telling me about. 'Just go in and look round,' I'd been told. 'You'll love it!' So I did – and I did love it. It was an Aladdin's Cave: there were shelves packed with just about everything cheap and cheerful, most of it imported from the Far East. It was the kind of stuff we see in bargain discount shops today. But back then there weren't any. It was a wholesale business, and the owner was a little bloke who sat in a dark corner behind a high wooden desk surrounded by box files and invoice books. Papers were strewn all over the place in a setting straight out of Dickens. I hung about listening, and watched him serve his customers. Some of them bartered with him when the goods were damaged, and more often than not he'd say, 'Well, just give us a couple o' quid then.' I'd already noticed a damaged box of clip-on parking lights for cars. Two nights before a few cars had got nicked for parking without lights outside one of the pubs in Dewsbury, so I ambled up to the desk with the broken box. 'How much for the damaged box of lights?' I asked.

'Give us three quid.'

'I've only got two, honest!'

'Give us two then.'

I wasn't lying either – two quid was all I had in the world.

When I got to the pub that night, the talk was still about having to leave your lights on and the ensuing flat batteries. So I joined in the conversation. 'I'm not bothered,' I said. 'I've got a parking light. There's no way my battery will go flat.'

'Really? Where do you get them? How much are they?' Everybody was asking. I sold the whole boxful at a quid apiece in no time.

The following week I went back to the little warehouse and spent ages poking around looking for something else to sell. There was plenty of stuff but most of it was either no good to me or too expensive. Then I spotted a large packing case that had split open: dozens of little pink kewpie dolls were spewing out of it. Somehow I knew there was potential – but I didn't know what at the time. So I made him an offer . . . 'Couple o' quid?'

'OK.'

What am I going to do with these? I was thinking all the way home.

I heaved the big box out of my Morris 1100 into the house and showed them to my mother. 'What are you going to do with them?' she asked.

'Dunno.'

She picked up one of the naked two-inch dolls by the loop of plastic string attached to its head. 'They might be all right for hanging on Christmas trees,' she suggested. 'Or as stocking fillers.'

'Hang on a minute,' I interrupted. I went into the shop and came back with a sweet bag, an assortment of chews and some small lollipops. I chucked a few chews, a lollypop and the doll into the bag with just the loop sticking out. Then I screwed the top of the bag up and held it up. 'How does that look?'

Mum wasn't convinced. 'You can't see what's inside,' she pointed out.

So the next day I hunted round town for some see-through plastic bags. I managed to get some, and the next time I presented the package to Mum she was sold on it. The doll, surrounded by a lollypop and a few brightly coloured chews, looked really attractive. I gathered the bag at the top – leaving the loop outside – and sealed it with a staple. Mum called them dolly bags, and going up to Christmas they sold as fast as we could make them.

Feeling pleased with myself, I went back to the warehouse and bought the remaining cases of kewpie dolls. Wasn't I clever? Too bloody clever as it turned out. The problem was, after Christmas the dolly bag sales ground to a halt and so did my bit of spare cash. It also left me with hundreds of little dolls on my hands!

So I started experimenting with them. I painted hair on some of them, using modellers enamel paint. Trouble was, they all looked like George Best. This gave me another idea. I added a red jersey, white shorts, black socks, and hey presto I had the Manchester United football team. They looked great. I did some more in the colours of my team – Huddersfield Town – and the blue and white stripes looked even better. I ended up doing loads, and in no time I had dolls of every colour all over the house hanging up to dry. The smell of paint became unbearable and began to upset Mum, so I was ordered to take my footballers elsewhere.

Round about this time I'd renewed my acquaintance with Bill – an ex-member of the band. He was always experimenting with tape recorders and such, and he'd found some rooms with the view to setting up a recording studio. There was also a room going spare – so I took it. I put a sign that read 'MASCOT DOLLS' in the window and set to work sending samples of the dolls to all the clubs in the football league. In the meantime I was painting dolls – lots of dolls. I ended up dreaming about the blasted things. I received a few acknowledgements from clubs to say they would consider them, but I got the feeling that they weren't taking me very seriously. It called for direct action. I started by visiting the shop for my team, The Town. They thought the dolls looked great and I managed to get them to take a dozen – sale or return. The following Monday they rang me back and ordered six dozen more. The fans had bought them to pin to their hats and scarves, and were coming back for more. Some of the girls even wore them as earrings. Once I saw a woman walking around town with one swinging from her shopping basket. But the icing on the cake came when I went to get my money: they gave me two free tickets for the next home game as well!

Leeds United didn't have a shop in those days: Jack Charlton had a sports shop and he had the concession for the scarves and such. I went to see him and he was really nice. He couldn't believe that I was a one-man business and had painted all the dolls myself. Anyway, although he managed to sell quite a few Leeds dolls, it was the big Town orders that kept me going. In the meantime it became apparent that the reason I hadn't heard from the other clubs I'd written to was that, like Leeds, most of them relied on the local sports shops to stock their scarves and hats and such. So I sounded out some of these shops, and one of them came up with a good suggestion: why not do boxes of assorted dolls, including rugby teams as well? So I did.

It was quite successful too – but I still had quite a few dolls left.

One day I was in my office when two official-looking blokes came in carrying briefcases. One of them opened his case and took a sheet of paper out. 'Is this one of your invoices?' he said, handing me the paper.

I looked at it and nodded.

'Well, we're from Her Majesty's Custom and Excise. Are you a registered business?' He rattled on, quoting regulations and stuff I couldn't understand. Oh God, I thought. I'd better act dumb. He looked around at the masses of dolls hanging up to dry. 'Are these all yours?'

I sensed trouble and decided to bluff my way out. Remembering Jeff – from the G Ward Co-operative – I put on my best doleful expression. 'Yes,' I said (thinking to myself I'd better lay it on thick.). 'I've just come out of a mental hospital and I have to paint them to keep my mind occupied. It's a sort of therapy.'

'But according to this invoice you sell them!'

'Well, yes,' I stammered.

'Tell me, do you declare the profits you make on these dolls?'

'No.'

'Why not?'

'Because I don't make any profit!' I lied.

'Well, why do you sell them then?' he asked, looking puzzled.

'To get money.'

'What do you do with the money?'

'I go to Leeds.'

'What do you go there for?'

'To buy more dolls!'

I tried to look as vacant as possible all the time he was speaking to me. Eventually he looked from me to his companion who was standing by the door. After a brief pause he shook his head and raised his eyes towards the heavens. 'OK, Mr Twohig,' he sighed. 'I don't think we need trouble you any further.'

He began to leave, and as he opened the door he turned and added, 'Oh, by the way, if you decide to go into this in a big way, please inform us, will you? Good day.'

Phew, I thought as the door closed. That was a close one.

But it put an end to the mascot doll enterprise.

Anyone want to buy a few gross of dolls?

When needs must

So what was I to do? I was skint and had no prospects; I was medicated and mixed up. Life was fast becoming a treadmill again. Sometimes I gave Dot a lift home from the pub, and kept her sitting in the car until the early hours listening to my tale of woe. Before I went into hospital I wouldn't speak – now you couldn't shut me up! But she never complained and always very understanding – unlike me: she had to get up for work in the morning, whereas I didn't.

Another great friend, John Hartley, also pitched in to help. He was resident organist at a large pub called The Angel, and he talked the landlord into hiring me to play guitar alongside him. The pay wasn't great, but it helped me to get back in front of an audience without being under pressure.

I'd known John for quite a few years. Strangely, he was one of the few people I didn't like at first meeting – but when I really got to know him he became one of my closest friends. Later he turned to acting, using the name Barry Hart. He played the original policeman, Ted Edwards, in the soap *Emmerdale* for a while. Other parts followed, in *Last of the Summer Wine* and lots of other TV shows. He made his film début acting alongside Dustin Hoffman – again as a police detective – in the movie *Agatha*. Like me he was a passionate Huddersfield Town fan. Since his death a few years ago, going to the match has never been quite the same.

Anyway, I managed to get by doing bits of jobs, which included selling vacuum cleaners and taxi driving – virtually anything. Dot managed to get me a part-time job driving a big delivery van at her place. I had to smile one day when I pulled up in the delivery bay of a large engineering firm in Harrogate. One of the guys unloading said, 'Do you know something – you're the spitting image of that club turn Sammy King!'

'Who?' I said, winding my window down.

'That singer Sammy King.' He looked at me closely again. 'You sure you're not 'im?'

I shook my head as another bloke signed my note. 'Sorry,' I said, in a thick Irish accent, 'I've never heard of him.'

In the meantime I was writing the odd song, and I started to get Bill to put them down on tape for me. By this time he'd moved his studio to his home after the rooms he rented caught fire. (It's a good job the mascot dolls had been moved too: with the paint fumes, the place would have probably exploded!)

But 'kismet' was still eluding me. I was like a spare part drifting round a zeppelin factory – uncertain of where to go or what to do. Scratching out an existence wasn't much fun. My financial status was somewhere between zilch and zero, and I was still prone to intermittent mood shifts. As the saying goes, drastic circumstances call for drastic measures. But had I the guts to take them?

Bill suggested that we should form a duo and go back on the boards. He worked out a way of playing backing tracks on stage by using a tape recorder. In essence he came up with what's now known throughout the world as karaoke. It's worth bearing in mind that this was the latter half of the '60s. If he'd patented his idea back then he'd probably be a billionaire today.

I talked the idea over with my folks, and as I expected they told me that whatever I decided they'd back me to the hilt. But I wasn't sure if I was ready to face an audience head-on: my confidence was low and my bottle showed no signs of returning.

One evening I decided to pop along the road to the Batley Variety Club (now known as the Frontier). I'd worked there on a number of occasions with the group, and they'd always received us well. My old mate Tommy Mitchell was one of the bouncers on the door and Dot had got a part-time job there in the cloakroom, so I thought I'd pop in and bore them both to death with my doubts and fears for a while. I was becoming quite close to Dot. She was a good listener and I was an incessant talker, so we had more in common than I'd first thought!

From time to time I suffered recurrences of my past psychiatric problems and lapsed into deep depressions, usually at a time when I was trying to cut down on my medication. My strategy was to reduce my intake by one tablet every week, over a period of months getting right down from nine pills a day to one but then came the hard part. Sometimes I could manage three days without taking anything, only to fall back into the deep fit of depression and back to square one and the nine tablets again. Dot saw it all come and go and her lack of intervention, whether intentional or otherwise, helped me through. When I was with her I enjoyed a stability that had been lacking from my life for such a long time. And when we started seeing each other on a regular basis, a lot of people – including my family – were not very pleased but it seemed to suit us and we were happy enough. By this time I was getting used to going with the flow, and viewed the whole thing as part of my destiny.

As I walked towards the entrance of the club the owner, James Corrigan, was coming out. 'Hello Sammy,' he said. 'How are you these days?'

'Not so bad, thanks,' I replied.

'Come on. I'm going for a little walk round, to get a bit of fresh air and to mull things over. Join me and we'll have a natter.'

So we walked round the car park and chatted away. He seemed to be genuinely interested in my well being. After he inquired about my health I told him the hard facts about the medication. I also mentioned that I was thinking of going back into show business with Bill.

Without hesitation he said, 'As soon as you do, let me know — and you can do a fortnight here.'

I was a bit taken aback. 'But won't you want to see what our act is like first?'

'I don't need to,' he said, shaking his head. 'If you're in it I'm sure it'll be OK.'

I was made up. His faith in me gave my low esteem an almighty boost, and chipped a huge chunk from the doubts I'd been harbouring about re-entering the business. What more did I need to make up my mind? Here I was, being given the green light by one of the most successful businessmen around. Deep down I knew I had to try again. I'd got to do it sometime, and this was as good a time as any. So Bill and I set to work making the backing tracks for the act. Among other things it helped to occupy my mind and gave me something to focus on. We decided to base the act on the music and comedy we'd been doing with the group before it disbanded.

True to his word, James Corrigan gave us a booking at his famous club, and I was determined to justify his faith in us. Bill was certain that everything would be OK but I wasn't as confident as he was. So we fixed a gig at a club in Hoyland Nether (on the outskirts of Barnsley) to test the new act out.

On the way there I was nervous, very nervous, no, extremely nervous. So nervous, in fact, that it felt like little bulldozers were working overtime in my bowels, pushing unpleasant stuff towards the exit. But I needn't have worried. When the lights went on and the music started the old automatic pilot kicked in and I was away. And when I got my first laugh things began to flow. We had a great evening. And when the guy came in with the lovely loot at the end of the night, it was sheer Bliss — with a capital £!

We managed to fit in a few more engagements before going to the Variety Club, and by the time we got there everything went smoothly and we went down a treat.

Between 1966 and 1977 Batley Variety Club was one of the foremost venues in the UK. I had the good fortune to work there alongside stars like Shirley Bassey, Cliff Richard, Jimmy Ruffin, Louis Armstrong, P.J. Proby, Tiny Tim, Guy Mitchell, Johnny Mathis, Gene Pitney, Roy Orbison – just about everybody who was anybody.

Chapter Fifteen
'PENNY ARCADE'

As the date-book for our act began to fill and my financial problems began to ease I still found time to write a few songs. My old recording manager at HMV (Wally Ridley) used to tell me that song-writing might one day provide me with a pension later in life, but I never took his advice seriously; I just enjoyed writing them. One song in particular stood out from the rest. It was a foot-tapping up-tempo song and sounded as if it might be OK as an entry for the Eurovision Song Contest, in which the UK had been enjoying quite a bit of success. The inspiration for the song originally came to me on a camping holiday in North Wales. I'd been invited by my old friend George to tag along with him and his wife Val, and we ended up on the island of Anglesey, where we stayed at a wonderful spot with a beautiful view across Trearddur Bay. Once again the choice of location was strangely inspirational. Val had retired to her sleeping bag and George and I were enjoying the final moments of an unbelievable sunset. The setting sun turned the becalmed sea into a pool of liquid gold, waiting to be consumed by the lengthening shadows of dusk. And moments before darkness was complete a series of tiny coloured lights suddenly appeared on the headland opposite. They began to twinkle, and within a matter of moments I had the first two lines of a song:

A light shone in the night, some way ahead.
Blue, turned into green – then it was red . . .

So an anonymous Welsh person switching on lights became the inspiration for a song that was soon to change my life. When I got home I finished the song, which I called 'Penny Arcade'. And it didn't stop there: I began to churn out song after song, in the end knocking out quite a few decent tunes. The only trouble was, now that I'd written them what was I going to do with them? I was no longer making records myself, and I was totally out of touch with people in the music industry. Fortunately the answer lay on my own doorstep – the Batley Variety Club! Why go to London? The big recording stars were all coming up here. If only I could meet just one of them, it might give me some indication of whether my songs were any good or not. Fortunately I soon got the chance to find out.

There was great excitement around the town with the news that Roy Orbison was to appear at the Variety Club for the very first time. He had always been one of my heroes. I must have spent a fortune playing his records on jukeboxes, especially 'Blue Angel', my all-time favourite. And when the chance came to meet him I was there with bells on. Derek Smith – our ex-manager and group member – was on the management team at the club and paved the way for me to meet him, so Bill and I went down to the club one evening. We already knew the compère, Jerry Brooke, and he took us backstage to introduce us to him. I was totally in awe of the man. The 'Big O' was just as I'd imagined him to be – tall, dressed in black and wearing those famous dark glasses. The only thing that surprised me was that he was constantly smiling and not as serious as publicity would have us believe. He was also very polite and well mannered.

Roy being a highly successful songwriter himself, I hadn't actually planned to pitch any of my songs to him. I just wanted him to listen to them and give me his professional opinion. He said he hadn't time at that moment as he was about to do his show, but suggested we should meet him afterwards at a restaurant up the road. I was completely overwhelmed – very grateful and nervous at the same time.

So later on, after leaving plenty of time for him to finish his meal, Bill and I went up to the restaurant. When we got there I was a bit taken aback. I'd only expected his wife and maybe his manager to be there with him, but we were met by his whole entourage and his backing group, the Art Movement. Roy came to greet us, and I was impressed by the fact he remembered my name.

Everyone arranged their seats to face the table where Bill had placed the tape recorder. These were all people at the top of their trade — talk about feeling nervous! I hadn't really been prepared for all this, having wrongly assumed I'd sit with Roy in a corner with headphones and play him a couple of songs without disturbing anyone. It was not to be . . . Bill cued up the first of my songs and set the tape recorder going. It was a slow ballad called 'After Tonight'. I really thought he would like it as it was definitely in his style. Although Bill had made a good job of the recordings there were a few bloopers here and there, which I tried coughing over to try and cover. Roy listened intently, and occasionally turned to speak to the man sitting next to him.

Barbara, his wife, said straight away that she didn't think it was for him, and when it finished he said, 'Have you got any more songs on there?'

I nodded, and he told us to leave the tape running. There were six songs in all, and people were becoming concerned about my cough by the time we reached the last one, 'Penny Arcade'. When it finished he asked if he could have a copy of the tape. He told me he was going back to Nashville the following week and wanted his recording manager, Wesley Rose, to hear them. Before you could say 'God Bless America', the tape was rewound, boxed and in his possession. Maybe if he didn't want to record my songs someone else in Nashville might!

We left the restaurant in the early hours — 4.15 a.m. on 11 May 1969 to be exact — in a state of euphoria, having actually spent time with a legend. Not only that, but he'd shown interest in my work. It all served to bolster my enthusiasm for the business that I subconsciously blamed for my past troubles. But by the time I'd come down to earth a few days later, my old fears began to manifest themselves, and once again I began to doubt that anything would become of it.

Then out of the blue I was called to the phone by my mum one morning. 'There's someone wants to speak to you,' she said, handing me the receiver. It was Ron Randall, the head of Acuff-Rose Music in London. He told me that Roy Orbison was due to record four of my songs in Nashville on 10 July: I was speechless. He added that he'd be sending a representative to meet me. It didn't sink in straight away. I told my mother what the phone call was about and she seemed as shocked as I was. Neither of us seemed to know what to say or do. I think Mum went into the kitchen and put the kettle on.

Everybody I told seemed to be more excited than I was: I think the medication I was taking might have had something to do with this. Then a small parcel arrived with the post two months later. It containing a tape recording labelled 'Penny Arcade, Roy Orbison's next single - to be released on 20th of August'. I was still sort of calm and also a little bit surprised. Of all the songs on the tape I'd given him I never thought he would have chosen that one. It was completely different to anything he'd done before.

The Acuff-Rose representative eventually came to see me. He immediately extended an invitation to visit their London office with a view to signing up with them. This I did, and in return I was given a three-year contract and a nice hefty cheque for advanced royalties – which I duly split with Bill for his help in making the demo tapes. Soon the record was being played on the radio and the local press were knocking at the door. TV companies picked up on it, and soon I was giving interviews on the regional TV stations. All this served to elevate me to celebrity status locally, and in no time I found myself in great demand to open fêtes and functions. I found the whole experience really enjoyable, and before long I got quite used to being asked for my autograph in the street.

Dot and I had become engaged in the meantime, and she too seemed to enjoy the razzmatazz. My folks, although greatly pleased with my success, were not too happy about our engagement. There were also comments like 'of course now that he's about to earn lots of money . . .' floating about from people who ought to have known better. After all, Dot and I got together when I was on my uppers, which no one ever mentioned. But it didn't worry us and we carried on as normal.

Sometimes she would go with me to meet some of the celebrities I came into contact with. I always got a kick out of seeing the expression on Dot's face when she met famous people. She got really excited at the prospect of meeting Joe Brown; and when she actually sat next to Cliff Richard at dinner she was completely overwhelmed. At first there were a few empty seats between her and Cliff when we first sat down. He turned to her and patted the seat next to him, 'Come on then, don't be shy – sit

ROY ORBISON

A signed picture from the 'Big O' to my mother.

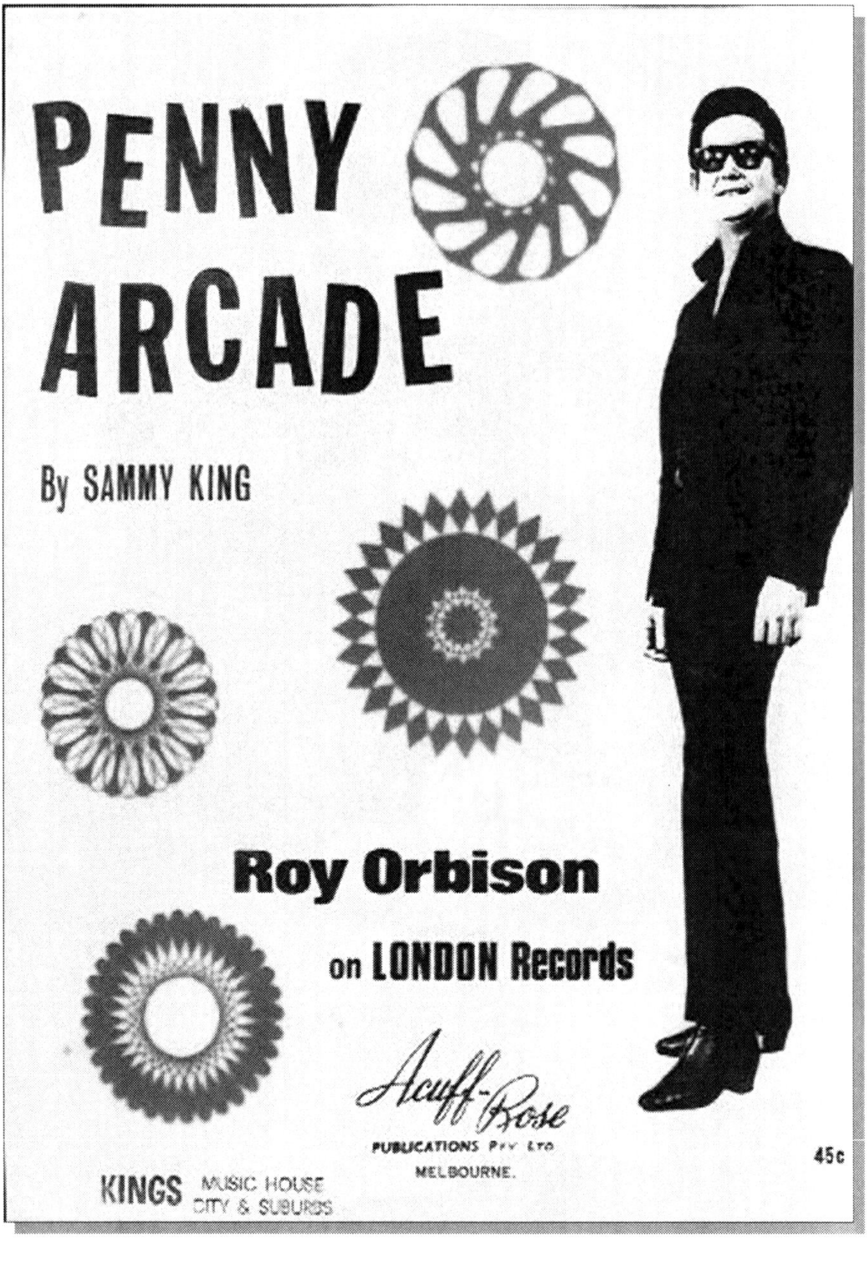
PENNY ARCADE
By SAMMY KING
Roy Orbison
on LONDON Records
Acuff-Rose
PUBLICATIONS PTY LTD
MELBOURNE.
45c
KINGS MUSIC HOUSE
CITY & SUBURBS

Gene Pitney. He never recorded any of my songs despite my sending many to him. What he always wanted to do was simply release my demos unchanged.

```
BD089 COC469 NEWYORK NY 45 19 427PM

LT
SAMMY KING
BOX MUSIC SERVICE 267 BRADFORD ROAD
BATLEYYORKSHIRE

TF BAT4675
INTERESTED IN USING WARM SUMMER EVENING AND SAY NO MORE AS
RECORD RELEASE PLEASE ADD VIOLINS ETC TO STRENGTHEN
PRODUCTION AND REMIX CONTACT ME WESTBURY HOTEL LONDON MARCH
7TH TO 14TH
     GENE PITNEY

COL 267 TF BAT4675 ETC 7TH 14TH
```

Trearddur Bay, Anglesey. This is the view that gave me the inspir or the line 'where a light shone in the night' in 'Penny Arcade'.

Cliff Richard.

next to me!' Needless to say she was in her element throughout dinner.

Cliff was a gentleman and a true professional. And although I have to admit to being more of an Elvis fan in those days, my respect for him soared to new heights when I was given the opportunity to work with him. Originally I was booked – along with Bill – as a supporting act when Cliff came to Batley, but I was also drafted into the resident orchestra to fill in on guitar, primarily for a rock'n'roll spot during his act. It was quite an experience. We rehearsed all afternoon and afterwards he thanked us all personally. Brian Bennett, his musical director – who for many years played drums with The Shadows – sensed that I hadn't done much orchestral work before, and went out of his way to make me feel at ease. He also added Alan Hawkshaw to the band who, apart from being a tremendous musician, was also a very successful composer. He has written some tremendous scores but his best-known work is probably the one that took only thirty seconds to write – the theme music for the TV series *Countdown.* Working with people like these was a truly humbling experience, and remains one of the high spots of my career. So for the next two weeks I was kept busy at the club doing my act, and after the interval backing Cliff Richard. The show was a sell-out and the place was packed every night. I seemed to be on the go all the time – which didn't go unnoticed by one particular lady in the audience one evening.

It was particularly busy, so I helped Dot in the club cloakroom before I started work. I remember checking this particular lady's fur coat in and later on, when I went on stage, I noticed her sitting near the front of the stage with her husband. She kept nudging him and saying, 'That's him from the cloakroom.' Then after I'd done my spot I changed into my tuxedo, popped my specs on and took my place in the orchestra ready to play for Cliff. When the curtains re-opened I could see her elbow digging into her spouse again. 'It's him again, him that's just been on – the one from the cloakroom.' All through the act she kept pointing to me: 'It *is* him, you know!' After the show I went to help Dot in the cloakroom again – and guess who was my first customer? 'It's *him* again!' she said, with a look of amazement. I only wish I could have found a way to have been driving the taxi that pulled up to take them home . . .

I didn't take Dot with me the first time I met Gene Pitney. It happened in similar circumstances to my meeting with Roy Orbison.

He too was happy to see me and listen to my songs, having heard of Roy's previous interest through Derek - our ex-manager. Once again I found myself in the presence of a '60s icon in the star's dressing room at the club. It's interesting to note that most of the really big stars I met back then were so down-to-earth and approachable, unlike the ones who were stars solely in their own mind. Gene could best be described as 'one of the lads': he was completely without edge, and friendly to the point that I felt I'd known him all my life within moments. It seemed perfectly natural to chinwag with the man who sang the soundtrack of the John Wayne film The Man Who Shot Liberty Valance; the songwriter who wrote 'Hello Mary Lou', 'Rubber Ball' and 'He's A Rebel' for Rick Nelson, Bobby Vee and The Crystals respectively. And I was completely won over by him when he admitted to finding the British comedian Max Wall (one of my heroes) hilarious. All I had to do was impersonate Max to send him into fits of laughter.

By this time Bill and I had turned out some pretty decent recordings of my songs in his home studio. Consequently Gene not only showed interest in the songs but also considered releasing the demos we'd done in their present state on an independent label in the United States. I was really flattered, but in my heart of hearts I knew I wouldn't be able to cope with the pressure of all that went with it.

I needn't have worried, for around the same time he was cultivating a strong business relationship with Mick Jagger and Phil Spector, which I assume took up most of his time. So, being in the lower echelons of such an illustrious pecking order, I guess the prospect of my becoming a US recording star was put on the back-burner.

As I got to know him better I became aware of his reputation for being slightly prudent where money was concerned. The first indication of this was when he was telling a few of us about his home in Connecticut. When he wasn't on tour he liked to relax by the side of his swimming pool and watch the apples grow in his orchard. As his was the only pool in the neighbourhood his children's friends were frequent visitors, and began to use it as a public amenity. 'I couldn't really put a stop to it,' he told us, 'so I've started charging them.'

But my lasting memory of him will always be associated with suits. When Gene was resting, he did just that – and it surprised us all when he told us he was prone to putting on weight in the process.

We'd grown used to seeing his slender build complemented by the blue mohair suit he regularly wore on stage. He wore a grey one too, and in order to fit into them he had to go on a strict diet before each tour. After working with him and seeing his show a few times, Bill and I came to the conclusion that he only owned two stage suits. This was a multi-millionaire we were talking about, and soon those two suits began to be a source of amusement to us. Before each performance we made secret bets as to which colour he'd wear: I'd take blue and Bill grey, or vice versa. One of us was always right, until the night Gene made fools of us both by wearing the grey jacket with the blue trousers!

Chapter Sixteen
THE MAGIC OF 'PENNY ARCADE'

Contrary to popular belief, 'Penny Arcade' wasn't a very big hit in this country. It hung around the Top 50 for three months, only creeping into the Top 20 for a few weeks – but it sold well considering that the record company had to rely solely on radio airplay to promote the disc. Roy Orbison couldn't boost the sales by doing TV and live performances, as he was on a world tour at the time. Nowadays, of course, this situation would have been covered by the use of a pop video. But it was a completely different story in the southern hemisphere. The release of the record in Australia and New Zealand was planned to coincide with Roy's tour there, and the result was amazing. The record shot straight to number one in Australia and New Zealand, and stayed there long enough to outsell even the Beatles and Stones records that had been released there. It became one of the all-time bestsellers in Australia, achieving gold-disc status. I was thrilled to hear about this on a popular radio programme, *Two-way Family Favourites*, one Sunday. Strangely enough it wasn't company policy to present the writer of the song with a gold disc at that time, only the artiste and the producer. To this day people think I'm kidding when I tell them I never got one! It's never really bothered me though. The prestige that the song brought me meant more than a hundred gold discs. I've lost count of the number of times people from all walks of life have told me it's their favourite song.

I remember sitting in my dressing room one evening at a club in Rotherham. Someone knocked on the door so loud that I thought it was going to fall off the hinges. I opened it with a degree of caution and was confronted by a group of young punk rockers. Oh hell, I thought. What's all this about? The leader spoke from behind an array of pins and tattoos. 'Are you Sammy King?'

'Er, yes. Why?' I replied – not knowing if I'd done the right thing by admitting to it.

'My mam says you wrote "Penny Arcade". Is that right?'

'Er . . . yes . . .' I stammered.

His face broke into a large grin. 'Can I have your autograph please? It's my favourite song!' He turned out to be a smashing lad, and he and his mates stayed chatting for ages. They wanted to know all about me, how I came to write the song and what Roy Orbison was like and so on. They were a great bunch. One thing learnt from that encounter was that you should never judge a book by its cover!

Apart from being recorded in many languages, over the years it's been adopted as a cult song in gay clubs up and down the country, and even today it still maintains its unofficial status as a kind of national anthem in the northern working men's clubs and on the Spanish Costas. Some people have even requested that it be played at their funeral in order to go out on a happy note.

But one of my proudest moments was when a young mother brought her three-year-old daughter into my dressing room, stood her on a chair and said, 'Go on then, sing for the mister.' And, God bless her, the little girl sang the song the whole way through word perfect. I was so overcome that if I'd been awarded a gold disc I'd have given it to that little girl there and then.

After the initial success of 'Penny Arcade', Roy returned to the UK on a number of occasions and sometimes he would stay at the Black Horse in Clifton near where I lived. The Black Horse was a popular base for a number of celebrities who came to work at Batley Variety Club, and Roy liked to stay in the annexe in the courtyard. Whenever I could I would pop up to play him songs and seek his opinion, which I valued greatly (many years later his son, Roy Kelton Orbison Jr, told me that it was on his father's personal insistence that 'Penny Arcade' was recorded in the first place. His advisors had tried to talk him out of it, in favour of a more authentic song but in Roy's own words he said 'the song has a magic quality about it')

Arriving at the Black Horse one afternoon, I met Roy's wife Barbara as she was about to step into a chauffeur-driven black Rolls-Royce. She was cradling Roy Kelton Jr, their young baby son at this time, in her arms. 'Sammy, I'm just going to do some shopping. Roy's just getting up, so go right in.' 'Just getting up' late in the afternoon, I came to learn, was the norm for Roy, who tended to stay up late to unwind after a show. I pushed the little cottage door open and stepped into the comfortable low-beamed room to be met by a vision that would stay with me for the rest of my life – Roy coming down the bedroom steps. It wasn't an entrance you'd expect from a superstar of the '60s. Rather than descending the stairs clad in a black silk monogrammed dressing gown, he was tottering down in blue and white striped brushed cotton jim-jams, smiling and yawning behind the famous black shades. No wonder everybody loved him, he was just so amazingly normal (and wearing Huddersfield Town colours too!) Anyway, after this episode I always made a point of calling in the late afternoon.

This was the beauty of the '60s and '70s. Apart from a few exceptions the stars weren't surrounded by security guards and such. Though they were held in awe they were also well respected, and – up to a point – approachable in private.

Roy wrote beautiful songs himself and to be honest I felt more than privileged that he had recorded four of mine ('Say No More', 'I Got Nothing' and After Tonight being the other three) so I never played him more than one or two songs at a time. Most of the time he would just encourage me to keep on writing and hand me the odd compliment but his reaction to one particular song I played him made my pulse rate go from zero to sky high. The contract with my publisher had run out, and acting independently I took along a 'rocky' song I'd written called 'Mississippi Fireball' for his appraisal. As always he gave it his full attention, and when the tape finished playing my hopes were dashed when he said that although he liked the number it wouldn't really suit him. My heart sank. I'd had a lot of faith in this particular song and I was more than a little disappointed. Then he added, 'But I think it would be great for Elvis!' My mouth went dry. I knew they were close friends; in fact it was well documented that Roy was Elvis's favourite singer. I couldn't believe it when he went on to say that he'd play the song to him the next

LONDON
AMERICAN RECORDINGS
DEMONSTRATION SAMPLE NOT FOR SALE
MADE IN ENGLAND
A
45 RPM
N.C.B.
HLU 10285
© 1969
TIME: 2.59
RELEASE DATE
22—8—69
Licensed by MGM Records A Division of Metro-Goldwyn-Mayer Inc.
Acuff-Rose Music
PENNY ARCADE
(King)
ROY ORBISON
Produced by Wesley Rose
Arranged by Jim Hall

PolyGram
polydor
PENNY ARCADE
ROY ORBISON

Roy
Orbison
Penny Arcade
Tennessee owns my soul
LONDON

PENNY ARCADE
ROY ORBISON
BREAK MY MIND
SO YOUNG
LONDON

PENNY ARCADE
LONDON
SIDE 1
GOLD 41
ROY ORBISON
EMI RECORDS NEW ZEALAND · AUCKLAND · WELLINGTON · CHRISTCHURCH

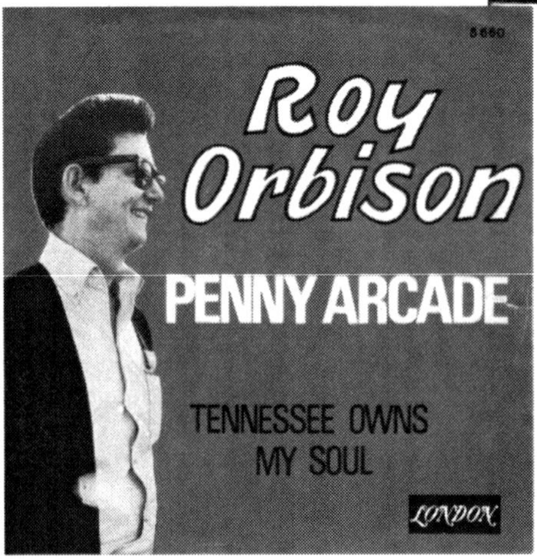
5660
Roy Orbison
PENNY ARCADE
TENNESSEE OWNS MY SOUL
LONDON

time he saw him. As you can imagine my journey home was 'lost in space', and by the time I reached home I had to keep pinching myself to make sure I wasn't dreaming. I wanted to tell everybody about it, but the cautious side of my nature took over and I decided to tell only a chosen few in case nothing came of it. And it turned out that nothing did happen, as is so often the case in the music world. Whether Roy forgot to play him the song, or the 'King' wasn't interested, I'll never know. Tragically it wasn't long afterwards that the news came through that Elvis had finally shaken his last leg, leaving the whole world in a state of shock. But this didn't stop me from dreaming that one day a dusty old tape recording of Elvis singing 'Mississippi Fireball' would be discovered at the back of a cupboard in some Nashville studio . . . ho hum . . .

Chapter Seventeen
THE IMPORTANCE OF BEING INDEPENDENT

Keeping busy helped with the continual struggle to wean myself off the medication, but it was harder than I had anticipated and Dot had to bear the brunt of it all. She must have had the patience of a saint to put up with my moods and insecurity. The burden eased somewhat when our social life began to thrive. We became friendly with one of Dot's friends, Ann. She and her husband Ken had recently married and were living in the nearby village of Ossett, opposite an ex-variety colleague of mine, Jill Summers. Jill popped into their house regularly to say hello and keep us up to date with her new career as an actress. She was doing quite a lot of television work at that time and eventually went on to become the *Coronation Street* stalwart Phyllis Pierce – the relentless pursuer of Percy Sugden during the 1980s. We got on well with Ann and Ken, and the new friendship seemed to give me a new spirit of adventure.

I also decided that it was time to cease being a burden on my family and friends and stand squarely upon my own two feet (no easy task, having one leg shorter than the other). Seriously, though, I needed my own space and above all to be independent. An opportunity was presented to me when a friend told me of a small cottage that was available for rent in Hanging Heaton – a small community on the opposite side of the valley. I loved it as soon as I saw it. It was tiny – just two rooms – and the toilet was at the end of the garden, but it was just right for me. I went to see Mr and Mrs Newsome, who owned the place, and the deal was done. It was going to cost me the princely sum of 12*s* 6*d* per week – this was 1970.

The cottage was perfect. It was remote without being out of touch and there was an atmosphere about it that was sympathetic to my creative needs. But above all it was the first home of my very own. I was truly happy there: it was such a welcoming place. It was there that I wrote, along with other songs, 'Ain't It All Worth Living For' – which became a hit in America a few years later. I always felt comfortable within the cottage's thick stone walls. Before I set off to work I banked the fire up with coal and covered it with a layer of nutty slack (coal dust). On my return a few stabs with a poker sent flames leaping up the fire-back, filling the darkened room with dancing shadows. How could a scene such as this not inspire me? Especially when viewed from an armchair with a cigarette in one hand and a brandy bubble in the other.

Living alone had many plus factors for me at first. But, like everything else in this life, there were just as many minuses that I hadn't considered – fresh laundry for instance. At home my cast-off garments disappeared from where they were left and miraculously reappeared washed, ironed and in my drawer. Now they lay in putrid piles around the bedroom. The one pair of bed-sheets I'd brought from home were long past their sell by date, and soon the small tear in one of them had become a major rip after I'd been chased by a gorilla in a nightmare. What was left of it smelt nothing like roses and it was in a pitiful state. So I decided to cast my fate to the wind and visit the nearby laundrette to rejuvenate a few things.

I'd never been inside a laundrette before but I wasn't put off. In the past I'd always been guided by my mother's philosophy: 'If you don't know how to go on – ask'. It was a spotless little place. There was a row of washing machines on one side and a row of seats facing them. Along the back of the room there stood a row of dryers. There was no one in when I entered, but as I closed the door behind me a lady came in through another door, which led to a backroom. 'Hello,' she greeted me. 'I haven't seen you in here before.'

'Er, no, I've just moved into the area,' I lied – having been there for over a month.

She must have sensed my helplessness. 'Do you know what to do?'

'No, I'm afraid I don't.'

She looked at my plastic bag. 'Is that your washing in there?'

I nodded, hoping that she wouldn't ask to have a look.

'Are they whites or coloureds?'

'Coloureds,' I quickly replied.

I don't think she was convinced. 'You know that you mustn't wash them together?'

I nodded confidently, thinking that I did now.

'Right - this machine should be big enough for your wash.' Opening the door of one of the smaller machines she twiddled a dial and beckoned me towards it. 'Put your washing in it, and after you've closed the door put your money in here.'

I got out a handful of change. She selected the necessary amount for me and placed it into the drawer-like slot. I furtively emptied the contents of my bag into the machine, hoping that she wouldn't see the state of it – the sheets in particular. 'Have you got any washing powder, please?' I asked – hoping at the same time to distract her prying eyes.

'The machine on the wall has got boxes of Persil. Have you got enough change left?'

'Yes, I think so.' I was now wishing she'd go away so that I could get on with revitalising my sad belongings.

'It'll take about twenty-five minutes, so if you want to do any errands you can leave it. It switches itself off. OK?'

I thanked her, and she disappeared closing the door behind her.

Good, I thought. Now I can get on with it. I pushed the drawer in, and then I remembered that I hadn't put any powder in. Fortunately the machine hadn't started, so I picked up the small packet I'd bought and checked to see how much I should use. There was no indication on the box, so I assumed that the contents must be the required amount. Anyway, even if it wasn't my stuff was a bit on the grubby side. I emptied the whole box into the hole marked 'For Powder', pulled the drawer holding the money and the machine whirred into action. It was easy! I left the laundrette feeling rather pleased and drove into town, promising myself that I'd make this a weekly event. I whizzed round town and the few errands I had to do didn't take long. Then I headed back for the laundrette, confident that I'd be there before my washing was finished.

My air of confidence was quickly replaced by a sense of foreboding as I approached the small establishment. The forecourt was littered with masses of soapsuds. As I made my way through them I caught sight of the manageress and two other ladies armed with mops and sweeping brushes. Between them they were attempting to remove the great clouds of suds surrounding my washing machine. 'How much powder did you put in?' the attendant asked, as I sheepishly peered through the door. I was too stunned to answer. Inside it looked more like the Klondike than a laundrette.

'Is it his washer?' one of her red-faced helpers scowled.

The three of them were going like the clappers, sweeping and mopping for all they were worth. The trouble was, the mass of suds didn't seem to be getting any smaller. I wanted to crawl into a tumbler and dry! (Sorry.)

'Can I help?' I asked, already knowing what the answer would be.

'I think you've done enough!' she replied. 'Just wait there till we've sorted this out.'

Eventually the situation was brought under control, leaving the floor of the laundrette sparkling and looking like new. Outside a slight breeze separated the great mounds of suds into smaller pieces, sending them tumbling into the road to be finally dissipated by the passing traffic. The lady in charge went into the back to put the mops and brushes away, while the older of the other two smiled at me, 'At least your washing should be clean, lad!' The other was red-faced and looked shattered.

I quickly emptied the contents of my machine into a basket and transferred them to a big drier. After setting it going I sat down, trying my best to be inconspicuous. Before long, though, the place began to fill up – and I was subjected to the most obvious scrutiny as the episode was recounted to everyone who came in. But if I thought that things couldn't get any worse I was wrong.

When the drier had finished its cycle I sprang from my chair. Let me get out of here, I thought, stuffing the washing into my plastic bag.

"Ere! Don't do that, lad.' The old lady who'd smiled at me got up from her chair. 'You'll get them all creased like that. Let me help you fold them,' she said, pushing me away from the drier and pulling out the sheet with the large hole in it. She gave me two ends to hold and unfurled the tatty piece of linen in front of the packed laundrette. I cringed with embarrassment as the row of seated housewives peered through the large hole in my sheet to see how their washing was doing in the machines opposite! There was a slight tear in the other sheet as well, which I hadn't been aware of. It seemed to take an age to fold everything up, and when I finally crawled out of the place feeling totally humiliated, I could only speculate about what the laundrette regulars would get from my first – and last – visit there!

I enjoyed my new-found independence but it didn't really go down too well with Dot, maybe because I appeared to be getting too well acquainted with the idea of living alone. And who could blame her? On the face of it I had everything I needed and wasn't beholden to anyone. But this didn't deter her in the slightest. She had other plans – which included looking for a house that would accommodate us both!

In the meantime our social life was getting into full swing. My financial situation was once more on a sound footing and I was ready to go out and see a bit more of the world. We got together with Ann and Ken, and on impulse we decided to buy a tent, load the car with camping equipment and set off for the Continent. We hadn't a clue what we were going to do when we got there: the plan was to get to France and take it from there. It turned out to be one of the best holidays ever. We drove down to Ramsgate where we boarded a hovercraft – an experience in itself – and crossed the Channel.

Apart from going to Ireland when I was quite young I'd never been abroad before; nor had Dot – so we had no idea what to expect. No doubt we were going to be in for quite a few surprises, and it wasn't long before we got the first one. When we landed in Calais ours was the first car off the hovercraft. An official waved us straight through the dock gates – no custom check, no nothing. I remembered to drive on the 'wrong' side of the road but I had no idea where I was going. Nor did those behind me, it seemed, because they all followed me down a cul-de-sac, which ended in a brick wall. Red-faced, I had to do a three point turn and drive back past the angry drivers, whose stationary cars now stretched from the cul-de-sac all the way back to the dock gates.

Eventually I found a main road and decided to follow it. It took us to St Omer, and along the way we were able to appreciate for the first time the beauty of the French countryside. The weather was exceptional, and the first thing we did on reaching St Omer was find a pavement café and refresh ourselves with a few cool drinks. To all intents and purposes the whole situation was idyllic, down to the last detail, as we sat in the warm sunshine watching the little town going about its business. But it didn't take long for reality to remind us that we were still in the real world . . . Ann, who had a working knowledge of French, went off to buy some fresh bread. We decided to stay and finish our drinks. Fifteen minutes later she returned, carrying a large loaf but looking mortified.

'What's the matter, Ann?'

'I've just been charged twenty francs for a loaf of bread!' she said in disbelief. A quick calculation of the exchange rate told us that one loaf had cost us a fortune. And considering we'd filled two shopping trolleys with groceries at our local supermarket in Batley for less than a fiver the previous day, our financial outlook looked pretty grim.

We decided to look around the market to see what the rest of the food cost. To our great relief everything else seemed to be reasonably priced. Ann spoke to one or two people and eventually twigged what had happened. Apparently there were two kinds of francs used at that time – ordinary francs and bread francs. The bread francs were old coins that were used solely for buying bread, and were only worth one-hundredth of an ordinary franc. The person who served Ann probably made her week's wage out of our loaf. We went back to the shop to confront the young assistant, but were met by the usual apathetic shrugs and 'Je ne comprend pas eengleesh!' The only redeeming fact was that the bread was lovely. But I've since ordered sandwiches at the Dorchester Hotel in London that didn't cost half as much.

We were determined not to let the episode spoil our adventure. We hit the road again and headed for the champagne capital – Reims. The cathedral there was awe-inspiring, as was the one in Strasbourg. These were just two of the many wonderful sights we saw in the next couple of weeks. Travelling light meant that we could move easily from place to place, and in the first week we drove through Germany, Liechtenstein, Switzerland, Monaco and Italy, before finally settling in Fréjus on the French Riviera.

After enjoying the best of what the Côte d'Azur had to offer, we made our way back home – stopping off in Paris for a bit of sightseeing. All in all it was a wonderful holiday – and it cost us twenty-five quid each. That included everything – food, petrol, crossing, and road tolls – the lot. If it hadn't been for that expensive loaf we might have been able to stay for another week!

Chapter Eighteen
TOO MUCH TOO SOON?

We returned from France refreshed, sporting a tan and with a few reservations. Four of us living in a small tent for a fortnight, even in idyllic surroundings, proved to be more than a little bit testing at times and I was glad to get back to the peace and quiet of my little cottage. I was perfectly happy living on my own but Dot wasn't. She told me, in no uncertain terms, that it was about time we should think about getting married. I told her that in practical terms the cottage was hardly big enough for me, let alone anyone else, and after that she made it her mission to find a place that was. In no time at all she did.

So that was that: I had no excuse to remain single. To be honest, getting spliced had never been high on my life's agenda, probably because I'd never been able to imagine myself married, but I didn't dismiss the possibility out of hand. In the past I'd always subscribed to the notion that if something's not broken don't fix it – but that old adage didn't allow for Dot's persistence!

When I first announced our intentions to my folks the initial reaction was one of indifference. But later, when it became apparent that we were serious, their attitude changed dramatically. To begin with, no girl was ever going to be good enough for me in the eyes of my doting mother. On top of this it was pointed out to me that it might be prudent to wait until I was off medication before making such an important decision. There was also the danger that it might get in the way of my career, which was rapidly developing at this time. So we were left with a situation that could hardly be described as wonderful.

After the initial hoo-ha and falling-out plans were made, and we were married on 2 September 1972 at St Joseph's parish church, Batley Carr. My childhood mate George was my best man, and afterwards our reception was held in the mayor's parlour at the town hall in Dewsbury. We received lots of good wishes, and there were telegrams from the Orbisons and from my old mate and comedian Charlie Williams – whom I'd recently been working with in the recording studio. Because of his popularity at that time it was felt Charlie should record an album. But he was petrified of singing with an orchestra – so I sang his parts for him until the tracks were laid down. Afterwards, when the orchestra had gone, my voice was lifted from the tracks and his was added at his leisure. This earned me his eternal gratitude, but he couldn't make it to our wedding – he was working at the London Palladium at the time – but his wife Audrey attended. After the reception we all finished up at the Shoulder of Mutton – a local hostelry – to complete a wonderful day.

I don't know why, but I awoke the next morning expecting to feel different somehow. I fully expected to be anointed by some great feeling of maturity, which would descend upon me from the heavens like the Holy Spirit in great tongues of fire; but nothing happened. I didn't feel any different to the way I felt the day before. Maybe it was the medication! But after I got out of bed and went downstairs the smell of the new carpets and furniture brought about a certain feeling that was hard to describe. After a while I began to realise that it might be the first stirrings of something previously unknown to me – unmitigated responsibility. I'd finally severed the umbilical cord and cast myself adrift into the real world. Responsibilities now rested firmly upon my shoulders. Marriage, I felt, was about to give me, among other things, a real purpose in life. I made up my mind there and then that I would pursue it in earnest.

But it wasn't going to be easy. I already knew that combining show business with the everyday pursuits of married life could be difficult. Many of my colleagues had tried and failed, but I was determined to give it my best. Dot still wanted to keep her daytime job, even though I could afford to keep us both. And though it proved to be inconvenient at times I didn't see any reason why she shouldn't if she wanted to. Meeting famous and important people often meant arriving home in the early hours. Dot enjoyed going with me, but it didn't make getting up for work a few hours later any easier.

Things went pretty well for us during the first year. We both worked hard to get the house how we wanted it, and Dot enjoyed the buzz of the celebrity scene – which occasionally was a source of great amusement to me.

Gene Pitney always kept in touch. I usually saw him when he visited the UK, and often received a telegram or phone call from him out of the blue. I remember Dot answering the phone the first time he rang, not long after we married. 'There's someone called Jean wants to talk to you,' she said suspiciously, noting the high-pitched voice. I took the receiver from her.

'Oh hello, Gene . . .' I turned to her and mouthed, 'It's Gene Pitney'. The expression on her face was priceless and the rest of the day she was in a trance, having spoken to *the* Gene Pitney.

Round about the same time I received word that one of the songs I had written a few years earlier, 'Ain't It All Worth Living For', had been recorded by Tompall and the Glaser Brothers and was in the American charts. A large cheque followed, along with an invitation to go to Nashville to receive an ASCAP award in recognition of the song's success. I graciously declined the offer, because of Dot's fear of flying, so the award was sent to London, where my publishers accepted it on my behalf at a reception in the PRS building in Berners Street. Jess Yates, who hosted the very popular TV show *Stars on Sunday*, was there, and, as he was returning north to the Yorkshire Television studios, offered to bring it back for me. He thought it would be an even better idea to feature it on the *Calendar* TV programme. so Bill and I were invited to perform the song and afterwards Richard Whiteley interviewed me. I never met Jess Yates so I was never able to thank him personally, which is a pity, because by all accounts he was one of life's true characters. Like his daughter Paula he was always in the news, and controversy seemed to follow in his wake. But he was a very astute man, and the success of *Stars on Sunday* has to be attributed to this.

The show was centred on famous people either reading a lesson, or singing hymns or songs in keeping with the Sabbath. Although Jess only had a small budget to work with, he had the knack of getting the most famous people onto the show. 'The Bishop', as he was affectionately known at Yorkshire TV, constantly visited Batley Variety club in an effort to persuade the big names to appear – and more often than not he was successful. But one superstar had been forewarned of his persistence and was ready for him – or so she thought! I was privileged to be appearing in the same show as Shirley Bassey when 'The Bishop' approached her to do his TV show. I heard through the grapevine the following chain of events. Miss Bassey knew beforehand that the show was run on a peppercorn budget, and so when Jess appealed to her generosity to do the show she agreed – but only on the understanding that a fifty-piece orchestra was provided to accompany her. Fully expecting him to be put off by the huge cost of her frivolous demand, she was surprised when he informed her that he'd be only too happy to comply with her request. I saw the show, and it was one of the best in the series: Shirley Bassey singing in her indomitable style, more than capably backed by the massed bands of the local Salvation Army . . .

Contrary to most people's expectations, our marriage seemed to work in the beginning, and my family – to their credit – put their initial reservations behind them. In retrospect I can fully understand their concern for me at the time – in particular from my mother's point of view. After all, my life seemed to have been a succession of disasters in previous years. I suppose that just like any mother she was being a little over-protective.

Regardless of whether or not Dot and I were compatible, our families got on well together, and this pleased me no end: harmony spells happiness in a Libran's book. So we seemed to get off to a good start – maybe too good. Most newly married couples at that time had to acquire things as and when they could afford them – but we were fortunate to be able to get things more or less straight away. Before long we were a two car household, and paying bills was the least of our problems.

I was extremely busy at the time working with the act. In between times I was writing songs, recording and travelling back and forth to London. I always considered my trips to London to be the high spot of my career as a songwriter. Thanks to the Beatles and others, the city seemed to be at the hub of everything that was happening in the pop industry. The excitement I felt of being a part of it all more than compensated for the loss of my original sporting ambitions. It was nice to be on first name terms with famous and influential people. And everywhere I went people knew about 'Penny Arcade'.

After the chart success of 'Ain't It All Worth Living For' in America, it was suggested that I record an album of my own songs for the giant ABC Dunhill Label. Plans were already in progress for me to fly to Nashville when the news came through that the deal had fallen through. To ABC's embarrassment they hadn't realised I was English; they'd assumed I was American. My album was to be aimed at the American country charts, and they felt that an English artist wouldn't have the necessary background to win over the very partisan country audiences. It was a great disappointment, but it wasn't the end of the world. Undeterred I continued to churn out my songs, and they began to find their way onto albums, TV and even into pantomime. One producer, whose name I could never remember, featured one of my songs – 'Crabapple Hill' – in every pantomime he produced until the day he retired. The song also featured on the hit album *Combine Harvester* by the West Country group The Wurzels. I was also invited to receptions and award dinners where I met and got to know people who could do me some good.

Dot missed out on much of this, much to her chagrin, but to preserve her independence she had to keep her own job. And conventional jobs meant conventional hours but if there was ever anything going on in our part of the country - she'd be there with bells on. One of the more notable occasions was when the great American singer/songwriter John D. Loudermilk was visiting this country. Ron Randall from Acuff-Rose brought him up to meet us and also to do some work in Bill's studio. As he was responsible for writing the massive hits 'Tobacco Road' and 'Indian Reservation', I was in awe of the man's talent. But I had no idea what he looked like. All I knew was that he was big and that he was part Cherokee Indian, so when we drove to the station to pick him up I half-expected to be looking out for a big bloke in a war bonnet! I needn't have worried: he was big all right, but he wasn't a bit like I imagined. He looked more like a friendly farmer and was dressed in ex-army gear, which back in the early '70s could hardly be construed as trendy. But it suited his persona, and I knew I'd like him straight away. John had a tremendous talent and his use of lyrics was extraordinary. As rich and talented as he was, he showed no inclination to conceit – in short, he was a star!

One evening Dot and I accompanied him, along with Ron, to Batley Variety Club to see my old mate Charlie Williams. The sound of a black man talking with a broad Yorkshire accent completely mesmerised the big American. He was also taken by the Yorkshire dialect and some of our colloquialisms – 'as fit as a butchers dog', for instance – sent him into hysterics.

It was a real bonus for me to meet people like John. I was eager to learn as much about song writing as possible, and unconsciously I took note of everything he said and did. One thing that intrigued me was his attitude to his musical instruments. He believed that a guitar, for instance, had only got so many songs in it. When he'd squeezed what he felt was the last one from his, he traded it in for a new one, and started again. I thought that was a wonderful idea, but one I'd personally find it hard to subscribe to. Being of a sentimental disposition, I like to hang onto things that have been good to me in the past.

John also travelled a lot, in the belief that changes of environment brought fresh ideas. I totally agreed with this, as I found I could get ideas no other way. The popular image of the archetypal songwriter bashing away at a piano in an attic could only be applied to me *after* the song had been conceived. I always wrote the song in my mind first – usually out walking or driving – and worked on it afterwards at the piano or with the guitar.

Acuff-Rose Music, which published my songs, was at that time one of the largest music publishers in the world. Their country music catalogue alone was second to none, and as many of my songs were country orientated I believed they'd serve my requirements best. Coupled with this, the demos of the songs – which we recorded at Bill's studio – always had an American feel to them. Bill was really into that kind of music, which also brought us an unexpected bonus.

The American country singer George Hamilton IV was due to tour over here and was looking for a band to accompany him. Before swapping over to the country music scene, George had been a teen idol in the late '50s, with a massive hit in the States called 'A Rose and a Baby Ruth'. But other than that I didn't know much about him. Ron suggested that Bill and I should put a band together; he was more than convinced that we could do the job. So I borrowed a bass guitar, and with Bill playing lead guitar we teamed up with an old friend of mine on drums – Norman Emsley. That's right, the one whose first words to me had been 'fuck off' at the art school dance many years before!

George's tour was scheduled to open at Batley Variety Club. The club management – whose perception of country music was ten-gallon hats and 'yee haas' – had arranged to have the stage decorated with bales of straw; there was even talk of having a few pigs running around. But when George arrived, dressed immaculately in a dark blue pinstriped suit with matching waistcoat, they soon dispensed with that idea. He looked more like a bank manager than a cowboy. Actually his dress sense matched his personality perfectly, for he was quietly reserved and his manners were impeccable.

George was accompanied by a pianist/arranger well known to us at that time – Jeremy Lubbock. He too was a gentleman in every sense, and talented too. These days he lives in Los Angeles and his CV has to be seen to be believed. The list of famous people who've sought his expertise is as impressive as it can get: Whitney Houston, Celine Dion, Barbra Streisand, Michael Jackson, Madonna, Sting, Elton . . .

So we got down to some serious rehearsal and it all went off smoothly. When the question of what we would wear on stage arose, I was grateful that it wasn't going to be overalls and a straw hat. It was suggested that we wear something not too flamboyant, so we plumped for black trousers with black polo-neck sweaters. When George saw us he immediately christened us the Yorkshire Mafia, and took great delight in introducing us as such to the audience each night.

We also did a spot on the lunchtime TV show *Pebble Mill at One*. It was the first time I'd done live television, and I was very nervous. Everything I'd done on TV before had been pre-recorded, so mistakes could be easily rectified. But it all went smoothly – although I nearly missed my cue when I got engrossed listening to an interview with Danny La Rue that preceded our spot. We met him afterwards in the hospitality suite, and he was a really nice bloke. Norman, our drummer, was in his element, and it really made his day when he bumped into his old friend Roy Castle outside the studios. There was a lot of backslapping and banter, and all in all it was a very enjoyable day.

Our next stop was Allinson's Theatre Club in Liverpool. Instead of checking into a hotel we stayed with my Aunt Evy. Having us about the place to fuss over she was in her element. It gave the lads a chance to savour her excellent cooking. Norman couldn't believe how good her roast potatoes were. At the end of the week we gave

Arkwright, featuring me (right) and Bill Clarke, 1975. Our song 'Where do we go from here' became Terry Wogan's Record of the Week, although what week in 1975 neither of us can remember!

Me with one of my two ASCAP (American Society of Composers and Publishers) awards.

The programme for the Country Music Association Dinner in 1972.

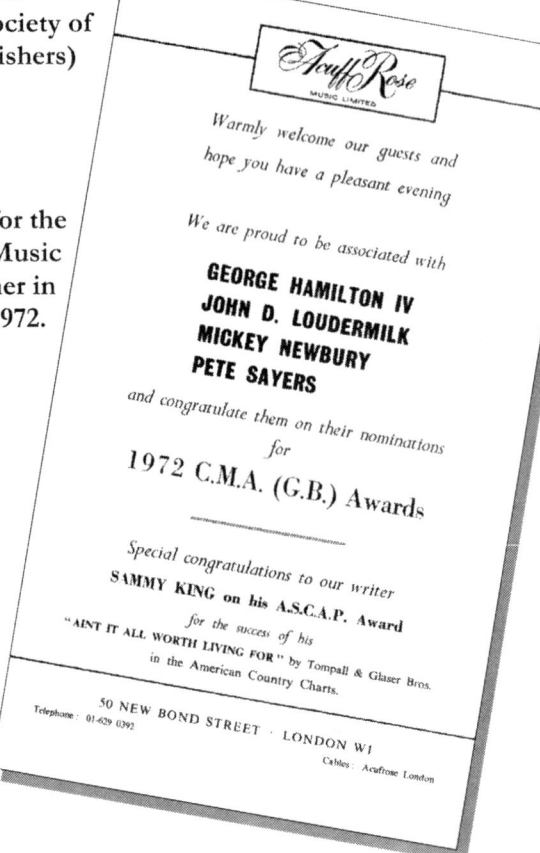

Acuff Rose
MUSIC LIMITED

Warmly welcome our guests and hope you have a pleasant evening

We are proud to be associated with

GEORGE HAMILTON IV
JOHN D. LOUDERMILK
MICKEY NEWBURY
PETE SAYERS

and congratulate them on their nominations for

1972 C.M.A. (G.B.) Awards

Special congratulations to our writer
SAMMY KING on his **A.S.C.A.P. Award**
for the success of his
"AINT IT ALL WORTH LIVING FOR" by Tompall & Glaser Bros.
in the American Country Charts.

50 NEW BOND STREET · LONDON W1
Telephone: 01-629 0392
Cables: Acufrose London

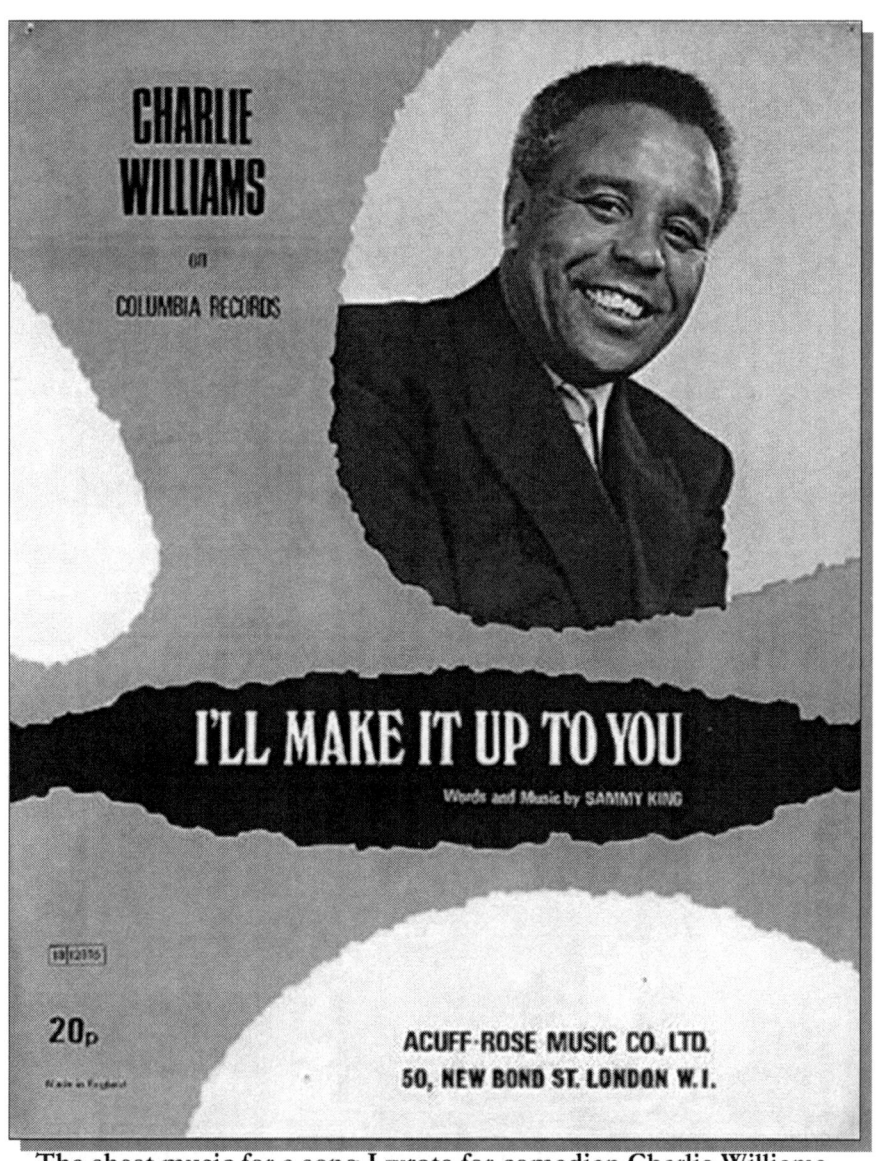

The sheet music for a song I wrote for comedian Charlie Williams, who was extremely popular in the 1970s.

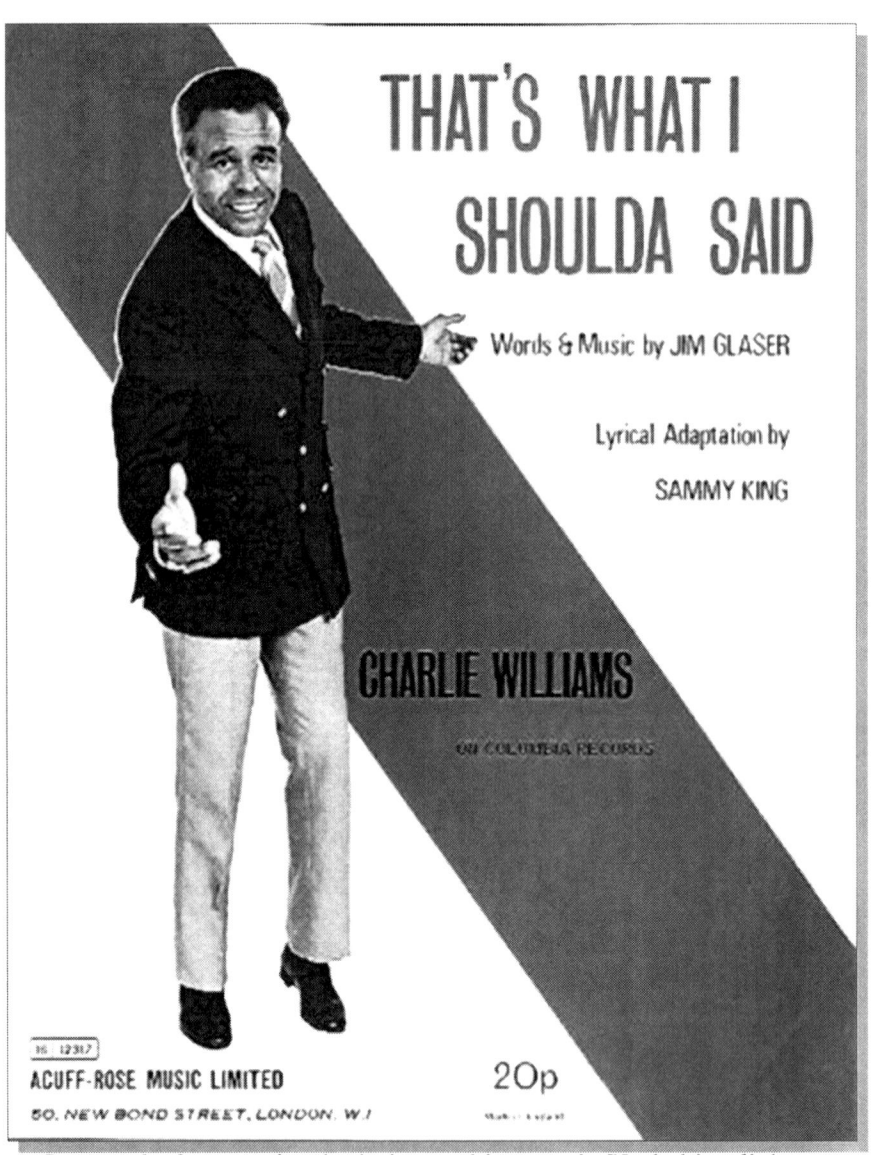

I was asked to rewrite the lyrics to this song in Yorkshire dialect. Charlie was from Barnsley and was probably the first black stand-up comedian on television. He appeared regularly on *The Comedians* and latterly on *The Golden Shot*.

George Hamilton IV and the Yorkshire Mafia. My good friend Bill
Clarke and I backed him on many occasions – and he referred to
us as the Yorkshire Mafia.

The Yorkshire Mafia. Left to right: Bill Clarke, Jeremy Lubbock and me. Jeremy went on to arrange and produce many songs in the US and featured on the Michael Jackson album *Thriller*.

Me and my nephew Daniel Twohig holding my **ASCAP** awards. Daniel has his own band these days.

My invitation to the ASCAP awards, 1975. Sadly I couldn't go as my first wife was frightened of flying.

Norman Emsley, drummer. He played in George Hamilton IV's backing band and was part of the Yorkshire Mafia. His first words to me when we were introduced were fuck off! I've never forgotten that.

Sheet music for comedian Little and Large's song 'Rock Steady'.

Sheet music for 'Ain't it all worth living for', which won me my first ASCAP award.

her the allowance we'd been given for our hotel bills. It amounted to a fair few quid, and she refused to take it. After being assured that it didn't come out of our own pockets, and after a bit of badgering, she reluctantly accepted it.

The tour finished up at the Wimbledon Empire in London. George was highly delighted with us and gave us a bonus, the only trouble being that the cheque was made out in dollars. But we got round that – although we did lose a few bob because of the exchange rate!

There never seemed to be enough time in the day for me during those first years of marriage. Along with work, there was the never-ending task of getting the house into order both inside and out. It was on a new development, so there was plenty of work to do outside. Fortunately most of our neighbours were newly married like us, and there was never any shortage of help when needed. If anyone had a wagonload of sand or topsoil delivered, an army of friends arrived with wheelbarrows and shovels and transported it to the rear of the house in no time at all. We helped and advised each other and really got on well. Those first residents, who've since moved on, laid the foundations of what is still today a happy and thriving little community.

So much was happening that I hardly found time to draw breath. When I wasn't decorating or building walls I was tripping down to London or was out nearly every night working with the act. And in between all this I somehow had to find time to lock myself away in the spare room that I used for an office to work on the songs that were queuing up to be written. This was all well and good for me, but looking back it couldn't have been much fun for Dot. Usually when she came home from work I was getting ready to go out. Reconciling the late hours of showbiz with her conventional nine-to-five job was nigh on impossible, so after a while she decided to accompany me less on engagements, thereby giving her more time to be with her own circle of friends. While this seemed to make good sense at the time it was probably instrumental in causing the first cracks in our relationship to appear. My creative powers were on a roll, and I saw this as a chance to secure our future. I dare say Dot realised this too, and as the rewards could have meant lasting security it was in her interest to give me my rein. The upshot of it all was that we ended up together but just about living separate lives – a title for a song if ever I heard one! But against all the odds (another good title?) we stuck it out for a while.

We also added a new member to our family – Sadie. Sadie, or Rubbish as her previous owner had affectionately called her, was a little fat mongrel puppy. She'd belonged to one of the local taxi drivers. Rumour had it that he had a fling with the late Jayne Mansfield and when he was kicked out of his home by his wife he had to live and sleep in his taxi. So he temporarily housed Sadie in a storeroom at Batley Variety Club. Unless he could find a home for her he was going to have to put her down. We heard of her plight and decided to go and see her. As soon as the storeroom door was opened there was a clatter of paint tins and a tiny bundle of fur covered in paint and dirt bounded towards us – tail going like a windscreen wiper at full pelt. Her tiny tongue lashed out at every inch of uncovered skin in sight. There was no way we could let her be put to sleep, so we took her home. She settled in straight away and claimed a corner of the kitchen as her own. The wall was panelled next to her bed, and when she got bigger her hind leg banged against the panels when she scratched herself during the night. Richard, our next-door neighbour, got up three times in the early hours to answer the door before he realised where the knocking was coming from.

But we were still saddled with the upside-down hours of showbiz. The worst times were usually in summer. Bank holidays and weekends saw families and couples setting off for the seaside or dales to enjoy the sunny weather. We, in the meantime, had to stay at home, usually because I had commitments in the evening that I dared not risk miss by getting stuck in a traffic jam or breaking down in the back of beyond. Maybe I was being too cautious, but I hated letting anyone down. In retrospect I guess I was letting the wrong people down – namely me and Dot. You know the old saying: all work and no play . . .

It wasn't that I was unaware of Dot's discontent. There were occasions when she expressed the desire for us to be just like an 'ordinary' couple for a change. So did I – but for some reason I couldn't ignore the creative forces within me. They seemed to have taken me over. And, considering my inquisitive nature, it's a wonder that I never seriously questioned where the inspiration for all these songs was coming from. I had no idea then, and I still have no idea today. They just rolled into my mind by the truckload – and I wasn't complaining. But it gradually became an obsession. My mind was constantly occupied with words and music. The buzz I got from developing a simple riff or phrase into a passage of music was intoxicating. After all they were *my* songs, *my* creations – no one else's. In a world of countless billions of people I was quite proud of the fact that I was the first to think of them. It was also very gratifying to know that I was creating something that would still be around long after I was gone.

Dot tried to take an interest in what I was doing, but for some reason I felt uncomfortable about outside input. I suppose I was frightened that the pipeline of inspiration might get obstructed and cease to function. Who knows what the reason was? At the time I couldn't explain half of what was going through my mind, let alone much of what I was doing. When it came to writing songs I displayed a single-mindedness that I never knew I had. I was completely deaf to criticism, and as far as I was concerned the things I wrote were set in stone. That'd probably why I've always preferred to finish a song before letting anyone listen to it.

Where do you go from here?
Most of my inspiration, musical or lyrical, came to me late at night or in the early hours of the morning. I never seemed to need much sleep, which meant of course that I was regularly plonking away on my guitar when Dot was in dreamland. I also got many ideas when I was driving the car: a tune could stem from the rhythm of the tyres on the road, or something else might catch my eye to start a lyric. Like the local estate agent's sign that read 'Holroyd Sons and Pickersgill'. The words kept rolling round my mind, and gradually Holroyd Sons and Pickersgill became Arthur Edward Pickersgill and gave me the first line of a song:

> Arthur Edward Pickersgill, working hard at t' mill
> Sorting out the bales – the ones to empty and to fill
> But Sat' day night he's rushing home to check his football pools
> Well . . . Chelsea won – and let him down – and so did Hartlepool . . .

I finished it, calling it 'Where Do You Go From Here?', and we made a demo at Bill's studio. Bill and I occasionally worked for a theatrical agency, with which Howard Huntridge, the TV producer responsible for *The Price is Right* and *Supermarket Sweep*, was involved. He also had connections with a small independent record label owned by the notorious Jonathan King. UK Records had a reputation for releasing unusual, one-off, low budget productions, and enjoyed a success rated envied by many of the larger labels. So Howard took it down to UK Records for us, and it was received favourably. Within the next couple of weeks we were all sitting in UK's London office planning its release. We had to find an image to complement the concept of the song – which was very northern. Eventually someone came up with the idea of flat caps, mufflers and the name Arkwright.

It worked! After a few plays on Terry Wogan's radio show the first pressing was sold out the first day of release. It became Wogan's record of the week, which meant it received extra air time. Jonathan King rang up. 'We've got a hit on our hands. I want you to start thinking of a follow-up, and maybe come up with enough new songs for an album . . .' Bill and I were stunned – and excited at the same time. I began writing songs in earnest. There's nothing like success to breed more success. This is it, I thought. This is going to be our year! We were all set for the big push. The press came round and Yorkshire Television sent a film crew. We spent a full day filming and interviewing, which culminated in an extended feature on *Calendar*. It all seemed to be happening – but then came disaster.

The oil crisis in the Middle East stopped the movement of oil tankers through the Suez Canal. When the west took steps to conserve their resources the knock-on effect was a stockpiling of oil-based raw materials – which included vinyl for pressing records. The major record companies, who owned the pressing plants, hung onto what they had and would only press their own records, leaving the independents out in the cold. The upshot was that the demand for our record couldn't be met. Everybody wanted it but nobody could buy it. People even wrote to Terry Wogan, and the situation became a talking point on his show. Eventually the problem was sorted out by using recycled vinyl, but in the meantime the chance had passed us by. By the time the presses started rolling again we were yesterday's news.

This was a big let-down, of course, but my disappointment was short lived when Dot gave me some news that would compensate for it a hundred times over – I was going to be a daddy! Yes, 1975 was going to be a good year after all – the best in fact. I was absolutely elated. In the weeks that followed I couldn't concentrate on anything. Both our families were thrilled at the news and looked forward to the prospect of the new addition.

In the meantime I was busy writing songs for the Arkwright album, which unfortunately, didn't materialise. But I wasn't too disappointed; after all, I'd accumulated a bunch of songs that were a little bit different. I left some of them at my publishers for scrutiny, and Bryan Johnston, who sang one of our first Eurovision song entries – 'Singing High High High' – happened to hear them. He thought they were very good, and suggested that strung together they would make a good musical. I immediately adopted the idea, and for years afterwards it became one of my many ongoing projects.

Months followed during which I found it difficult to apply myself to anything. The prospect of being a father overshadowed everything. I was in a dream half of the time, which is probably why I can't remember much about the early stages of Dot's pregnancy – only the latter part. I was working away from home with George Hamilton IV at Aldeburgh in Suffolk, and even though Dot assured me that she was all right it didn't stop me from feeling a little concerned. We were recording a series of concerts for BBC television at The Maltings – an old industrial building that had been converted to a concert hall. George was hosting the shows and the Yorkshire Mafia were there to provide the musical accompaniment for him and the guest artistes, which included two American songsters, Billie Joe Spears and Tanya Tucker.

Billie Joe was a darling, and a character to boot. Four times married, she just lit up the whole proceedings with her banter and personality. At rehearsal she just walked in and said, 'Howdy, boys! Just give us a 'G'.' And we sailed through her hit song 'Blanket on the Ground'. But Tanya Tucker was a totally different story. She was young, very beautiful – but unfortunately for us very temperamental. Her record ' Delta Dawn' was currently in the American charts, and it must have gone to her head. We'd been sent a copy of the disc weeks earlier in order to learn it, so by the time she came to rehearsal we all knew the arrangement backwards. Norman even had a metronome with him to make sure he set the tempo correctly. We'd incorporated two more friends into the band – Tony Cervi on keyboards, the musical director at Batley Variety Club, and Teddy Platt, lead guitarist with the original Voltaires. Both were very talented and both excellent musicians. But unfortunately it wasn't good enough for Miss Tucker. Try as we might we couldn't please her. First it was too fast, then too slow; too loud, then too soft. In the end we all trooped off to the canteen for a drink. Her manager came after us and apologised for her conduct, putting her tantrums down to the fact that she was missing her boyfriend (Glen Campbell), and was feeling very lonely. We, in typical Yorkshire fashion, pointed out that this had nothing to do with us. He agreed, and begged us to reconsider. Eventually we all went up to the hospitality suite and she apologised. This seemed to break the ice, and afterwards she was a totally different person. We all seemed to get on better, and Tanya's spot on the show went down a bomb.

It was a wonderful experience for us all to see the work that goes on behind the scenes during the making of these TV shows. One of the nice things was putting a face to the names of the technicians, many of whom I'd become familiar with after reading their names on the credits of other shows.

We also had time to wander around the little Suffolk resort of Aldeburgh, which at that time of the year we had practically to ourselves. George Hamilton (the fourth) and most of the 'top dogs' in the unit, stayed at one of the large hotels courtesy of the BBC. We, being of a thriftier disposition, spent our generous accommodation expenses on a smaller, more homely, residence – and pocketed the balance! Four of us bunked in one large room while our drummer Norman – who snored like a buzz saw – was confined to a small single room. It was a really comfortable place and we all settled in well. The first night we were all sitting on our beds chatting about the day's rehearsal when Norman came in. 'Hey, fellas, come and look at this!' he said, beckoning us to follow him. His little room was on the ground floor, and as he led us downstairs he was grinning from ear to ear. He ushered us through his bedroom door and threw open the cupboard doors that made up three sides of the room. 'What do you think to this lot?' he chuckled. Each cupboard was filled with bottles containing every kind of spirit under the sun. There was enough booze in that room to float a battleship. Norman loved a drink, of course, but he was a pint man at that time – and an honest one at that.

The next morning we were all having our breakfast – except for Norman, who was still in his room snoring for England. The landlady was chatting away as she was serving us. 'I do hope your friend doesn't mind being on his own,' she said.

'No,' I replied. 'It couldn't have worked out better, really, because he's not been out of hospital long. The peace and quiet will do him good.'

'Oh, really.' She looked concerned. 'What's been the matter with him?'

'Norman's a recovering alcoholic . . .' Before I finished the sentence she dropped the tray she was carrying and dashed out of the dining room. Shortly afterwards she returned, looking more than a little relieved. Fortunately she saw the funny side of it when we revealed the joke. Norman wandered in soon afterwards, bleary eyed – having just being woken up by a panic-stricken landlady. She was a really nice lady and we gave her some complimentary tickets for the show for her and her family. After that she couldn't do enough for us.

This really was a wonderful time for me. I was enjoying my work, I was making a good living and, with a baby due, the world seemed a mighty fine place.

Where there's muck there's brass

The journey back from Aldeburgh seemed to take an age. Suffolk is a lovely county but those little country roads seem to go on for ever. By the time we reached the M1, having crossed Cambridgeshire, I thought I'd seen enough of the Fens to last me a lifetime. But after just one hour on the boring M1 it was a case of 'Come back Fens – all is forgiven!' The motorway's only redeeming factor, I suppose, was that it got me home quicker. I'd enjoyed my time at the Maltings but I was eager to get back up North and back to reality. Dot was nearing her time and I, naturally, wanted to be on hand.

The whole prospect of becoming a father seemed to take precedence over everything – in particular my writing. In retrospect I should have found the experience sublimely inspirational, but for some reason it had the opposite effect on me. Every day my thoughts were completely taken over by a constant stream of speculation. Would the baby be a boy or a girl? Would he or she grow up to take an interest in sport or music? And who would the child take after? The questions were endless. I began to take a marked interest in the logistics that were involved. Dot had most things under control, but I still found myself looking at prams or staring in baby-shop windows, taking note of what might be needed. Even before the list was completed the result was surprising: it was endless. I started to wonder how parents managed in the past. I can't recall seeing a bottle-sterilising unit or a baby alarm when I was young, let alone a baby bouncer. But I didn't care. So far as I was concerned he or she could have whatever it wanted.

When I set off for work in the evening it was with a much greater purpose. For very soon, God willing, there was about to be someone added to our family, someone completely dependent on us. From now on there was no comfort zone. I could no longer be choosy about which venues I played. If the bad venues paid then I'd be there. Fortunately the really bad gigs were few and far between, and most of the clubs we worked were OK – but that didn't stop us falling foul of technical hitches occasionally.

Using taped backing back in the early '70s was very innovative but, like anything else controlled by electricity, it was prone to glitches. We used a large reel-to-reel tape machine, which on the whole was very reliable – although hauling it round from venue to venue in all conditions really tested its mettle. On the few occasions that it succumbed to gremlins it provided us with situations that, though not funny at the time, gave us a chuckle afterwards. Like the time Bill and I set up for a private party at a club in Doncaster. Everything was switched on and ready to go – except the tape machine. It was as dead as a dodo. So that was it! No tape, no show. Our machine was a large, expensive, professional model – not the kind of thing you find lying about the average person's front room: most people at that time favoured cassette recorders anyway. We didn't hold out much hope of finding a replacement machine among the punters and in the end all we could muster was a battered old Sony belonging to the chairman's daughter. On reflection we really shouldn't have bothered. It played all right, but the tape speed was slower, much slower, which meant the music was much lower – and I spent most of the time singing down in my boots. But there was a slight plus. When I came to the very high notes, which I normally approached with clenched buttocks and protruding veins, I found I could handle them without breaking sweat! The slower speed also meant that the spots were longer – what was normally a thirty-minute spot ended up lasting nearly forty. So at least they got their money's-worth.

It's amazing how much voltages varied in different areas. It might only have been slight but I was aware of it. The fact that I could hit the last note in 'My Prayer' easier in Sheffield than Leeds was no coincidence. But so long as it was consistent it wasn't so bad. It was only when it fluctuated that the pantomime began. Like the club in South Yorkshire that was not only affiliated to the local colliery but also relied on its independent power source for electricity. This had its advantages, of course, for if the surrounding area was hit by power cuts the club was unaffected. But unfortunately for us it wasn't conducive to trouble-free tape backing.

The lights in the concert room would suddenly dip and there'd be cries of 'Ey up! T'cage is off down t'shaft.' But not only did the lights dim – the tape would slow. And if the cage stopped three times on its way to the bottom then the audience was treated to a song with three key changes!

Chapter Nineteen
MANDY

When I finally made up my mind to put these memories down on paper I really didn't know how to go about it. Even though I enjoyed English at school I always seemed to be lacking in the vocabulary department. Much to my regret, I'm ashamed to say that I've never been an enthusiastic reader. Having spent most of my time trying to cobble original songs and lyrics together, I never seemed to get round to look at what the great writers had been doing. So I thought it might help if I joined a creative writing class at our local college of further education – and, indeed, it helped enormously. I received lots of encouragement and advice and at the same time added a number of wonderful people to my list of friends. One of them, my tutor, Gladys 'Goldie' Armitage, coined a phrase: 'No one ever said you were put on this earth to be happy.' Ironically it never seemed to apply to her, for she always seemed to be happy and lived life to the full, but it did seem to sum up the contrasting fortunes of my early life.

It's long been my opinion that for every modicum of success I've managed to lever from the Jaws of Destiny, there's always been a price to pay in return. And in my own case I felt I was paying dearly. By some people's standards I'd enjoyed a pretty successful career in show business; I'd written a few hit songs and appeared on telly. I suppose it was OK, but somehow nothing really compensated for the ungainly limp I was stuck with and the fact that I'd never play football again.

But all this changed in the early hours of the morning of 17 November 1975. Not long after Bill and I parted company and I was working on my own, I arrived home tired and hungry having done battle with an uncompromising audience somewhere in South Yorkshire. The house was in darkness, which was a bit strange; Dot usually left a light on for me. As I doused the headlights and got out of the car our next-door neighbour Mary came out of her house in her dressing gown. 'Dot's gone in,' she said, smiling. 'It's nearly time.' I started to get back into the car. 'No, no, everything's fine. They said they'll ring you when something starts to happen.'

'Are you sure?' I croaked.

'Yes. It'll be all right, Sam. The best thing you can do is get yourself off to bed and get some rest.' Mary was always good in these situations. She had a way of bringing calm to any predicament.

I went in the house, made a cup of tea and rang the hospital – just in case there'd been any developments. The nurse assured me that everything was fine.

Although I was dog-tired I couldn't sleep. I just lay in bed staring at the phone. Eventually I must have dozed off, but it can't have been for long – maybe a few minutes – when the phone rang. Half asleep, I picked it up.

'Mr Twohig?'

'Yes.'

'Your wife's given birth to a baby girl.'

I was dazed. 'Really? How is she – they?'

'They're both fine.'

'Can I come up?'

'Yes. Just tell the nurse who you are when you get here.'

'Thank you.' I was suddenly wide-awake.

The next thing I remember was being shown into a little room and being given a mop cap, surgical gown and white shoe covers. 'Please put these on and then I'll take you in to see your wife and baby,' said a young nurse – or words to that effect. I was still in a state of 'Is this all really happening?' The whole situation seemed bizarre, yet exciting and wonderful. After I'd slipped my arms into the gown the nurse tied it at the back. Then I slipped the shoe covers on and stretched the cap over my head. I must have looked a sight –

God knows, I felt one! Me being only five foot three, the dark green gown nearly reached the ground. It left just enough room to expose the embarrassingly oversized covers on my shoes. I was assured the mop cap was mandatory – as I had long hair at the time. I looked ridiculous – for all the world like one of those covers tied with string that they put on top of pots of home-made jam at church fêtes. As I followed the nurse down the corridor I caught sight of our reflection in a glass panel: Florence Nightingale being pursued by a large jar of greengage jam shod in a couple of doilies! 'Oh God,' I gulped. 'I hope I don't bump into anybody I know!'

For some reason I had a nagging feeling that I was being set up: you know, first-time father and all that. Could this be an initiation or something? After all this was the maternity wing – the domain of women. Visions of going through a door to be met by hoots of laughter and finger pointing crossed my mind. But the scene that awaited me laid all my fears to rest. There they were: Dot, looking remarkably well, and the little bundle that was going to change my life for ever. I'd been told that all new-born babies looked like Winston Churchill, but she didn't – she was absolutely beautiful.

'Now then, Daddy!' Dot grinned.

I was dumbstruck. I didn't know what to say. Outwardly I knew I looked ridiculous but I've never been able to describe what I felt inside. To do so I'd have to invent a brand new vocabulary. Already I was thinking ahead as I looked at our sleeping daughter. This little person is here now, in this world, with her mum and dad. Your dad's going to do everything in his power to make your life on this earth as happy as he can. I'll work hard, and you'll never want for anything – I promise.

We didn't choose a name for her straight away, and when she left hospital she was still known as little 'Baby Twohig'. Amid all our excitement and preparations her name, for some reason, had been completely overlooked. When we finally got down to choosing it, our choice was narrowed down to three names – Amanda, Samantha and Martine. The first name to be eliminated was Martine – a lovely name, but it just didn't seem to suit her for some reason. So it was between Samantha and Amanda. We finally chose Amanda, reasoning that Samantha would probably be shortened to Sam and two Sams in the same household would create confusion. So Amanda it was, or Mandy for short. She could make up her own mind and use whichever she preferred later on in life. We used both.

If she was good it was 'Mandy' and if she was naughty it was 'A-MAN-DA!'

Dot chose to bottle-feed Mandy, for reasons best known to her. I didn't know anything about all that stuff, but later I had my suspicions. When I arrived home knackered from a gig in Mansfield at half past two in the morning, no sooner had I opened the bedroom door than my yawning wife said, 'Oh, while you're still up give her, her bottle. There's some made up in the fridge.' And went back to sleep! By this time the rapid little intakes of breath that precede the inevitable infant wail were gathering momentum. I nipped downstairs, weary as I was, to collect her bottle. After sticking it in the bottle warmer for a while I squirted a little on my wrist to test the temperature, and headed back to the bedroom just in time to avert the impending eruption. Cradling her in my arms, I sat at the end of the bed and watched in wonder as she fastened onto the teat. Although I was really tired I couldn't help smiling to myself as she hungrily set about draining the bottle. Every so often she slowed down and looked as if she was going to fall asleep. Then, just as I was about to withdraw the bottle, she fastened back onto it and started furiously sucking again. Sometimes this happened two or three times before the last drop was gone. Then it was burping time. I must confess that this was the only activity I had difficulty with. It requires a certain penchant for manipulation, more evident in women than men, for getting someone to part with something unwillingly – even a commodity as insignificant as wind! And when it finally came up it was sometimes accompanied with what you'd just put down there. So when I helped with feeding duties, I had more than my share of baby honk deposited on me. I didn't really mind, and looked upon it as a kind of badge: 'We have a new baby . . . and sick happens!' Baby honk is unique. Apart from the fact that it stains everything it comes in contact with, its unmistakeable blend of sour milk and talcum powder stays with you for ever. It evokes instant memories of sleepless nights, early mornings and nappy changing.

Now that's one thing that sorts the men from the boys! For while some of the guys I knew at that time would have had a go at feeding baby, most drew the line there – some even confessed to feeling ill at the thought of full nappies. But I didn't mind doing it at all: I found the whole activity quite fascinating. I'd watched Dot do it and I soon got to grips with it – although sticking the pin in was a bit frightening. But once I'd got the knack of it, armed with a Moses

My daughter Mandy, who once asked me if I could buy her a moon!

basket bursting with nappies, creams, baby wipes, lotions, pins, cotton buds, cotton balls, kitchen sinks and so on, I could make our little daughter happy and comfortable in no time at all.

I just loved looking after Mandy and seeing to her needs. Even pushing her round in a pram was a joy, and in the months that followed I experienced to the full the whole concept of fatherhood. I began to appreciate the fact that the kind of work I did enabled me to spend my days with Mandy, unlike many other fathers who had to go out to work. I was there to witness at first hand the progress she made in her early years. Watching our little girl grow was something really special. During this period, of course, my creativity was put on the back boiler, and I had no regrets about swapping it for domesticity. I was soon aware that a lot of guys were missing out on something wonderful. I was totally overwhelmed by our baby and everything about her. She completely took over our lives, and I began to think that this was what life was all about. I was fascinated by the little cooing sounds she made when she was content, and devastated when she cried in discomfort. I'd willingly have cut off my right arm to ease the pain she felt when she was teething or when she suffered

One of my more formal portraits.

the other nuisances' babies have to contend with. More than once I questioned my faith and belief in the God of goodness and compassion when something nasty made her cry.

We became aware that Mandy was gradually becoming more conscious of us, and the usual topics came up for discussion: 'I wonder what her first word will be?' or 'Who do you think she looks like?' Needless to say the speculation changed from day to day, as it does with every baby. Babies bring a lot of love, they say, and Mandy certainly endorsed this. Her grandparents doted on her, as did the rest of the family, and the earlier misgivings about me and Dot – particularly my mother's – seemed to soften. Our baby was looked upon as something very special.

So what's your proper job then?
I found it nice to experience what could be termed as a normal life for a while. Now that a baby was added to the equation we had to make changes in our way of life to accommodate her. Before she'd had Mandy, Dot had had a nine-to-five job, which meant we often had difficulty fitting a social life into the time between my show business commitments. Showbiz folk seem to go out when everyone else is at work and work when everyone else goes out! Consequently, if ever we went out with friends, more often than not it was to see me work. And when people in 'normal' professions saw me performing with a huge grin on my face, seemingly having the time of my life on stage, they always thought I was lucky to be able to enjoy myself while working. Well, sometimes it was true, but there were other times when I operated on automatic pilot in order to survive.

I remember years before when we (the Voltaires) had to drive through the night after a gig in Cardiff, to fulfil a lunchtime date the next day in Doncaster. This was before motorways, and the journey seemed to take for ever. We arrived a few minutes before we were due to go on. Tired and hungry, having barely slept or eaten, we'd just enough time to change into our suits – which were still damp with perspiration from the gig the night before.

After we'd just finished a difficult first spot with an uncompromising audience, the entertainment secretary at the club – fully aware of our epic trek – asked me, 'How do you manage to keep smiling after all that?'

To which I replied, 'I wasn't aware that I *was* smiling!'

'But you were,' he insisted. And suddenly I realised I'd been infected by a phenomenon prevalent throughout the world of entertainment – the showbiz smile. I must confess that my first reaction was one of slight shock. My mind had been overridden by a cheesy grin. Being an up front kind of person I wasn't exactly comfortable with this. It was like being told that I was one step up from being a charming second-hand car salesman who'd just sold a pile of junk. But after a bit of consideration I grew more comfortable with it. After all, I wasn't selling anyone a pile of junk, and my jokes aren't *all* second-hand! On further reflection, I realised that this was indeed part of the anaesthetic that had seen me through some tough nights.

Much later I developed a theory about the showbiz smile. It must have been fabricated from the same stuff as the cannon used in the making of a Victoria Cross. And in a way I believe it's borne as a symbol like the bandanas worn by Japanese kamikaze pilots. It carries a message to all those on the other side of the footlights: 'So what if I die? At least I'll do so with honour!' Come to think of it, there are more than a few similarities between the armed forces and us. I know it's rather a dubious analogy but there are those among us who consider certain places of entertainment as battlefields and approach them accordingly. Sadly many artistes have died in the line of duty, metaphorically speaking.

Believe it or not, showbiz is often looked upon by the public as a duty rather than a profession. Forgive my cynicism, but if I'm ever invited to a party, for example, guess who's always asked to 'sing us a song' or 'give us a tune on the piano'? Right first time: yours truly. They'd never ask a soldier to shoot a few people or lay mines if he went to a do, or goad the local bricklayer to get his trowel out for the girls and show them his Flemish bond. 'But it's my night off,' I always tried to explain. And what happens? The inevitable mutterings of 'Miserable sod . . .'

You see, entertaining has never been looked upon by the public at large as being a proper job, but believe me it is – at least to my way of thinking. Like any other profession, we provide a service and expect to be paid for it. We have to pay our bills and taxes just like anyone else. But it's comforting to know that we're not on our own in this situation. I read somewhere that a doctor found himself faced with similar circumstances. Whenever he attended a social gathering people always pestered him about their ailments and illnesses. He got so fed up with it that he sought advice from a lawyer who was attending the same function. The lawyer told him that the best way to stop them doing it was to send them a bill. 'What a great idea!' said the doctor. 'Why didn't I think of that?' The next day he received a bill from the lawyer . . .

I don't blame people for thinking showbiz is a doddle, but the majority don't seem to realise how stressful the business can be. You've probably heard the saying that you're only as good as your last show? It's so true.

I've never found it easy to switch off from my profession. This is quite commonplace and happens at all levels – even the big stars don't have impunity, as my next story illustrates. For years my mother ran a market stall in Dewsbury, selling fruit and later sweets. The market was just a stone's throw from the Dewsbury Empire Theatre. All the big stars came there, and occasionally Mum took us to see some of the shows. I remember seeing Morecambe and Wise doing pantomime when they were just starting out, as well as old-time music hall acts like Frank Randle, Old Mother Riley and Albert Modley. What I admired about them most was that they could stand in front of all those people without fear, and make them laugh; but now I know it wasn't always the case.

Among the actors who joined the Empire's repertory company to learn their trade was the actor/entertainer, and ex-husband of Joan Collins, Anthony Newley. Sometimes he wandered round the market on his day off and often called at my mother's stall to buy sweets and chat. She even got his autograph for me and I was 'made up', having previously seen him at the cinema playing the Artful Dodger in the film *Oliver Twist*. This prompted me to follow his career with interest, and I read everything I could about him. Many years later I saw him doing an interview on television and something he said evoked a great surge of empathy inside me. He said that when he had an engagement in the evening it coloured his day. I knew exactly what he meant. It's as if your mind's permanently distracted: you can't devote your full attention to what you're doing. This to me was one of the less endearing aspects of showbiz. A lot of people are able to start work when they get there and forget about it when they leave, but my gig starts the moment I wake up. The countdown's already started before I get out of bed. Whatever I do during the day the clock's always ticking; every second is a step nearer to something that could end in complete satisfaction or absolute humiliation.

Accompanying the clock there is, more often than not, a little voice constantly planting little seedlings of doubt. 'I hope they'll be a good audience tonight – not like the other night . . .' I try to ignore it, and concentrate on something else, like a new joke or song, but still the voice continues. 'After all, there've been a few redundancies in that area. Folk won't be in the best of spirits . . .' I try to steer my thoughts in another direction, but it's hopeless. Nothing can ever be taken for granted in showbiz, because the shadow of insecurity is a constant companion. This is why so many personalities turn to drink and other distractions to get them through. So I bumble through my day, and by the time I'm humping my equipment into the car I can sometimes be so wound up that I could readily exchange responsibilities with a toilet attendant in Addis Ababa. It's even worse when there's a long drive to the venue: there's more time to stew in your own insecurity.

What's the worst scenario? I'll give you an example. I arrive at a club to find the gig is upstairs, and there's no lift. So I lug a few hundredweight of gear up two or three flights to be greeted by the sight of the stage (if there is one!) at the far end of the room. The tables and chairs are set out at random, so before I can get to my place of work I have to navigate my way through a maze of furniture. And these situations are never without incident. More than once I've swept ashtrays off tables with my suitcase or towed a chair with the strap of my shoulder bag.

Eventually my gear's safely deposited on the stage and it's time to face my next ordeal – finding the dressing room. The first door I try is locked. The next one is filled with chairs stacked to the ceiling, leaving just enough room for two industrial vacuum cleaners and a polisher. There's a sink, but it's hidden behind a stack of plastic containers containing bleach and disinfectant. Sometimes, to add a touch of surrealism, a newly opened carton of bingo cards is casually placed on top of a mop bucket. So, where do I get changed? My wardrobe case slung over my left arm, I gingerly walk along the back drapes of the stage, prodding at intervals in the hope of detecting a recess that might contain a nail, even a mirror. No such luck. My quest is interrupted by the arrival of the club steward. 'We don't use them any more, lad. You'll be getting changed in the committee room downstairs. Hang on, I'll get you the key and show you where it is.'

A few seconds later I'm carrying my bag and wardrobe case

down the same stairs I've just carried them up. I follow the steward down a passage into a games room where the regulars view me with apprehension. I can almost hear them thinking out loud as they pot their snooker balls and shuffle their cards, 'Huh, another one who doesn't know what hard work is!' And I'm thinking, isn't show business wonderful?

My mouth is dry, of course – fear? So I dump my belongings on the committee room table and make my way to the games room bar to order a soft drink.

'Anything else?'

'No thanks.'

The steward hands me my drink and punches the till. 'That'll be seventy pence.'

I reach into my pocket. Shit, I've only got a tenner – he's going to love me. I hand him the note. 'Sorry, I've got nothing less.'

He doesn't believe me. His look says it all.

I return to the 'dressing room', my trouser pocket bulging with damp pound coins, fifty pences, twenty pences, five pences and coppers. Thank heaven the farthing went out of circulation. Waiting for me is the concert chairman. 'I want three spots from you tonight – the first at eight o' clock.'

'But it's five to already!'

'Well, you'd better start getting ready then, 'adn't you?'

'But there's only four people in – and two of them are behind the bar.'

'Don't worry. They'll start to come in once you've started.'

So I begin to undress, with a mental picture of hundreds of people milling outside the club, patiently waiting for me to burst into song so they can enter. And just as I'm enjoying my brief moment of self-deception a member of the committee enters, leaving the door open to all and sundry. 'Need to get some raffle tickets,' he mutters, beginning to open cupboards. The snooker players treat the sight of me standing there in just my underpants with complete indifference. I close the door and begin to dress. The raffle tickets are collected and carried away, and once more the door is left wide open.

I feel I must make a few observations on what some so-called mannerly people consider to be adequate facilities for the use of artistes engaged to entertain them. Back in the '60s there was great jubilation surrounding a club in South Yorkshire that had been rebuilt at great cost. The group I was with at the time, along with two other acts, was booked for the grand opening. The committee placed great emphasis on the facilities provided for the members to enjoy. No expense had been spared.

We arrived to find that there wasn't even a dressing room, leaving the five in our group and the two other acts with nowhere to change. I pointed this out to the president of the club, who in turn directed me towards the architect – busy quaffing the free champers placed at his disposal. Amid all the backslapping and mutual high regard that was going on between him and the rest of the committee, I mentioned our problem to him. I can't say I was really surprised by his reply. 'The toilets are right next to the stage. Get changed there!'

We actually got changed in the van. And we also set up our own sound system. Groups at that time usually carried their own set-up, which was fortunate for us: unbelievably, the club had re-installed the system from the old club – a thirty bob mike plugged into a five watt system driving two six inch speakers: a 'state of the ark' set-up if ever I'd seen one. All this to serve a room seating five hundred people!

Surprisingly, very few clubs provided what could be termed first-class dressing rooms. Most were too small and hot water was a rare commodity. The bigger, more affluent clubs were often the worst offenders. Those subsidised by the National Coal Board were usually pretty good; occasionally we even had the luxury of a shower at our disposal.

It's something I could never understand. Union men, who quite rightly fought for better working conditions over the years, ran most of the working men's clubs, but for some reason seemed oblivious to the conditions we were subjected to. My own union (Equity) held no sway in the northern clubs, and was as useless as men's nipples so far as I could see.

I remember inviting a good friend to come and see my show at the Miners Welfare near to where he lived. He was the top union official at the local pit and only used the club on odd occasions. I was in the dressing room when he came backstage to greet me. He looked around in disbelief. 'What's all this?' he asked, looking horrified.

'All what?' I replied, thinking I was missing something.

He shook his head. 'Is this where they expect you to get changed?'

'Well . . . yes,' I shrugged – slightly surprised.

'Where's the shower?'

'They're probably sitting in the committee room,' I replied – being my usual flippant self.

'Do you mean you've got nowhere to get showered when you've finished working?'

'Listen, I'm lucky to have a nail to hang my clothes on.'.

He walked over to the sink, which was coming away from the wall. 'This is a disgrace . . . And they expect . . .' He broke off to examine the hole in the windowpane. After a few moments' reflection he turned and walked out, shaking his head, leaving me to wonder why. It couldn't have been anything I said, could it?

Minutes later he returned with half a dozen shame-faced characters shuffling behind him. They hung their heads as he berated them for allowing conditions like this to exist under their stewardship. One by one he pointed out each shortcoming. 'No soap – no towel – no hot water – no plug – no carpet – no heating. Call yourself union men? One look at these conditions and you lot would've walked out o' t'pit. And you expect this lad to . . .' On and on he went – and with every word their heads sunk lower and lower until they'd have hidden under the rug if there'd been one.

Without wishing to dwell on the lack of integrity of others, I've never lost sight of the fact that showbiz has been a great learning curve for me. Years of confrontation and compromise have toughened me up in more ways than one, and taught me to face up to the misuse of authority. Like the time I was about to go on stage to entertain a packed house during the festive season. It was a very popular local club and people were swinging from the rafters. There were no coat hangers or nails, so I placed my stage clothes on the only chair in the dressing room and began to get changed. I'd only just removed my sweater when the door opened and in walked a stocky individual. Without so much as a by your leave, the cheeky sod picked my clothes up, dropped them on the floor and grabbed the chair. 'What do you think you're doing?' I shouted, pulling my sweater back on.

'I need this for my wife,' he said, without even looking at me.

I snatched the chair back and snapped, 'Well, bugger off and get one from somewhere else!' He glared at me. 'You've got no right to come barging in here – this is my dressing room!'

'Well, I'm telling you I've got every right – I'm the president here!'

'I don't give a bugger who you are. This room's for the artiste and it's off limits to you.'

He pointed his finger at me and hissed, 'Listen here, you. You're the paid servant, and you'll do as you're . . .'

I didn't wait for him to finish. I put the chair down and grabbed my belongings and case. 'I'm nobody's servant, mate – and you can stick your precious club up your arse.' I pushed past him and began weaving my way through the crowd. He stood open-mouthed at the dressing room door, and I called to him over my shoulder, 'I'll pick up the rest of my gear tomorrow.'

The audience, well aware by now that there'd been some kind of altercation, began to buzz with speculation. I could hear whispers of 'Where's he going?' and 'What's happened?' as I pushed through the doors.

I was making my way to my car when the club secretary caught up with me. 'Where're you going, Sam? What's the matter?' He looked at me inquiringly and I stopped. He was a really nice bloke, and I felt I owed him an explanation. He shook his head as I took him through the chain of events leading up to my abrupt departure. He was incensed by the way I'd been treated and sympathised with me completely, but appealed to my better nature by pointing out that a lot of people (including my own fans) were going to lose out on a full night's entertainment because of one dick-head. 'It isn't their fault,' he pleaded.

I relented, of course – but not before I'd received a full apology from the president.

Chapter Twenty
SWEET REALITY, AND BACK DOWN TO EARTH

Meanwhile, back on the home front . . . The '70s were in full swing, and fortune seemed to be smiling on me for a change. I was as happy as could be and my mood must have animated my creative side. Music and lyrics were pouring forth constantly. I had ideas coming all the time, and my music publisher Ron Randall at Acuff-Rose was well pleased to say the least. Coupled with this, the act was in demand and the date book was full. The only drawback was that there never seemed to be enough time to do anything else. Everything seemed to be happening at once, which at times could be very frustrating. And I was constantly being warned by a voice inside me that things were heading in the same direction as they had been when I'd had my breakdown.

Within a couple of years of being married I was writing, recording and performing, in between popping down to London to meet people and pitch songs. Added to this, I desperately wanted to be near Mandy, to dote on her every moment. But life doesn't always go along with what you want, and many's the time when you disregard the wake up calls that are tossed into what you think is a perfect situation. Trouble is never far away. The moment you take your eye off the ball your feet can be swept from under you. While I was distracted by concerns over my mental fortitude, and my ability to cope with the pressures of providing for my family, situations closer to home escaped my notice.

All marriages come under pressure, and ours was no exception. Although I didn't realise it, most of my time was taken up with my work. The music business is like that. Everyone wants everything now – not tomorrow or three weeks next Wednesday, but now. Maybe this is because there's always that feeling in the back of your mind that it could all end at any moment. So while the ideas were coming I had to see them through. And this began to take its toll. Sometimes I was so mentally exhausted that I wasn't fit for anything – but I never felt I'd crack up again. I always seemed to know when to say whoa.

Mandy also helped. Her presence seemed to have a calming effect on me. On occasion her energy seemed to make up for my lack of it. I made it my task to bring a little order into my life, so I was able to enjoy first hand those memorable little moments. Months before her first birthday she was walking unaided, and I'm sure if I'd left the keys in the car she'd have had a go at that too! Tripping over teddies and wooden toys didn't bother me much, and there was always an element of comedy in trying to fit a rigid-legged infant into a high chair. And who can forget Tommee Tippee mugs and plastic bibs with the trough at the bottom containing soggy rusks floating about in goo? The memories will last for ever . . .

Even our dog Sadie seemed happy with everything – I suspect the main reason being that there was always food being scattered or dropped from Mandy's high chair. Sadie must have thought it was worth being hit by a plastic spoon or dish because she was always beside her at meal times. In fact as time went on she became quite protective of her secondary food source and followed her just about everywhere. Just as well she did, too. On one occasion Mandy, who'd not long been walking, disappeared from the garden. She was playing with her toys on the front lawn when the phone rang. I went inside and picked up the phone, which was in the lounge. As I spoke I glanced through the window to keep an eye on Mandy and saw to my horror that she was no longer there. With my heart in my mouth I raced into the garden: there was no sign of her. All the gardens around were open plan, so I could see down the road. Sadie was standing in the driveway of the house four doors down, which was having an extension built at the rear. She looked at me and then down the driveway. I tore round the back to find Mandy four rungs up a ladder propped up against the extension. Needless to say that from that day on we all went to answer the phone if it rang while we were in the garden —Sadie too!

So there I was, thinking the '70s were being good to me . . . I had a few songs on a couple of best-selling albums and another version of my song 'Ain't It All Worth Living For' by Mack White had just gone into the American country charts, again earning me another ASCAP award. The resulting royalties from their chart success meant I didn't have to go out working on an evening as much either – and I got to spend a few evenings relaxing with my feet up in front of the telly. I enjoyed being at home in the day, as it meant I was always on hand to see to Mandy and give Dot time to escape the drudge of everyday routine. She started having a few nights out with her friends too. I wasn't bothered about going out in the evening, as I found it too much like work. The only trouble with this arrangement was that we eventually found ourselves living separate lives. While I was busy directing all my attentions to our little daughter and my work, I completely overlooked the fact that my wife might need some attention too. And when an attractive young wife isn't getting enough attention at home, there's always someone in the away team ready to score.

Having always been a bit naïve where women are concerned I never saw it coming, and when I was eventually told that she'd met someone else I couldn't believe it; I thought it was a joke. But when the cold truth dawned I was left with a feeling of utter dejection. In the past I'd written songs about betrayal without understanding it, but now I was beginning to experience its true meaning. As I was the injured party, friends and family rallied round and were very helpful, but this didn't restore my busted ego. To compound matters, it came when everything seemed to be going in my favour. It happened not long after I had returned from a reception at the Performing Rights Society in London, to receive my second ASCAP award. Everyone who was anyone was there, and I really thought the door of opportunity was beginning to open. I was introduced to top record producers who were anxious to hear my work and was given an open invitation to call and see them without even having to make an appointment. I'd grown to love writing and enjoyed being involved in the recording industry, but I had no hesitation in deciding that my ambitions would have to be set aside for a while. This wasn't just about two people losing their way: it was about Mandy. As far as I was concerned she had to be the first priority. Our little one was blissfully unaware of what was happening, and I'd made a promise to her when she first came into the world: a promise I intended to keep no matter what. Unfortunately, more often than not these situations can't be resolved without some upset or ill feeling, and this was no exception.

It was doubly sad because initially things were quite amicable. I've always been a realist, and it was obvious to me that Dot was totally besotted by the new man in her life. She'd gone to live with him, and there was no way we could carry on the way we were. The only issue up for discussion, as far as I was concerned, was Mandy's future. To begin with, we agreed that Mandy should stay with me. Everything seemed to go smoothly: I re-mortgaged the house and settlements were made to what I thought was everyone's benefit. There was very little for the solicitors to do, which I've since suspected could have been the catalyst behind the ensuing chain of events. I've never had much regard for solicitors. I'm sure there are some who try to uphold the principles of true justice, but in my experience the smell of a few bob to be made can completely overwhelm the delicately refined fragrance of integrity.

Out of the blue, after I thought that everything was settled, the custody of Mandy became an issue. There followed a very unpleasant battle, the details of which I feel are not worthy of mention in a book that's supposed to be a celebration of life. Baskets of dirty washing were washed in public, benefiting no one and ultimately serving to make what had been an endurable situation completely intolerable. A lot of bad blood and bitterness followed, along with the inevitable sleepless nights. This only served to put up barriers that weren't originally there, and created an atmosphere of mistrust. Fortunately little Mandy wasn't old enough for this to have any effect on her, but the fact that it might in later years frightened me to death. It's an ordeal I never wish to go through again: I'd rather have someone stick pins in my eyes than suffer the nightmare of that hearing.

But with the benefit of hindsight, coupled with a lot of soul searching, I feel sure that the right decision was made. The authorities opted to maintain the status quo and let Mandy stay in her own home, with me looking after her. It meant, of course, that I wouldn't be running back and forth to London every five minutes any more, which would probably affect my song-writing career, but I wasn't bothered. I felt that I'd got my priorities right, and have never wavered from that opinion.

Although she may not realise it, even to this day, Mandy was the catalyst that brought changes in the lives of many different people. Everyone went out of their way, sometimes acting completely out of character, to ensure that she wouldn't witness any bitterness or bad feelings. Prejudices were put aside when opposing parties came into contact with each other. Both families rallied round to make her life as happy as could be – and in doing so many of us discovered more than a few hidden virtues! Today we're all a bit older and a lot wiser. We had the good sense to ignore our differences and make sure that Mandy would grow up in the knowledge that she was loved and protected by all of us. There were no barriers or prejudices. There were no grudges borne. Mandy helped a lot of grown people to grow up.

It's you and me against the world, kid
Heartened by the knowledge that Mandy would now not have to face any major upheaval, I settled down to get on with things as best I could. After the custody hearing I didn't celebrate. Nothing had been won or lost. Only time would tell if the judgement would be vindicated, and all I could do was make sure it was.

I vividly remember the first time I was alone after everyone else had gone. The house was strangely silent. Mandy was in her usual place – sitting in the crook of my arm – and we stared out of the back window. There's always been a nice view out there, one that I'm drawn to whenever I have anything to mull over. I pulled out a chair, and Mandy clung to my neck as we sat down. 'Well, it's just you and me now, kid,' I said, giving her a little squeeze with my arm. Just then I felt a little nudge as a moist nose nuzzled my hand. Sadie gently poked her face under my other arm. She looked up at me with such sympathetic eyes that I felt ashamed for ignoring her. 'Sorry, girl, I forgot about you, didn't I? You'd have missed her too, wouldn't you? All those tasty titbits falling from her high chair!' As I made a fuss of her, I said, 'So here we are, then – the three musketeers.' Sadie gave a little sigh in agreement. I didn't know whether to laugh or cry; and I settled for the tears.

But of course it wasn't just the three of us. Help came from everywhere. Michelle (Mandy's cousin) elected to sleep in her room with her a few nights of the week. Mandy enjoyed this and gained much from it. It was like having a surrogate big sister around and I'm sure Michelle benefited too, for today she is an excellent mother. My sister-in-law June (Michelle's mother) was always on hand too. Having three children of her own, she gave me plenty of much-needed advice during the years that followed. And there were always four doting grandparents to fall back on. I was also very touched by the support I received from friends and neighbours. I know it's a natural reaction, and in most cases has a tendency to be temporary, but I can say in all honesty that never once did it wane. Whenever I'm told I did a good job bringing up Mandy I'm flattered, but I can't deny that I had a lot of help from a lot of good people.

Dot, to her credit, never tried to buy Mandy's affections. She continued to see her regularly, and resisted the temptation to spoil her or refrain from disciplining her if it was ever needed.

So, where did this all leave me on the showbiz front? I still had to earn a living, but it was now limited to two gigs a week — during which I also had to run the gauntlet of gossip! Things felt different in many ways. My wife jokes didn't seem to have the same impact, as the punters knew we were no longer together. News of my marriage break-up had spread like wildfire: I was well aware of the whispers and nudges in the audience. Songs began to take on a new meaning. Bobby Vee's hit song 'Take Good Care of My Baby' nearly brought me to tears when I was singing it, because for the first time it brought to mind what would have happened if I'd not been given custody of Mandy. I'd never allowed that possibility to enter my thoughts: she was the whole focus of my life and I couldn't imagine being parted from her.

There'd been the chance to go to Nashville to join Acuff-Rose as a staff writer, or go to work in Australia on the back of the success of 'Penny Arcade', but I don't think this would have served any purpose. True, I might have been a success, I might even have 'made it', but I now know for certain that I'd have been totally miserable. All this speculation was academic, though. The die was cast, and I just had to get on with life. Financially I wasn't on the breadline, but electing to do fewer gigs meant I had less money to chuck around. Even so, this didn't stop me lashing out a few bob at holiday time and during the festive season.

The first holiday we went on was to Torquay (I told you expense was no object!). I don't know how it came about, but Mandy and I — along with Grandpa Twohig and my brother's family — booked into a hotel. It might even have been the one that inspired *Fawlty Towers*. I suspect it had been designed by Heath Robinson after a night on the sauce, and it was fraught with staff problems. The chef was prone to going on strike, which meant the proprietor had to take the helm in the kitchen. It was obvious to us all when this happened because the soup was tasteless and the dessert was always arctic roll. The only person not put out was Mandy. She was just 'happy to be' and she adored arctic roll (I'm not sure she still does, though). Like me, she's always had a sweet tooth and is easily seduced by calorie-packed ice cream and gooey cakes. On that particular holiday she showed to what extent she'd go to get either of them.

We were all sitting in a quaint little café called the Copper Kettle having afternoon tea, my brother's treat. Mandy, perched in a high chair, had just made short work of a buttered scone, and watched as a waitress parked a trolley next to her bearing a huge black forest gateau, neatly sliced into sections. Instinctively she reached out to grab it. Quickly I grabbed her hand, only for her to try to grab it with her other one. I grabbed her other hand but even that didn't deter her. With mouth wide open she lunged toward the trolley and buried her face in the magnificent confection. Chaos descended, but not before the whole café was reduced to fits of laughter. The sight of Mandy's face covered in glazed cherries and cream will stay with me for ever. So too will the expression on my brother's face as he paid the bill, which included nearly half a gateau.

There were many more unforgettable episodes during the years that followed. Any designs I'd held of trying to crack the big time were forfeited without any regret, for now it was blatantly clear where my responsibilities lay. Watching Mandy grow into a happy little girl was worth more to me than anything the music business had to offer. For most of my life I'd bumbled along without really knowing my true purpose – and on many occasions I've been accused of lacking ambition. This I've always countered with the excuse that I didn't really know what I wanted! But now, at last, I'd found something I *really* wanted to do – and to succeed in. But it wasn't easy.

Mandy was only eighteen months old when her future was entrusted to me. Who and what she would become, when the time came for her to take her place in society, was my responsibility. The first few years were sprinkled with the obligatory sleepless nights and worry, usually brought on by the pain and frustrations of childhood ailments, whereas the need for eyes in the back of my head and an unrelenting intuition were a necessary requirement. The list of things to remember and to do was endless, but even the most taxing day could be rewarding. A big hug for Daddy followed by a sloppy kiss in payment for a bedtime story was all that was required. And regardless of the accolades I've received over the years, if anyone asks me what my greatest achievement is in life I'd have to say my daughter.

The most memorable occasion during those early years was a Christmas that marked an awakening for me. I was awoken by the sound of Mandy stirring in her bedroom. A prolonged yawn was abruptly interrupted by what I assumed to be her sudden realisation that it was Christmas! This was immediately followed by the sound of little footsteps tearing down the stairs. My concern for her safety was soon quashed by the sound of wrapping paper being torn to shreds in the lounge below. The tearing stopped, the pitter-patter of footsteps returned and my bedroom door, which had been slightly ajar, was flung open. 'He's *been*!' Mandy sighed, her eyes shining with excitement. 'And he's brought me a pram!' Pitter-patter, pitter-patter, down she went again, and once more wrapping paper was torn apart. Pitter-patter, pitter-patter, up she came. 'And he's brought me a doll!' she gasped, hardly able to contain herself in her excitement. Pitter-patter, pitter-patter, up and down she went. The stair carpet must have been scorched for the next half-hour, as I was given a running inventory of every single one of her presents.

It was a wonderful Christmas. Everybody seemed to have put aside their differences, and Mandy's happiness was evident. She played and played, and come bedtime she offered no resistance to being put to bed. Although it was obvious she was tired, a beaming smile never left her face as I tucked her in. She didn't ask for her usual bedtime story, but instead lay quietly staring out of the window into the night sky. I sat on her bed and looked out across the frost-covered landscape twinkling below. Moonlight tinged everything in sight with a silvery glow. The whole scene was reminiscent of a classic Christmas card. It was one of those moments that must have inspired the line 'God's in his heaven, all's right with the world.'

We sat quietly for a few moments, basking in a wonderful feeling of contentedness, until Mandy's questioning voice broke the silence. 'Daddy,' she said, without shifting her gaze. 'What's that?' She pointed out of the window.

'That's the moon,' I said, tucking her blankets in. 'Now it's time for you to go to sleep.'

She still had one of those faraway looks on her face as I walked away. Before I reached the door her little voice piped up inquiringly, 'Daddy . . . will you buy me a moon?'

It stopped me in my tracks. In her innocence she didn't realise the magnitude or significance of what she'd said, but it still had a profound effect on me. Maybe it was an emotional time of year and the feel good factor was in full flow, but it still elicited something inside me that made me feel really special. My little girl, in one sentence, had put me on a par with Superman! All the applause, awards, plaudits and rewards I'd received over the years couldn't live up to the feeling I experienced that moment. To someone else it might just have passed as a lovely thought or nice sentiment, but for some reason it had a marked effect on me. Not only did it make my eyes moist, but for the first time I knew the true meaning of the phrase 'made it in life'.

The next few years were spent trying to ensure Mandy was put on the right track and given a good start in life. Like all children she had her moments, and finding the right punishment was usually harder on me than her. I had to play good cop/bad cop all the time. When she was naughty she had to be punished. It broke my heart to hear her sobbing in bed alone, with no one else to turn to. Measuring the time before I went to cuddle her better never got any easier, and I know I suffered more than she did.

But as time went by we settled into a routine that seemed to suit us both. Mandy was always a quick learner, and as she grew older she became a great help to me, making her own contributions to the running of our home. This also gave me more time to catch up with my music.

A good friend and neighbour at that time – John Wagstaff – came round to see me one day. He ran a management agency at that time and was responsible for launching the pop group Black Lace and later took over management of Smokie. Knowing my position with Mandy, he came up with a wonderful idea. One of the London agencies had asked him for acts suitable to entertain families of holidaymakers abroad in the 'Pontinental Holiday Complexes', and he wondered if I'd be interested, adding that I could take Mandy along too. After being assured that provisions would be made for her to be well looked after, I agreed.

What followed was a wonderful adventure for both of us. By this time Mandy had started school, so we arranged to fly out to Greece and later Tenerife during the school holidays. Not only was it the first time she'd been abroad, it was the first time she had flown. Mandy grew up a lot during that holiday: meeting people from different places and backgrounds seemed to add to her confidence.

It was good for me too. I was used to working alone, but out there I was working with other artistes including the American vocal group The Platters and a young Frenchman who had the massive international hit 'Born to be Alive' in the '70s – Patrick Hernandez. The shows were first class, and it was certainly no hardship to perform to people who were already seduced by the exotic atmosphere.

Tenerife suited my act to a 'T' and I was offered a permanent job there. The money wasn't a fortune, but it would have cost nothing to live there as everything was included. They said that Mandy would be found a place in school, and was guaranteed to be bilingual within a couple of years. Though greatly tempted, I declined because of a number of factors – the main one being that my daughter would be separated from her extended family. Fortunately it turned out to be the right decision: the company changed hands and policy within eighteen months.

Never judge a club by the punter

So it was back to school for Mandy, with lots of exciting tales to tell (like climbing to the top of Mount Tedie, Tenerife's extinct volcano), and back to the grind for me.

Over the years, more often than not I've been blessed with audiences who listen and enjoy – but there are plenty who didn't. Some weren't even prepared to listen. Others listened but seemed determined not to enjoy. I remember telling a joke to what I was beginning to think was an all-Japanese audience. To my surprise a very nice lady burst out laughing, only to receive a sharp dig in the ribs from the man sitting next to her. She immediately clammed up, and that was the only laugh I got all night. It begs the question, 'Why do these people come in at all?' The only theory I can come up with is that they must have been forced in at gunpoint. A comedian once told me that he was sitting in the loo after doing his spot when he heard two members of the audience discussing his act.

'What do you think of the comedian?'

'I suppose he's all right – if you like laughing.'

There's nothing worse than sitting in a strange club waiting for someone to come in to be entertained. After you've broken your neck to get there on time, you're all set up ready to go – and there's no one in. The clock ticks on and on and the only sign of life is a spider weaving its web across the handles of the concert room door. Though this rarely happened to me in urban clubs it frequently happened in the rural areas: at harvesting time it was sometimes ten in the evening before anyone appeared. But you learn to take it all in your stride, and find something to amuse yourself with in the meantime.

Sometimes the process of the club filling up can be quite entertaining in itself. Long-standing patrons (especially female ones) often lay claim to certain seats in the concert room: 'the one I was sitting in when I won the jackpot at bingo' or 'the one I've sat in since the club opened'. So woe betides anyone who's unwittingly sitting in it when she walks in. The withering look the poor unfortunate would receive could be worthy of Medusa. It's happened to me on more than one occasion, and I've always moved in order to be exonerated. It can be an intimidating process.

But there are times when the 'it's my chair' scenario can apply for totally different reasons. When I was working solo, after Bill and I had parted company, Eric – my brother's brother-in-law – was helping with my equipment at a gig. Once he'd set everything up, Eric always preferred to sit near the dressing room door; I'd get a couple of drinks and would join him. The club was a bit out in the sticks (where men are men and sheep are grateful), and we'd been waiting for someone to come in, but an hour had passed and still there was no sign of life. 'They'll be coming in later,' the barman reassured us, polishing glasses at the same time. This particular evening we were sitting on an upholstered seat that stretched along the wall the length of the room. Before long the doors opened, then closed . . . but no one came in. At least we thought no one had – but from the partition that hid the lower half of the doors emerged a very small man and woman. As soon as they saw us they fixed us with a glare of disapproval as they clambered onto the seat further along from us. Eric and I looked at one another, shrugged and carried on with our conversation. Whenever we stopped to drink I looked towards the wee couple out of curiosity. I'd already noted that thanks to the shortness of their arms and legs they'd had difficulty climbing up onto the land saddle. And each time I looked I was met by the same stare.

Presently we heard chattering from behind the door. It opened – and they started to come in. We exchanged looks of disbelief as in walked the unlikeliest bunch of characters I'd ever seen. There was a young Chinese punk girl complete with safety pins and multicoloured spiked hair, a man so tall he had to duck to get through the door, a huge lady who was literally bursting out of one of the biggest frocks I'd ever seen, and bringing up the rear a woman who abused the right to be ugly. Then a Tarzan look-alike strutted in, with a bald-headed character with muscles on his muscles. 'It must be fancy dress night,' I surmised.

'No,' Eric fired back. 'There's definitely a circus in town.'

Soon the concert chairman came over to introduce himself, and we learned that neither was the case. 'They might look a bit odd but they're all OK – just a bit eccentric.'

'What about them two?' I asked, nodding towards the wee pair. 'They've been giving us mucky looks since they came in.'

'Ah, well,' smiled the chairman. 'You're sitting in their seats.'

'If that's all it is, tell them we don't mind moving.'

With that he went over and muttered to them. Immediately their faces lit up and they clambered down from their seat. Eric and I budged up, and they gave us a huge smile as they went to their seat – after bending down to pull out a step that was built in beneath it. This allowed them to climb up without any effort, and gave them something to place their feet on.

Despite our initial apprehension it turned out to be a great night and, being out in the sticks, the bar didn't close until . . . well, it didn't!

It's amazing how diverse social clubs can be. Tastes in music and comedy can vary from town to town. As I've mentioned, what goes well in one place can bomb out a couple of miles away. It can take years to 'read' an audience, and then just when you think you've got the hang of it you can fall flat on your face.

Right up to retirement I never stopped learning. It's been hard work at times, but it's provided a rich source of memories to look back on. It's also brought me into contact with a lot of good people, many of whom have become close friends.

I always enjoyed working the pit villages. For some reason most of the time they took to me – probably because I worked hard and saw to it that they got their money's worth. I think they appreciated that – and also the fact that I'd sit with them in between spots and chew the fat. I made lots of friends in the process, many of whom I still keep in touch with today. Getting to know the people of the mining communities gave me an insight into the many fine qualities they have that are so often overlooked by the majority of people in other parts of the country. Sure, they can be hard-headed, bolshie and militant. But in fairness, you'd need to have a certain uncompromising approach to life to do their job. And there's always another side to the coin. Let's not forget that these communities have produced their fair share of athletes, sportsmen, artists, poets, writers and conservationists, not to mention a wealth of musical talent – the Grimethorpe Colliery band, for instance.

I've always loved brass bands. For some reason they seem to be able to tap into sentiments within me that a philharmonic orchestra can't reach. How can anyone listen to the 'Grimey' rendition of Rodrigo's *'En Aranjuez Con Tu Amor'* and not fail to recognise the passion and feeling behind every note that stems from a history fraught not only with joy but also with more than its fair share of adversity. Grimethorpe! Who the hell gave the place that name? Like it or not it's now very well known after it featured in the hit film *Brassed Off*. Personally I love the place – and the surrounding villages. OK, so there are a few dick-heads who give the place a bad name now and then, but by and large most of the folk are great. After all, didn't they tell me not to leave my car round the back of the club when I performed there? Of course they did – and I'll be eternally grateful to them for doing so. They could have said nothing and let my car be set on fire, like those belonging to some of the other acts! Yes, it's little acts of kindness like those that I'll never forget – along with a few other things, of course.

Come to think of it, the first time I worked at the Grimethorpe working men's club the stage was being rebuilt: someone had set fire to the old one. Along with brass bands, pyromania must be a popular pastime too. I found it an awkward stage to work: as it was high and stretched across one corner of the room, I never seemed to be able to face the audience square on. It also had a raised edge running across the front, which hid your feet. I could have gone on barefoot and no one would have noticed. But it's just as well that I didn't one night, when, although the stage wasn't easily accessible, one young lady joined me on it. This was in the 1990s, when I'd been working solo for a number of years. She was celebrating her hen party, and it was quite obvious that she and her friends were three sheets to the wind. When I started my dance spot I wasn't surprised when they all got up to dance. Almost immediately I was inundated with slurred

Who could forget Black Lace, with such pop classics as 'Agadoo' and 'Vino Collapso'? I did the art work for the dance moves that featured on the record sleeves.

In 2007 Linda and I visited a club in Nashville, and I got called up on stage to sing with current country star Brenda Best. It seems the courier we were with had told the management that they had a celebrity in the audience. I looked around to see who they meant . . . it was me.

Me and my lovely wife Linda, 2009.

Me and my 'minder' Tommy Mitchell. Tommy became my roadie following an illustrious career as the bouncer at Batley Variety Club.

Still playing today. This was taken in the Pile Bar in Bradford. where the first Rock'n'Roll reunions took place.

My 'fame' took me to many events, and I am seen here with snooker legend John Virgo at a charity match.

My 'minder' and friend Tommy Mitchell with Roy Orbison at Batley Variety Club requests for this song and that song, which I did my best to comply with. But obviously my programme wasn't to their taste, and midway through a Drifters song I was horrified to witness the bride-to-be being hoisted onto the stage by her friends. Oh no! I thought. That's all I need.

She staggered towards me, resplendent in tight miniskirt and high-heeled shoes. A bridal head-dress decorated with objects and a rude message swept down to her jacket, which was bedecked with dozens of condoms containing what I hoped was condensed milk. I ignored her to begin with and, moving away, continued to sing. 'You're more than a number in my little red book,' I twittered. 'More than a one night date . . .' When I turned round she was swaying and grinning at me.

''ets twist again . . .' she seemed to slur above the music.

'Don't know it,' I quickly replied, and warbled on. 'All I had to take me was just one look . . .'

''wist missain!' she slurred, louder this time.

By this time I was getting really fed up, so I broke off singing. 'Look! For the last time I don't know "Let's Twist Again".'

'No,' she said, pointing to the floor. 'Av PISSED mi'sen.'

And she had. Around her feet was a pool that was getting larger as she spoke. On seeing the look on my face her mates began to cheer. This brought on a fit of giggles from the bride-to-be, which made the pool get even bigger, engulfing the cables and footswitch lying around the stage. Her mates lifted her back down from the stage and dispatched her to the toilet, cheering and shouting on the way.

I finished my spot and paddled back to the dressing room. I took off my boots, placed them on a radiator to dry the soles, and sat down to savour the aroma while I gathered my thoughts. I could still hear the hen party laughing and singing in the concert room over the shouts of 'Come on you lot. Sup up and fuck off. It's time to go home!' from the club steward.

Tommy, my roadie, had gone onto the stage and was dismantling the equipment. I'd better warn him about the piddling pool, I thought. Too late! 'Aaarrggghh!' I could hear swearing coming from the stage. Tommy came into the dressing room, winding one of the wet speaker wires around his arm. 'Some silly get has spilt beer all over the stage, and the leads are sodden,' he complained.

'I'm sorry, mate,' I apologised. 'I meant to tell you about that. Er . . . it's not beer . . . well, not now it isn't.'

Tommy selected an appropriate swear word, muttered it under his breath and continued to wind the cable around his arm.

Tommy

Good old Tom: one of life's true characters. He was one of those people you could never forget once you'd met him, which in my case was back in the 1950s when I liked to hang around the local coffee bars, listening to the jukebox and playing the pinball machines. My best mate George was well into rock climbing and other outdoor pursuits at this time, and as I was still dabbling about in the music business our paths didn't cross as much.

I was in 'Ma's' coffee bar in Batley putting an Elvis song on the jukebox for the umpteenth time when through the door bustled this burly character whose face looked as if it had been around a bit. He ordered a tea and looked round to see who was in. Spotting a few acquaintances, he fired a few 'How do's' across the room, collected his tea and came across to where I was sitting. 'Y'all right?' he asked.

I nodded. He sat down and started talking to me as if I had known him all my life. And strangely enough, after a few minutes it felt as if I had. He prattled on about how he'd just finished his national service and was going to make up for lost time. I liked him straight away. He seemed confident, and laughed and smiled a lot as he went on to tell me about his time in the Army boxing team – which accounted for his craggy looks and the absence of half of his front teeth.

But these minor alterations to his looks didn't seem to bother him; in fact nothing ever did. He had a capacity to block out anything remotely connected with worry or apathy. His greatest asset was his confidence – which knew no bounds. This, most definitely, accounted for the numerous women he was involved with over the years. He loved them all – tall ones, short ones, fat ones, thin ones. Whether it was the most stunning of beauties or the unfortunate 'stick-fetcher', it didn't matter to Tom. In his eyes they were all fair game. One of his favourite sayings was 'I've had women every colour except green – and that's only because I haven't met one yet!'

Born under the sign of Cancer, he was always on the move, and he loved the company of people. Occasionally he liked to throw parties. They were usually boozy and noisy affairs and his house could easily have been mistaken for the local bus station, such was the volume of traffic going in and out. The local off-licence usually did well when Tommy had a do, as the beer always seemed to run out before the revellers did. One year, on top of the usual quota of beer, he added a nine-gallon barrel. It made no difference. The revellers turned on the tap, took turns lying underneath it, and in no time it was empty.

One of his mates, a little guy called Johnny, was a very amiable person – until he started drinking. Then it was Jekyll and Hyde time. After a few drinks he wanted to fight everybody, and became a real pain in the arse. Tommy got so fed up with him one time that he gave him a slap, picked him up and hung him by his coat on a hook on the back of the front door. He was still there the next morning snoozing away, swinging backwards and forwards every time someone left or entered.

In the time I knew Tommy, which was over forty years, he only harboured two ambitions. The first was to meet a green woman . . . the second - which he had right up to the day he died - was to return to Hong Kong where he did most of his national service. They were the happiest days of his life but also, tragically, the saddest.

Being in the boxing team, for some reason he was granted special dispensation to stay off camp. He took up with a Chinese girl, who eventually bore him twins. He regularly visited her in a flat he helped her to rent outside the barracks. One day when he went there he found the twins missing. His girlfriend's lack of concern rankled with him and after a lot of screaming and shouting it came to light that she'd sold them. Having heard he was due to be posted back home, she'd decided she wouldn't be able to support them. Tommy went mad. He smashed every stick of furniture in the flat, piled it in the middle of the room and set fire to it. It was only the intervention of neighbours investigating the fracas that stopped him throwing her on the top of it too.

This episode had a marked effect on Tommy. He had children from two later marriages, which failed, but lost touch with them when his ex-wives moved away. This is probably one of the reasons why he made a great fuss of kids wherever he went. Tommy doted on kids, and they in turn loved him. He went out of his way to amuse them by doing little tricks with coins and things. Maybe it was his way of compensating for the loss of his own children.

During the '70s Tommy became head doorman at the famous Batley Variety Club, meeting just about every big star who appeared there. He was extremely proud of a photograph album he kept, in which he was pictured rubbing shoulders with the likes of Shirley Bassey and Tom Jones. He loved being involved in show business. For ten years he acted as my roadie, and was in his element strutting round the clubs wearing a t-shirt emblazoned with the words 'ON THE ROAD WITH SAMMY (Mr PENNY ARCADE) KING'.

On top of being a very good roadie, Tommy was also a very good minder and was adept at dealing with troublesome punters. I recall one particular notoriously rough club where I was appearing. While I was on stage a couple of yobbos sneaked into my dressing room. This escaped my notice, but not Tom's. Seconds later my opening song was interrupted as the dressing room door was flung open and the two yobs were ejected. They slunk out of the club and didn't return – but after the show, we went outside to find my car's two electric wing-mirrors ripped off and smashed, which prompted Tommy to lament, 'I should have broken their fuckin' arms before I slung 'em out!'

Tommy died from a heart attack in 1999. He'd been suffering from angina for a while and could no longer pursue his duties as my roadie – but that didn't stop him coming along for the ride. He loved the showbiz life more than I did. Thankfully the last gig we went on was a good one. The club was nice, the people were friendly and receptive and Tom even won a game of bingo – after borrowing a quid from me to buy a ticket!

Going on a gig was never the same without Tom – God bless him. Even so, the car responded a little quicker, and it drove differently – probably because the nearside suspension was no longer sitting down.

So where did this leave me? Long before Tommy died I'd given a lot of thought to gradually cutting out performing on stage altogether. My bad leg was giving me a lot of pain, but simple economics put paid to any of that. I just had to carry on.

Mandy, apart from the usual mandatory teenage blips, was doing well at school without causing too much trouble, and, being an independent soul, seemed quite capable of making more of her own decisions. So apart from being the source of interest free loans, there wasn't much for me to worry about on her account. My responsibilities as a single parent were diminishing rapidly and I thought it might be a good time to start writing songs again.

My good mate Waggers (John Wagstaff) was in the process of launching the group Black Lace to fame with 'Superman' and

'Agadoo'. He'd made a few good connections and said he'd be only too pleased to promote my stuff wherever possible —as I'd done him a few favours — like the artwork for the cartoon characters on the Black Lace record sleeves, and a few other bits and bobs. The relationship proved fruitful when Waggers was instrumental in a song I'd written being picked up by the popular TV soap *Emmerdale*. 'Just This Side of Love' was sung in the show by the actress Malandra Burrows (who played Kathy), and proved to be a big hit. It shot up the charts, despite the BBC refusing to play it on Radio 1. The reason they gave was that it 'didn't fit the format' required of the station' – a rather crass statement seeing as they were playing 'Kinky Boots' by Patrick Macnee and Honor Blackman at the time. Perhaps the fact that our record was on the Yorkshire Television Label might have had something to do with it! More positively, the record brought a few quid in, and I was able to take time off to get my bad hip fixed. It had got to the stage where I could neither walk, sit nor stand without being in excruciating pain. Trouble was, I was in my late forties and replacement hips were only recommended for people over sixty. Coupled with that, the X-rays showed that my joint was in such bad shape that a replacement might not take. But a brilliant young surgeon, Peter Angus, took my case to a seminar of colleagues and came up with a solution – a brand new type of hip. And though I still retained a slight limp after it was fitted, the pain had gone and it was ecstasy.

Six months later I was back at work, and one of the first engagements was a cabaret spot at a private function. To our mutual surprise I found myself facing Mr Angus, sitting at the front table. My opening line was directed to him. 'You had me in stitches. I hope I can reciprocate.' Fortunately I did. But for most of my act he stared at my leg more than me. I guess some people can never get away from their work!

The success of the Malandra Burrows hit started things moving again. I was invited to do a few TV interviews; a producer dug out an old feature about the Arkwright record; and I sang 'Penny Arcade' on the Bill Maynard series *Maynard's Bill*. An invitation also arrived from the local police, to play John Virgo in a charity snooker game along with my old mate Stan Richards (Seth, the old gamekeeper in *Emmerdale*). It was a hoot, but it didn't stop me getting a parking ticket soon after . . .

The act was in demand and life was ticking along nicely. Mandy left school and before long she'd settled into a job. She worked hard, and it was the sight of her reversing a motor car out of the drive – instead of a pedal car – that prompted me to reflect on what might have been.

But what's the point of 'what might have been'? It's of no importance now. One thing's for certain: never once have I had any regrets. During the writing of this book I've come to realise that fate dealt me a winning hand. True, I could perhaps have earned lots more money if I'd taken a few different directions, but there's not enough money in the world to buy the precious memories I have at my disposal every moment of every day.

I was there for Mandy's first proper smile (not wind!), her first word and the first shaky step unaided. I can still meet old friends and schoolmates to relive the old times. And once a year the old Bradford bands get together to play for the fans. Maybe we're getting on in years, but the wonderful thing is that once the music starts in our minds we're sixteen all over again. Mick Sagar still belts out rock better than ever, Richard Harding's guitar skills still mesmerise everyone, Garth is still 'Shaking All Over' (not age-related), Drew's still buzzin' on the keyboard, Mel's solid as ever, Dougie remains unperturbed, Dave Butts is still sexy and Andy's drums still drive the rest of us along. (Smudge – our original drummer now lives in California.)

. . . And my mind drifts back to that night when I was standing all alone on my first gig with The Dingos, when the pretty young blonde called Linda took pity and invited me to sit with her and her friends. It was an act of kindness I've never forgotten – and am never likely to. For every day when I wake up she's there beside me – and she's still as beautiful. We're married now, and I couldn't be happier!

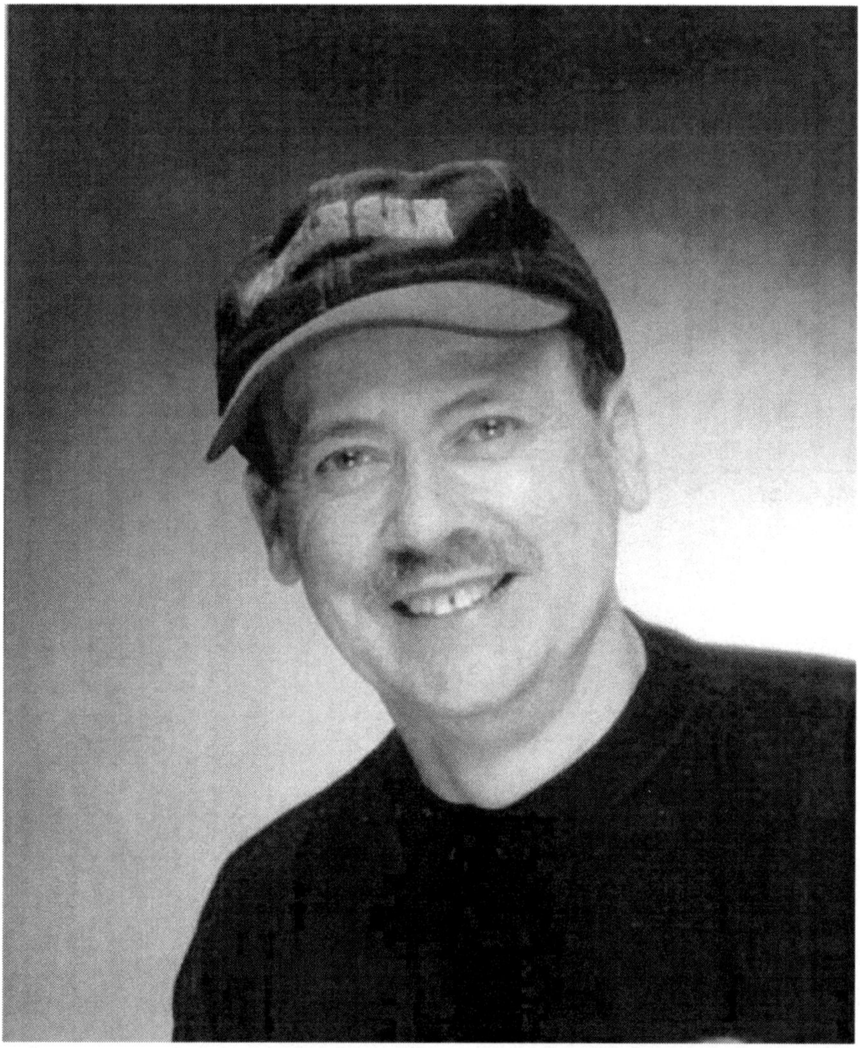